Neonatology for the MRCOG

Peter Dear
MD, FRCP, Consultant and Senior Lecturer in Neonatal Medicine
Regional Neonatal Intensive Care Unit and Department of Paediatrics
St James's University Hospital, Leeds LS9 7TF

Simon Newell
MD, FRCP, Consultant and Honorary Senior Lecturer in Neonatal Medicine and Paediatric Gastroenterology
Regional Neonatal Intensive Care Unit and Department of Paediatrics
St James's University Hospital, Leeds LS9 7TF

Series Editor: Peter Milton
MD, FRCOG, Consultant Obstetrician and Gynaecologist
Addenbrooke's and Rosie Maternity Hospital, Robinson Way, Cambridge
CB2 2SW

RCOG Press

First published 1996

ISBN 0-902331-82-5

Published by the **RCOG Press** at the
Royal College of Obstetricians and Gynaecologists
27 Sussex Place, Regent's Park
London NW1 4RG

Registered Charity No. 213280

Designed by Geoffrey Wadsley
Printed by Latimer Trend & Co Ltd, Plymouth

Contents

	Preface	vii
	Introduction	viii
1	The effects of birth on the fetus	1
2	Care of the normal infant	25
3	The preterm infant	37
4	Intrauterine growth retardation	49
5	Nutrition and infant feeding	59
6	Jaundice	73
7	Common congenital abnormalities	81
8	Infection of the fetus and newborn	89
9	Blood disorders	99
10	Hydrops fetalis	107
11	Inborn errors of metabolism	113
12	Neonatal effects of maternal disease	121
	Suggested references for further reading	132
	Index	134

There is not much to learn about holding a baby.
There are 152 distinctly different ways – and all are right!

Heywood Broun
Collected Edition (1941)

Acknowledgement

We are indebted to our many colleagues in obstetrics for teaching us so much about their art and we are pleased that the Royal College of Obstetricians and Gynaecologists has given us the opportunity to repay that debt.

We would like to thank our secretaries, Janice Keville and Maureen Corbett, for uncomplainingly staggering through the preparation of this manuscript. The table of drugs in breast milk was prepared by Stephanie Glendinning, pharmacist on our neonatal unit.

Preface

Possession of the MRCOG is an essential prerequisite for higher training within our specialty, both in the United Kingdom and in many countries overseas – the MRCOG has a high standing not only in the UK and the Commonwealth but increasingly within Europe. At the present time there are Fellows and Members of our College in over 80 countries throughout the world and the number of candidates taking the MRCOG examination continues to rise.

Preparing for the examination involves not only working in carefully monitored training posts but also a substantial amount of academic preparation and, from 1998, the submission of a 5000–8000 word dissertation on an obstetric or gynaecological topic.

In carrying out such studies candidates have traditionally used major standard works ranging from 'Jeffcoate's' and 'Donald' in my days during the 1970s to the present large, excellent, multi-author textbooks.

Whilst the use of such texts is likely to continue as candidates quite rightly appreciate the comprehensive nature of these books and the invaluable source references contained therein, the Publications Committee felt there was a need for a series of smaller, cheaper and more regularly updated texts on particular topics which need to be revised for the examination.

I think it is particularly appropriate that *Neonatology for the MRCOG* is the first of these books, dealing as it does excellently with what is after all the ultimate aim of safe obstetric practice – a healthy baby along with of course an unharmed mother. I am sure it will prove invaluable not only to MRCOG candidates but also to practising obstetricians, midwives and others concerned with perinatal care, including paediatricians in training.

Peter Milton FRCOG
RCOG Publications Committee
May 1996

Introduction

Increasing knowledge and technological advancement in both obstetrics and neonatal medicine are bringing the two disciplines closer together for the purposes of joint decision making. Growing possibilities for prenatal diagnosis, the assessment of fetal well-being and fetal therapy combined with improvements in the outlook for babies receiving intensive care mean that choices about the timing, manner and place of birth are now much better informed than was once the case. Although there are still many occasions on which there seems to be no alternative to just 'get the baby out', increasingly there is the opportunity to choose between different courses of action. Of course, with the opportunity to make informed choices comes responsibility for the chosen action and that is why it is increasingly desirable that the responsibility is shared between the obstetrician and the neonatologist.

In order to have a meaningful dialogue, the neonatologist must understand something about obstetrics and the obstetrician something about neonatal medicine. A six-month SHO post in the complementary specialty is ideal but changes in the pattern of postgraduate medical training are likely to make that more difficult to achieve. Joint meetings are a valuable mechanism for learning some of the practical issues but at some stage there is simply no substitute for sitting down with a good book.

We hope that this is such a book. It is written with the trainee obstetrician very much in mind and is unashamedly eclectic in its choice of material. It is not meant to be a comprehensive text on neonatal medicine. It concentrates on those aspects of the subject that we believe obstetricians ought to know about, either because they are relevant to obstetric decision making or because they are important things for the obstetrician to have a view on when there is no neonatologist to ask.

1 The effects of birth on the fetus

> *'Sir,' replied Dr Slop, 'it would astonish you to know what improvements we have made of late in all branches of obstetrical knowledge, but particularly in that one single point of the safe and expeditious extraction of the foetus.'*
> Laurence Sterne, *Tristram Shandy* (1760–1767)

The transition from intrauterine to extrauterine life requires a remarkable functional adaptation in virtually every organ system. In general this proceeds reliably and uneventfully, so that birth is properly regarded as a natural event not requiring medical intervention. In the individual, however, the potential for things to go disastrously wrong is ever present and it is the joint task of the obstetrician and neonatologist to try to anticipate such problems and to plan appropriate action. Details of the family history, the progress of the pregnancy, the gestation, the results of fetal assessment and so on may allow prediction of problems but often unexpected problems arise to put the fetus at great risk. This chapter will begin by reviewing the major physiological events occurring in the fetus around the time of birth and will then focus on some of the more common problems which arise.

Physiological changes at birth

The most dramatic sequence of events occurs in the cardiovascular and respiratory systems. During a short period the circulation changes from the fetal to the adult pattern as the newborn infant switches from placenta to lung as the organ of gas exchange. The major phenomena involved in this transition are set out in Table 1.1(see also Figure 1.1). Difficulties in accomplishing some of these will be referred to later in this chapter.

Table 1.1 Major cardio-respiratory changes at birth

Phenomena	*Effects*
Stress of labour stimulates catecholamine and steroid responses in fetus	Prepares lung for air breathing by curtailing lung liquid secretion and stimulating surfactant release
Uterine contractions impede villous space blood flow	Deteriorating trend in fetal blood gas status
Compression of fetal thorax by birth canal	Expulsion of some lung liquid
Thorax recoils on leaving birth canal	Proximal airway fills with air
Blood gases deteriorate following clamping of the umbilical cord	Initiation of breathing
Bombardment by sensory stimuli, e.g. cold	Initiation of breathing
Air enters lung and raises interstitial pO_2	Pulmonary vascular resistance falls, so increasing pulmonary blood flow, arterial pO_2 and left atrial filling
Low resistance placental circulation stops	Systemic vascular resistance increases and venous return to right atrium falls
Pressure gradient between atria reverses	Foramen ovale closes functionally
Direction of ductal shunt reverses and ductus is perfused with oxygen-rich blood	Ductus arteriosus closes

Less dramatic, but no less critical to survival and health, are the changes that occur in the renal, gastrointestinal, endocrine and haematopoietic systems. Some of these are outlined in Table 1.2.

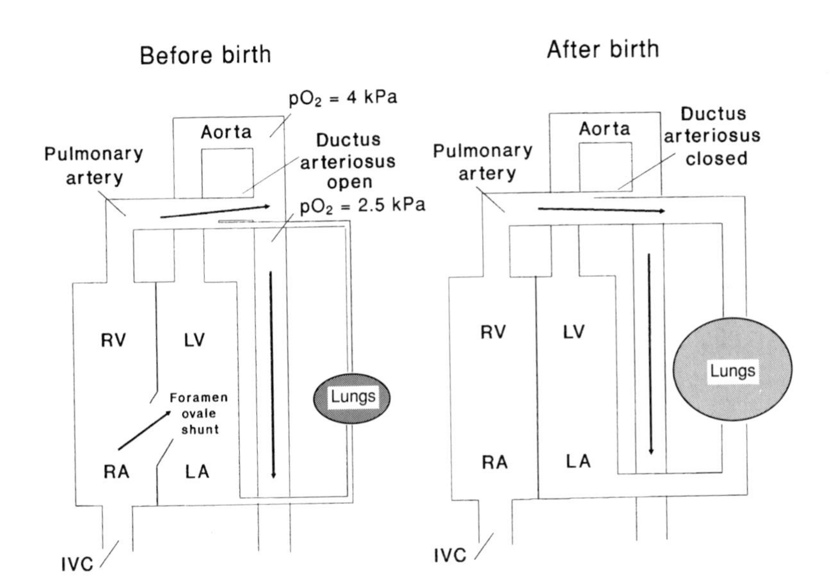

Figure 1.1 Circulatory changes at birth

Table 1.2 Physiological changes at birth

System		*Changes with birth*
Renal	*From:*	no excretory function and large volumes of dilute urine (5 ml/kg/hr)
	To:	full excretory function and fluid conservation (1 ml/kg/hr)
Gastro-intestinal	*From:*	minimal digestion, absorption or peristalsis
	To:	full functional activity to support enteral nutrition
Endocrine	*From:*	relative quiescence and the inactivation of many hormones
	To:	full homeostatic functioning
Erythropoietic	*From:*	high concentration of HbF (17 g/dl)
	To:	a lower concentration of HbA (11 g/dl at six weeks)

Table 1.3 Fetal adaptations to hypoxia

- **High haemoglobin concentration** (17 g/dl at term) – increases the oxygen carrying capacity of the blood at low pO_2. This mechanism is exploited by the fetus up to the point of diminishing returns, beyond which any further increase in haemoglobin would result in a large increase in blood viscosity.
- **Fetal haemoglobin** (HbF) – the dissociation curve of HbF is steeper than that of adult haemoglobin (HbA) over the range of pO_2 found in fetal life, allowing better delivery of oxygen to the tissues (see Figure 1.2).
- **The fetal circulatory plan** – the anatomy of the fetal circulation ensures that the pO_2 of blood in the ascending aorta is about 30% higher than that in the descending aorta. As a result, the fetal brain and myocardium receive a better supply of oxygenated blood than most other tissues.

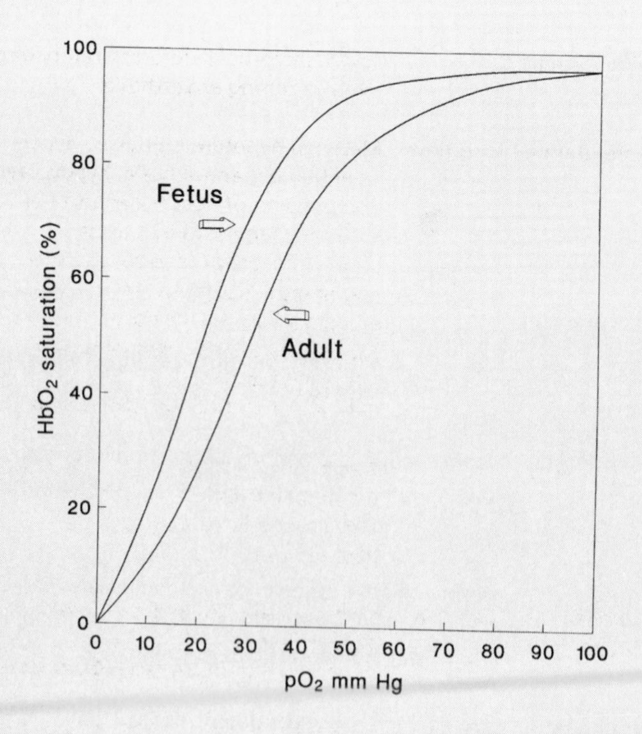

Figure 1.2 Fetal and adult oxyhaemoglobin equilibrium curves

Problems arising out of the transition from intrauterine life

Birth asphyxia

The partial pressure of oxygen (pO_2) in umbilical venous blood at term is of the order of 3–4 kPa, a value similar to that found in the adult at the summit of Mount Everest! The only reason that the fetus can meet its tissue oxygen requirements at this pO_2 is that it is especially adapted to hypoxia as outlined in Table 1.3.

It is important to realise that not all fetuses have these adaptations in place, for example the anaemic fetus (see Chapter 9), and even for

Table 1.4 Requirements for adequate fetal oxygenation

Requirements	*Potential threats*
Normal maternal pO_2	Severe maternal cardiorespiratory disease Hypoxia during anaesthesia
Adequate uterine blood flow	Maternal hypotension due to hyperventilation, anaesthesia, hypovolaemia Compression of abdominal aorta or inferior vena cava by uterus Maternal vascular disease (e.g. pre-eclampsia, diabetes) Prolonged or obstructed labour Excessive uterine activity or spasm (e.g. syntocinon) Uterus contracting on second twin
Healthy placenta	Placental infarction Placental abruption Intrauterine infection Post-maturity
Unobstructed umbilical cord blood flow	Cord compression by fetal parts Cord prolapse Cord knotted, or damaged by traction
A normal fetal haemoglobin concentration	Rhesus haemolytic disease Twin-to-twin transfusion Feto–maternal transfusion

the vast majority who are well adapted the situation is precarious and a small drop in pO_2 occurring antenatally or intrapartum can threaten the oxygen supply to the brain and other vital tissues. Some of the factors on which adequate fetal oxygenation depend are set out in Table 1.4, along with some of the potential threats to fetal oxygenation.

Some of these problems are relatively common, and even normal parturition exposes the fetus to a degree of hypoxia. It is not surprising, therefore, that physiological mechanisms have evolved to help maintain the oxygen supply to vital organs such as the brain during birth. These mechanisms allow the fetus to withstand exposure to hypoxia which would be lethal to the adult and the most important ones are shown in Table 1.5.

As a result of these and other mechanisms, the vast majority of fetuses escape hypoxic injury at birth even when there are major obstetric complications. In a small minority of fetuses the depth and duration of exposure to hypoxia during birth cannot be compensated for by the adaptive mechanisms described and, through the sequence of events outlined in Figure 1.3, biochemical changes occur within the brain that may result in permanent brain injury.

Table 1.5 Fetal reserves against hypoxia

- **Maintenance of the circulation** – the fetal heart has high glycogen stores, allowing it to maintain an output during hypoxia as a result of anaerobic glycolysis. Unless cardiac output is maintained during hypoxia brain damage rapidly ensues.
- **Redistribution of the circulation** – the hypoxic fetus preferentially perfuses its brain, myocardium and adrenals at the expense of the rest of the organs and tissues. There is also redistribution of flow within the brain to the advantage of the brain stem and central structures.
- **Brain 'shutdown'** – early in the course of a significant hypoxic episode the brain ceases all but maintenance functions and switches to anaerobic glycolysis. These mechanisms, along with the inherent resistance to hypoxia of the newborn infant's brain, make an important contribution to the infant's ability to survive intrapartum asphyxia intact.

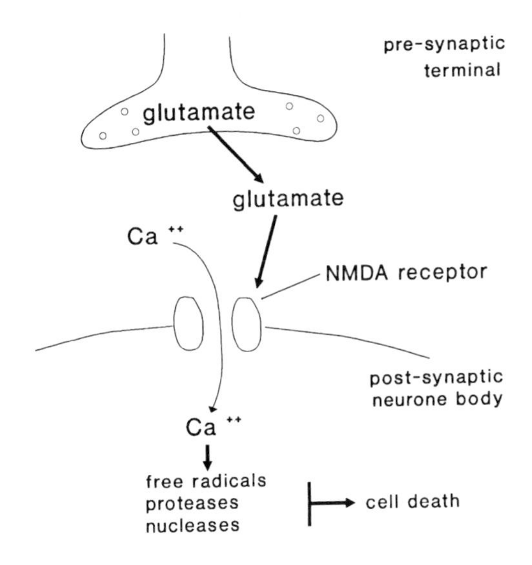

Release of glutamate opens calcium channels through activation of the NMDA receptor. Influx of calcium into the neurone results in changes which may lead to cell death.

Figure 1.3 Glutamate in post-asphyxial cell damage

Recognition and management of the asphyxiated fetus

The best hope is that the midwife or obstetrician will recognise asphyxia in the fetus and either remove the cause (e.g. stopping syntocinon) or effect delivery by the most rapid means. This is an important goal of modern obstetrics, utilising the available means of fetal assessment. As well as detecting and rescuing the asphyxiated fetus it is also the responsibility of the obstetric/midwifery team to ensure that the facilities and staff for skilled resuscitation are present at every delivery where fetal asphyxia is anticipated. This is one of many reasons why communication between the labour ward and the neonatal unit should be efficient.

Neonatal resuscitation

The baby who has suffered significant asphyxia during the hour or so immediately preceding birth will almost invariably have difficulty in making a normal respiratory adaptation at birth. This is because even modest hypoxia has a depressant effect on neonatal respiration. This is in contrast to the situation in the older child or adult where hypoxia elicits a sustained increase in respiratory activity. Since the cascade of cardio-respiratory events outlined in Table 1.1 depends critically on aeration of the lung, asphyxia-induced apnoea at birth must be corrected by artificial ventilation as soon as possible. Except in the most extreme cases, effective ventilation of the lungs will result in a rapid improvement in heart rate and skin colour as the pulmonary circulation opens up and oxygenated blood starts to reach the myocardium and systemic circulation.

The clinical condition of the asphyxiated baby at birth is determined primarily by the direct effects of hypoxia and acidosis on the tissues but it is partly a reflection of the acute responses to hypoxia outlined in Table 1.5.

Assessment of the infant at birth

The condition of newborn babies is traditionally defined in terms of the Apgar score as illustrated in Table 1.6. If this is performed and documented conscientiously it provides a reasonably objective and useful statement about the baby's condition at birth and during the subsequent minutes. It should be appreciated, though, that the Apgar score can be influenced by too many factors other than asphyxia for it to be regarded as a specific indicator of asphyxia. For the purposes of deciding whether or not a baby requires resuscitation the

Table 1.6 The Apgar scoring system

		Score	
System	*0*	*1*	*2*
Heart rate	Absent	Below 100/min	100/min or higher
Respiratory effort	Nil	Slow, irregular	Regular, with cry
Muscle tone	Limp	Some tone in limbs	Active flexion of limbs
Reflex irritability	Nil	Grimace only	Cry
Colour	Pallor or generalised cyanosis	Body pink, extremities blue	Pink all over

respiratory activity and the heart rate are of most immediate use. Any baby who does not breathe within 30 seconds of birth, or who exhibits slow and irregular gasping requires help. Bradycardia indicates hypoxia.

Resuscitation procedure

1 Take steps to minimise heat loss

Place the baby on the resuscitaire. Make sure that the radiant heater is switched on. Rapidly dry the baby with a towel. Cover the top of the head and the lower body with a towel or blanket. Start the clock on the resuscitaire if you have not already done so.

2 Evaluate the baby's condition

The only practical tool for this is clinical observation of the adequacy of breathing, the heart rate, skin colour, muscle tone and responsiveness to stimulation (the components of the Apgar score). In most cases it is obvious whether or not resuscitation is necessary but occasionally it is difficult to decide. **It is preferable to intervene unnecessarily than to fail to do so when it is necessary.**

3 Resuscitate

(a) Suction, stimulation and oxygen

Use a suction catheter to clear the upper airway of secretions and to stimulate breathing. If the baby does begin to gasp in response to this, direct a gentle stream of oxygen towards the nose and mouth. Do not blast a forceful stream of cold gas at the face as this causes cooling and increases oxygen consumption. Further stimulation of breathing can be given by rubbing the baby's body with a towel or gently flicking the soles of the feet with the back of your finger.

(b) Bag and mask ventilation

If spontaneous breathing does not begin within 30 seconds of suction and stimulation it will be necessary to provide artificial ventilation. If the baby is in very poor condition, and if you have the skill, immediate intubation is desirable as it is the most efficient way of ventilating the lungs. In less extreme cases, and certainly if you are unsure about intubation, intermittent positive pressure ventilation using a facemask and resuscitation bag is an acceptable alternative.

The facemask chosen must make good contact with the baby's face so that a near-perfect seal is created. The latex rubber masks produced by Laerdal (complete set infant bag and masks, ref. 850001,

Laerdal, Stavanger, Norway) are good and come in a variety of sizes, all of which should be available on the resuscitaire. Place the mask over the baby's nose and mouth, lift the jaw and press firmly (Figure 1.4).

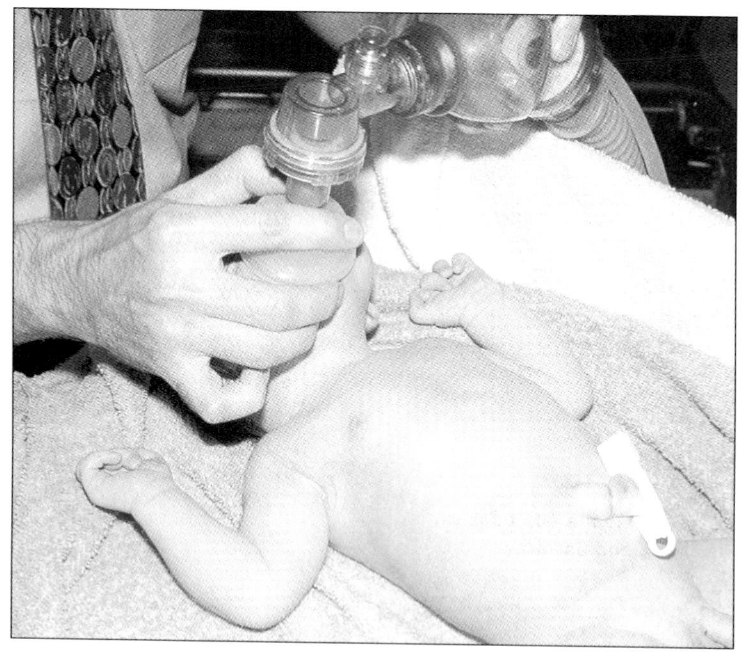

Figure 1.4

Resuscitation bags vary in design but have in common the facility to control or limit the pressure applied to the lung. For routine resuscitation a maximum pressure of 30 cm of H_2O should be used. This is usually high enough to provide an adequate tidal volume (of about 6 ml/kg) but low enough to minimise the risk of creating a pneumothorax. Make sure that you understand how the bag that you are using works so that you can employ it properly.

Connect the resuscitation bag to the oxygen outlet on the resuscitaire and turn the oxygen on to about 4 litres per minute flow rate. The concentration of oxygen delivered to the baby's lungs will depend on the design of the resuscitation bag. High concentrations of oxygen are usually used for neonatal resuscitation. All modern resuscitaires incorporate either a pressure-limitation mechanism or else a pressure measurement gauge as an added line of defence against the use of excessive pressures.

Once the bag-and-mask system is in place, squeeze the bag gently at a rate of about 50–60 times per minute. Remember that the tidal volume required by the average term baby is only about 25 ml and try to visualise this volume of displacement when you squeeze the bag. Use your thumb in opposition to two or three fingers and allow equal times for inspiration and expiration. Look at the baby to see that the lower chest and abdomen are rising and falling with your efforts. As a rough guide, the lower sternum should lift by 1–2 cm with each squeeze of the bag.

(c) Intubation

Intubation is learnt by watching and then doing under close supervision. It requires considerable practice if it is to be accomplished quickly and successfully. Figure 1.5 shows how the epiglottis is lifted out of the way by placing the tip of the laryngoscope in the vallecula. For a baby weighing more than about 2 kg use a 3.0 or 3.5 mm endotracheal tube. For smaller babies a 2.5 mm tube may be used for

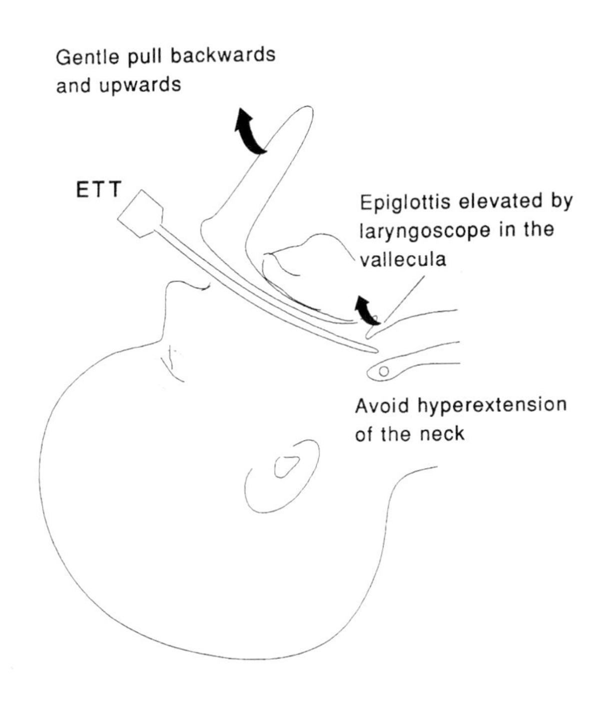

Figure 1.5 Neonatal intubation – use of the laryngoscope

resuscitation but should be replaced by a 2.7 or 3.0 mm tube for longer term ventilation. Whether you use shouldered or non-shouldered tubes is a matter of local preference. The authors prefer unshouldered tubes as they can be left in place for long-term ventilation.

Always check that the laryngoscope light is bright (it should be painful to look at when held 6 inches from the eyes) and that the bulb is well screwed in. Ensure that the suction apparatus is turned on and that a suitable size of suction catheter suction is connected and at hand. Also at hand should be a pair of McGill's forceps and one or two flexible endotracheal tube introducers, just in case! Either the oro-tracheal or the naso-tracheal approach can be used for resuscitation from birth asphyxia; it depends on what you are used to. The SHOs at St James's University Hospital, Leeds, for example, mainly use naso-tracheal intubation because that is what is used in the hospital's neonatal intensive care unit. Once intubated, the same guidelines for ventilation as described for the bag-and-mask technique are appropriate for most cases. However, once an endotracheal tube is in place there is the opportunity to apply the inflating pressure with a T-piece. This allows longer inspiratory times to be used (up to 2 seconds) than are possible with the bag and mask. This technique is of value in improving alveolar ventilation when there is retention of lung liquid, as after pre-labour Caesarean section, or when there is surfactant deficiency.

4 Re-evaluate

Resuscitation is an iterative process of evaluation and action. You must ask yourself if the baby is responding as expected and if not what are you going to do next.

Effective pulmonary ventilation almost invariably causes a rapid rise in heart rate, closely followed by a rapid improvement in skin colour.

If this does not occur it is most likely that there is a technical problem. Consider:

(a) the endotracheal tube is in the oesophagus or the right main bronchus
(b) the pressure release valve is faulty and will not allow an effective pressure to be produced
(c) the oxygen supply is not connected or turned on.

If (b) and (c) are excluded, then, regardless of what you hear with the stethoscope, always assume that the tube is the problem and re-intubate! **Do this until you are sure that the tube is in the trachea.**

MOST BABIES WHO ARE GOING TO RESPOND TO RESUSCITATION WILL RESPOND TO VENTILATION ALONE.

Failure to improve with intermittent positive pressure ventilation (IPPV) is very rare but causes will include the following:

- **Congenital abnormalities** – such as diaphragmatic hernia, major congenital heart disease, pulmonary hypoplasia or malformation of the lung, laryngeal or tracheal atresia. These either prevent resuscitation or else are diagnosed radiologically after resuscitation has eventually been successful.
- **Gross ascites** – as part of generalised hydrops or due to lymphatic or urinary leakage. In these cases it may be necessary to drain some of the fluid in order to relieve thoracic compression. Do this by passing a 21-gauge butterfly needle (or similar) into the peritoneal cavity; either in the midline, halfway between the umbilicus and the symphysis pubis or else in the flank. Attach a 50 ml syringe via a three-way tap and aspirate as much fluid as you can. Save some for analysis.
- **Pneumothorax** – this is a rare finding during resuscitation at birth. It may occur spontaneously or as a result of resuscitation. Clinical clues are mediastinal shift, reduced breath sounds on the affected side or abdominal distension. Immediate management involves inserting a 21-gauge butterfly needle into the second interspace in the mid-clavicular line on the suspected side. If there is a tension pneumothorax there will usually be an audible hiss of gas through the needle and ventilation will improve. As long as positive pressure ventilation is continued there is no need to create an underwater seal. A definitive chest drain procedure can be performed after transfer to the neonatal unit.
- **Severe hypovolaemia** – massive, acute blood loss from events such as feto–maternal haemorrhage or twin–twin transfusion (see Chapter 9) can prevent improvement with ventilation alone as tissue hypoxia cannot be reversed in the presence of severe hypovolaemia. This diagnosis is difficult to make as all severely asphyxiated babies look very pale, but if such a situation is suspected, and in the absence of any other more likely explanation for failure to respond to IPPV, it is reasonable to give a rapid infusion of 20 ml/kg of uncross-matched O-negative blood.

If improvement is unsatisfactory despite adequate effective ventilation; and the pulse remains below 80 bpm

1 Begin external cardiac massage (ECM)
This is best done by an assistant. Grasp the baby around the thorax with both hands; fingers along the thoracic spine and thumbs on the sternum (see Figure 1.6). Squeeze the chest so as to depress the sternum by 2–3 cm, about 120 times per minute. There is no need to synchronise this with IPPV. An alternative technique for external cardiac massage, which is the only one that you can employ single-handed, is to depress the sternum with the fingers of one hand just below the intermammary line (see Figure 1.7).

2 Reassess
If the response to ECM is inadequate, and ventilation is satisfactory, the infant may benefit from drug treatment.

3 Drug treatment
Give 0.3 ml (0.1 ml/kg) of 1 in 1000 adrenaline mixed with 1 ml of normal saline down the endotracheal tube. Alternatively, catheterise the umbilical vein and infuse 0.3 ml (0.1 ml/kg) of 1 in 10 000 adrenaline and 5–15 ml (approx. 1–2 mmol/kg) of 4.2% sodium bicarbonate.

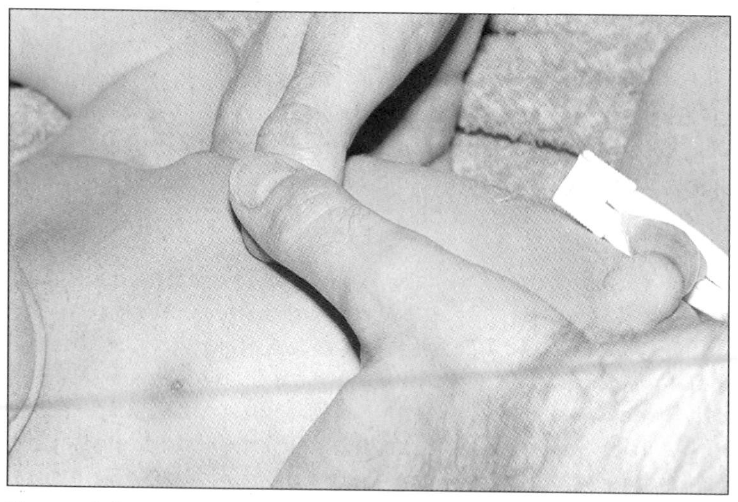

Figure 1.6

Whether or not dextrose should be infused in addition is controversial. Some animal experiments have suggested that dextrose can worsen the outcome by providing fuel for anaerobic metabolism, leading to lactic acid formation and worsening acidosis within brain cells. Other evidence suggests benefit.

The intracardiac administration of drugs is potentially hazardous and rarely necessary. It should be reserved for cases in which it proves impossible to gain any other form of vascular access. In the vast majority of cases simple measures, well executed, will bring success. Recourse to drugs is rarely necessary.

Birth asphyxia as a cause of cerebral palsy

Cerebral palsy has recently been defined as an 'umbrella term covering a group of non-progressive, but often changing, motor impairment syndromes secondary to lesions or anomalies of the brain arising in the early stages of development'. Among lay people it is still often assumed that most cerebral palsy has its origin in birth asphyxia but recent studies on the epidemiology of cerebral palsy have suggested that no more than 15% of cases are attributable to perinatal events and some large studies have produced a figure as low as 9%. The contribution of other aetiologies is shown in Figure 1.8. This information is reassuring for the obstetrician but in so far as some of the perinatal factors causing cerebral palsy are potentially

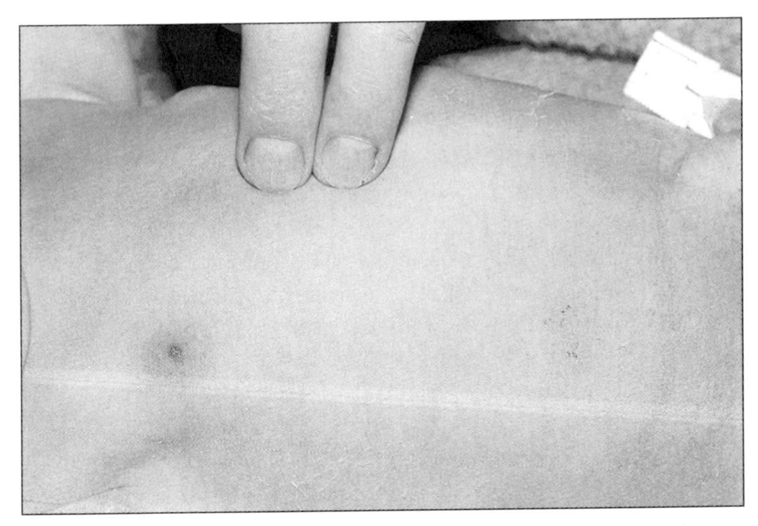

Figure 1.7

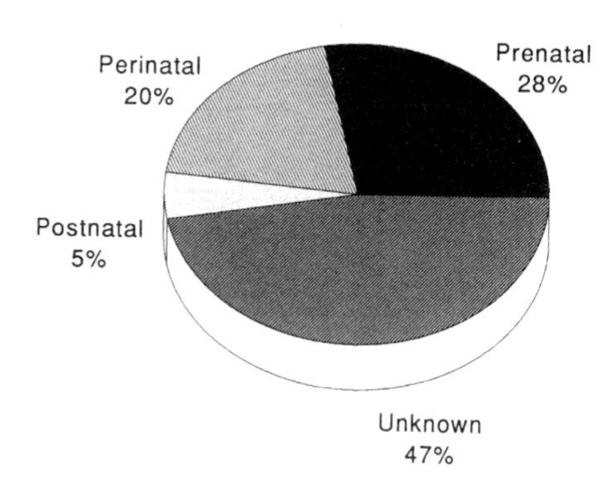

Figure 1.8 Cerebral palsy causation – current state of belief

avoidable, improvements in obstetric practice could contribute to a reduction in the prevalence of this devastating condition. In order to be reasonably certain that a case of cerebral palsy has its origins in perinatal asphyxial brain injury the following conditions should be fulfilled:

1 There should be unequivocal evidence of severe perinatal asphyxia. This can be from either observations made on the fetus, in the form of CTG, blood gas analysis, etc., or from observations made on the state of the baby at birth and its response to resuscitation.
2 There should be evidence of an acute neurological disturbance during the first few days of life, known as an hypoxic/ischaemic encephalopathy, and characterised by such features as seizures and abnormalities of consciousness and muscle tone. A baby who shows no neurological abnormalities after birth has almost certainly not sustained significant asphyxial brain injury.
3 There are often, although by no means invariably, signs of asphyxial injury to organs and tissues other than the brain, notably the kidneys.
4 Other causes of cerebral palsy, such as developmental brain defects and inborn errors of metabolism, should have been excluded by appropriate investigation.

Cases of cerebral palsy that meet the above criteria would currently almost certainly satisfy the criteria for causation applied by the medico-legal process although, of course, the mere fact of causation by perinatal asphyxia is by no means evidence of obstetric negligence. It will probably never be possible to prevent all cases of perinatally acquired brain injury.

Meconium aspiration pneumonia

Meconium is made up of the residue of gastrointestinal secretions, including bile, and swallowed elements. It has plastic properties and is extremely durable. In the healthy fetus large bowel peristalsis is absent. Meconium may, however, be passed antenatally or during labour, typically in the presence of post-maturity and asphyxia. Meconium staining of the liquor occurs in about 10% of all deliveries but in about 20% of post-mature deliveries. It is very unusual to find meconium staining of the liquor before 34 weeks' gestation and when it occurs infection, especially due to *Listeria monocytogenes*, should be considered.

As a sign of fetal distress the passage of meconium has poor specificity and sensitivity although when combined with the results of other tests of fetal well-being its value increases. Meconium aspiration syndrome is an important cause of neonatal mortality and morbidity in its own right. Meconium can cause a serious respiratory illness with major ventilation perfusion mismatch due to airway obstruction, so that the chest X-ray shows shadows and hyperinflation (Figure 1.9). It is often compounded by persistent pulmonary hypertension (see below).

Whenever there is heavy meconium staining of the liquor a paediatrician should be present at the delivery and should use a large-bore suction catheter to aspirate meconium from the mouth as soon as the head is delivered. Once delivery is complete the baby should be taken to a resuscitation platform and the upper airways should be aspirated once more. If by this time the baby is making vigorous respiratory efforts nothing further is indicated but if the baby has difficulty in establishing respiration, intubation and aspiration of meconium from the lower airway is indicated. Thick meconium requires a large suction catheter and if it is thought that a great deal of meconium has been inhaled it is a good idea to perform intubation directly with a large suction catheter and to replace this with an endotracheal tube for ventilation once the meconium has been aspirated.

Subsequent management of the baby who has inhaled meconium

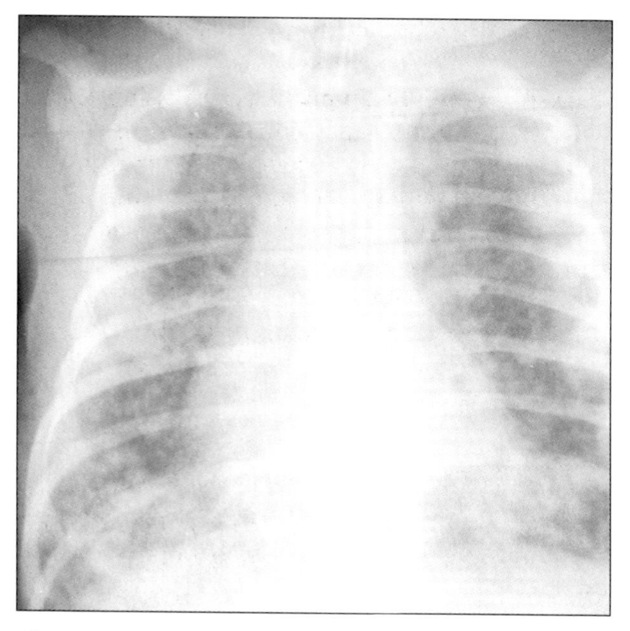

Figure 1.9

will depend on the severity of the resulting airway obstruction and the co-existence of persistent fetal circulation or asphyxia. Severe meconium aspiration pneumonia is one of the most difficult neonatal conditions to treat and prolonged ventilatory support and oxygen therapy may be required.

Persistent pulmonary hypertension of the newborn

This condition is also known as **persistent fetal circulation.**

During fetal life the pulmonary circulation is largely obstructed by constriction of the smooth muscle in the pulmonary arterioles. Under normal circumstances the first breath is followed by relaxation of this smooth muscle and the pulmonary vascular resistance falls rapidly. When this fails to occur the pulmonary vascular resistance remains above the systemic vascular resistance leading to right-to-left shunting of blood through the foramen ovale and/or the ductus arteriosus. The result is cyanosis that is unrelieved by oxygen therapy.

Persistent pulmonary hypertension is seen in a variety of circumstances but is most strongly associated with perinatal asphyxia, meconium aspiration and chronic fetal hypoxia. In the latter case there may be excessive musculature in the pulmonary vascular bed. In all cases it is desirable to exclude structural heart disease by echocardiography.

In some cases, persistent pulmonary hypertension resolves rapidly once acidosis has been corrected and the baby is well oxygenated. In other cases it is difficult to treat. Vasodilator drugs such as tolazoline, prostacyclin, sodium nitroprusside and magnesium are sometimes effective but they are all problematic because they cause systemic hypotension. Recently, persistent pulmonary hypertension in the newborn has been successfully treated with high-frequency oscillatory ventilation (HFOV) and inhaled nitric oxide therapy and it seems likely that this will emerge as the most effective treatment within the next few years.

Feto–maternal haemorrhage

Significant fetal blood loss across the placenta occurs in about 8% of pregnancies. Occasionally, however, the blood loss is substantial and it may occur acutely intrapartum. Affected infants appear pale and shocked at birth and are initially difficult to distinguish from those who have been asphyxiated without acute blood loss. It is often only after the circulatory failure has been treated with infusions of plasma that the anaemia becomes apparent. In all cases of unexplained anaemia at birth a Kleihauer test should be performed to look for evidence of feto-maternal haemorrhage.

To perform the Kleihauer test, a smear of maternal blood is examined after acid elution which washes the haemoglobin from the maternal red cells whilst the fetal cells remain intact. The fetal cells which contain haemoglobin can then be counted easily amongst the maternal ghost cells, allowing estimation of the size of feto–maternal bleed.

Acquisition of infection intrapartum

For the vast majority of individuals the passage down the birth canal provides the first contact with micro-organisms. Whether or not this results in infection depends upon the pathogenicity of the vaginal flora, the heaviness of the colonisation and a number of host factors including the maturity of the infant. The duration of rupture of the membranes is also an important consideration, with the likelihood of ascending infection increasing beyond 18 hours. Infection is dealt with in Chapter 8 but in the context of this chapter it is important to stress the value of effective communication between obstetrician and paediatrician if there has been prolonged rupture of the membranes or if there are any particular maternal factors which might predispose towards perinatal infection. Obtaining good microbiological specimens from the mother can also be very valuable in informing paediatric decision making and management.

Traumatic birth injury

In modern obstetric practice serious birth injury, such as tearing of the dura or spinal cord is rare, but evidence of lesser degrees of physical trauma is quite commonly discovered on routine examination. Birth trauma is predisposed to by factors such as a cephalo-pelvic disproportion, precipitate labour, mal-presentation and mal-position, prematurity and instrumental delivery.

Intracranial haemorrhage

Extradural, subdural, intracerebral, intracerebellar and subarachnoid haemorrhage can all be due to trauma. Intracranial haemorrhage due to trauma may be associated with other forms of injury such as cephalhaematoma, skull fracture, sub-galeal haemorrhage, retinal haemorrhage or peripheral nerve palsy. With good obstetric care serious intracranial haemorrhage ought to be very rare unless the fetus is unusually susceptible, for example as the result of thrombocytopenia or an inherited coagulopathy.

Nerve palsies

Several nerves are susceptible to traction or direct pressure injury. Usually these lesions recover as traumatic-induced swelling subsides, but minor disability persists in about half and a few are left handicapped.

Brachial plexus palsy

This is more common in the large baby and usually affects C5 and C6 roots (Erb's palsy), resulting in weakness or paralysis of deltoid, serratus anterior, biceps, teres major, brachioradialis and supinator. The affected arm lies straight and limp beside the trunk, internally rotated and with the fingers flexed (waiter's tip position) (as shown in Figure 1.10, in an infant who also has Down's syndrome). If the manoeuvre to elicit the moro reflex is performed, the affected arm does not respond. Less commonly the lower roots are injured,

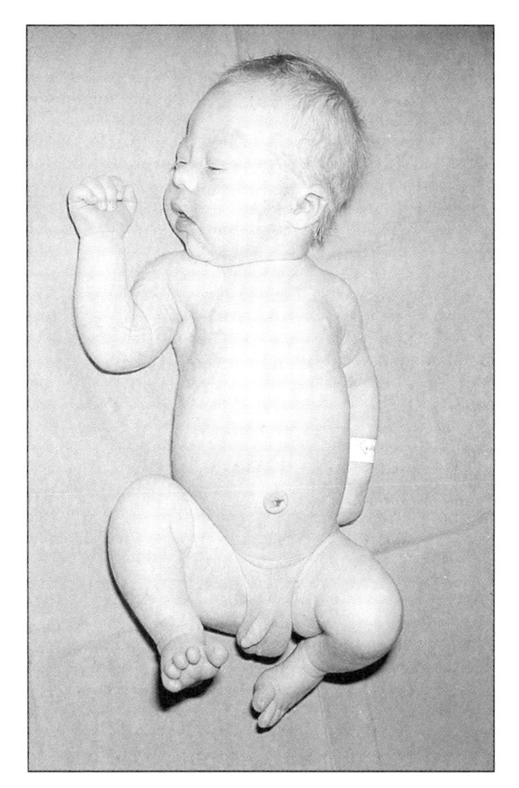

Figure 1.10

resulting in weakness of wrist extensors and the intrinsic muscles of the hand (Klumpke's palsy). Modern microsurgical techniques can be used to repair the brachial plexus, and indeed other traumatic nerve injuries, and referral for such surgery should be considered in cases which do not recover rapidly.

Facial nerve palsy

The facial nerve may be injured by pressure from the maternal pelvic bones or by forceps blades. It is a lower motor neurone defect, usually unilateral (Figure 1.11). The prognosis is good.

Phrenic nerve palsy

Infrequently, the cervical roots of the phrenic nerve, C3, C4 and C5, are damaged causing diaphragmatic paralysis and respiratory difficulty. If the problem persists surgical plication of the diaphragm may be necessary.

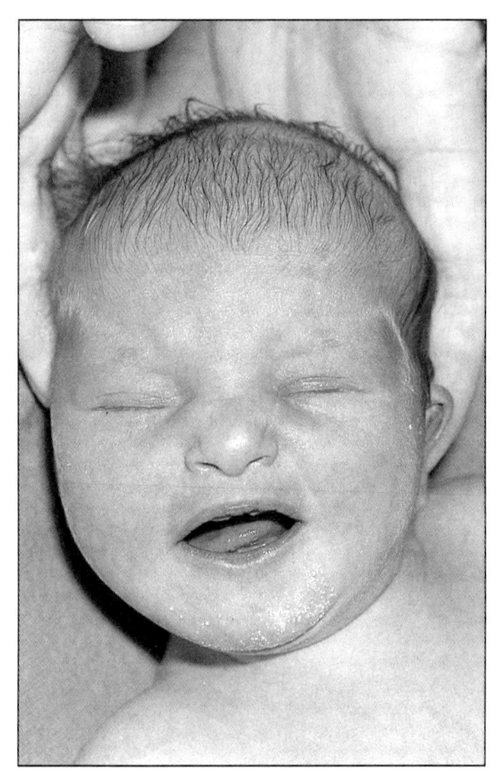

Figure 1.11

SYMPATHETIC PALSY

Damage to the first thoracic root may result in Horner's syndrome.

Skeletal injuries

SKULL FRACTURE

The skull of the newborn is remarkably resistant to fracture despite the considerable distortion that it undergoes during birth. Asymptomatic linear fractures of the parietal bone are commonest but depressed fractures sometimes occur and generally require surgical elevation. Neonatal skull fractures are predisposed to by certain congenital disorders, including osteogenesis imperfecta and Menkes syndrome.

CLAVICLE FRACTURE

This is the most commonly seen fracture and occurs where there has been difficulty delivering the shoulders. Complete breaks are painful and limit the baby's arm movement. Fractures of the clavicle heal well but often a large callus forms during the process.

HUMERUS AND FEMUR

Both fractures and epiphysial injury may occur in these long bones, usually during very difficult births.

Soft tissue injuries

CEPHALHAEMATOMA

In about 2% of babies sub-periosteal bleeding occurs, usually over the parietal bone (Figure 1.12) but occasionally over the occiput, where it may be mistaken for an encephalocele. The extent of the swelling, and therefore the amount of blood loss, is limited by the attachment of the periosteum to the margins of each skull bone. In 5% of cases, an associated linear skull fracture can be seen on X-ray. Cephalhaematomas require no treatment as the vast majority of them resolve spontaneously over a period of 1–2 months.

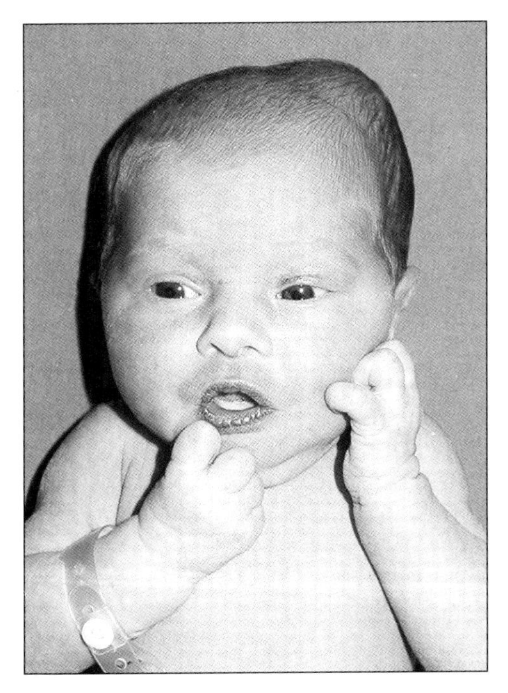

Figure 1.12

Sub-aponeurotic haemorrhage

In this case the haemorrhage occurs between the periosteum and the galea aponeurotica. As the swelling here is not limited in the same way as in a cephalhaematoma, serious blood loss can occur. This lesion is especially related to the use of the ventouse but improvements in obstetric techniques and the routine prophylactic use of vitamin K have rendered this a very rare lesion.

Sternomastoid tumour

This is a fusiform fibrous mass which may be palpable, and indeed visible, in the middle of the sternomastoid muscle. It is commonly thought of as being secondary to trauma although the precise aetiology is uncertain. It is sometimes associated with cranial or facial asymmetry. The mass usually disappears over a period of about six months and gentle physiotherapy to prevent shortening of the muscle is the only treatment required.

Bruising and abrasion

Difficult births are often accompanied by bruising, which in breech delivery may be extensive. Usually there is little serious harm done to tissues although the breakdown of extravasated blood may contribute to neonatal jaundice. Preterm babies are particularly vulnerable. Skin abrasions are portals of entry for micro-organisms and should be carefully observed for signs of infection.

Respiratory depression and altered behaviour from intrapartum drugs

The most commonly used drugs in labour which can affect the fetus are opiate analgesics. Opiates cross the placenta slowly but are also slowly metabolised by the fetus. The worst effects are seen with repeated doses or a single dose given 1–3 hours prior to birth. Under these circumstances Apgar scores are lower than in babies whose mothers have not received opiates and careful behavioural studies show abnormalities of fetal behaviour lasting up to a week. During resuscitation the respiratory depressant effects of opiates may be reversed by giving naloxone – 200 μg as a single i.m. injection.

2 Care of the normal infant

> *A bit of talcum*
> *is always walcum.*
> Ogden Nash 'The baby' in *Freewheeling* (1931)

On the labour ward

Keeping the baby warm

On the labour ward, priority should be given to ensuring that no serious drop in body temperature occurs. In the average labour-ward environment the naked newborn infant will lose heat, by evaporation, convection, radiation and conduction, faster than it can generate it and its temperature will inevitably fall (Figure 2.1). Hypothermia (defined as a core temperature below 35°C) predisposes to respiratory distress, sepsis, hypoglycaemia, bilirubin encephalopathy and cold injury. The ideal labour-ward environment from the baby's point of view would have still air, at 100% relative humidity and a temperature of about 34°C. It would have no large cold surfaces, such as windows. Such an environment would be intolerable to the mother and her attendants and so compromises have to be reached. As long as the baby is dried at birth and then wrapped in dry towels or blankets, including covering the top of the head, no harm should result as long as the room is not unduly cold or draughty. If the baby requires resuscitation, this should be carried out under a radiant heater. Heat loss is more rapid and its effects more devastating in the small or immature infant.

Vitamin K

Vitamin K is necessary for the hepatic synthesis of coagulation factors II, VII, IX and X, and for the conversion of inactive precursors to the

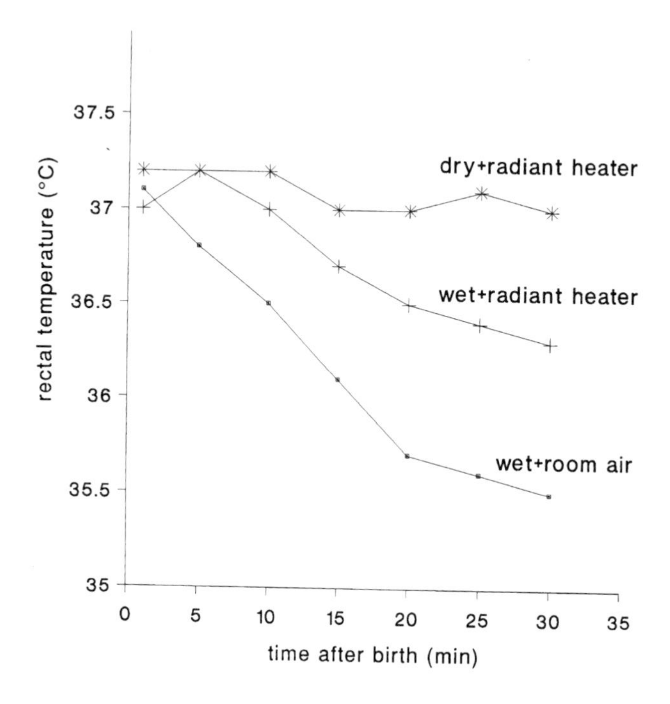

Figure 2.1 Prevention of hypothermia

active form. For reasons which are not yet understood the vitamin K concentration in cord blood is low and in the absence of intestinal synthesis by bacterial flora a vitamin K deficiency state easily develops. This is known as haemorrhagic disease of the newborn. Breast-fed infants are particularly vulnerable as the breast-milk content of vitamin K is very low compared with a standard proprietary formula.

The overall risk of bleeding for an unsupplemented breast-fed infant is in the region of 5%. Bleeding characteristically occurs between the second and sixth days of life. A wide range of manifestations has been reported, including gastrointestinal bleeding, vaginal bleeding, haematuria, bleeding from the umbilical cord stump, epistaxis, bruising and petechiae and, most serious of all, haemorrhage into major organs.

Haemorrhagic disease of the newborn can be completely prevented by the routine administration of intramuscular vitamin K at birth to all infants, and there is a lot to be said for this policy. An alternative, but less effective, approach is to administer oral vitamin

K, although in the case of breast-fed infants further doses at one week and four weeks of age are necessary. One epidemiological survey showed a statistical association between intramuscular vitamin K use at birth and the subsequent development of lymphatic leukaemia in childhood and led to an increased use of oral as opposed to intramuscular vitamin K. Other epidemiological studies have suggested that this association was unlikely to be due to a causal connection and more recent larger studies from Canada and Europe have found no evidence of a link between vitamin K and cancer.

The babies of women who have taken phenytoin or phenobarbitone during pregnancy are more prone to develop haemorrhagic disease of the newborn because of hepatic enzyme induction. In this situation maternal vitamin K supplementation and the routine administration of intramuscular vitamin K at birth are both indicated.

Oral anti-coagulants taken by the mother in late pregnancy predispose the infant to bleed during or after delivery. Heparin does not cause such a problem because it does not cross the placenta. Babies of women who have received oral anti-coagulant therapy should routinely be given intramuscular vitamin K at birth.

The umbilical cord

Apart from a possible benefit to the preterm infant of delayed cord clamping and a probable benefit for the polycythaemic infant of early cord clamping, there is little or no scientific evidence available regarding the optimum timing for cord clamping.

The cord should always be examined to see how many blood vessels are present. One of the umbilical arteries is absent in 1% of births and is associated with a 30% incidence of congenital abnormalities, particularly gastrointestinal and urinary tract malformations and chromosome abnormalities. It is probably a sensible policy to check the karyotype and to carry out renal ultrasound of all such babies routinely.

Routine care of the umbilical cord

The umbilical cord stump is one of the first sites to become colonised by bacteria after birth, and inhibiting the rate of umbilical colonisation reduces the rate of colonisation at other sites. This is particularly relevant with regard to *Staphylococcus aureus*. Very many agents have been used in cord care to prevent heavy colonisation by pathogens but, unfortunately, it is extremely difficult to draw clear conclusions about the risk–benefit ratio of any of the regimes. We currently use alcohol swabs and chlorhexidine powder and will continue to do so unless good reasons to do otherwise are produced by future research.

The umbilical cord usually separates at about seven days of age. Attachment of the cord beyond 14 days of age suggests an immunodeficiency state, particularly an inherited defect of neutrophil function.

Labelling

All newborn babies should have name bands attached to wrist and ankle before leaving the delivery room. This should be done under the supervision of the mother.

Passage of urine and meconium

It is important to note when the baby first passes urine and meconium. Often this occurs at or soon after delivery, but both are normally passed within 12 hours of birth (although passage of meconium may be delayed beyond this in some normal babies). Delay in bowel or bladder function should prompt a search for underlying pathology.

The routine newborn examination

All newborn babies should have a clinical examination within the first 24 hours of life, and a second check at about one week. The aims are to:

1. Detect:
   - (a) conditions that will benefit from early treatment, e.g. congenital dislocation of the hip, glaucoma
   - (b) conditions needing long-term supervision, e.g. congenital heart disease
   - (c) conditions with genetic implications for future pregnancies, e.g. Down's syndrome
   - (d) signs of systemic illness.
2. Discuss parental anxieties, and to take a brief medical, genetic and social history, seeking information that may be relevant to the future health and development of the baby.
3. Provide advice on matters such as feeding, attendance at baby clinics and immunisation.

4 Note and advise on minor abnormalities about which parents may otherwise worry (see Table 2.1).

Table 2.1 Common conditions of little clinical importance that may cause parental anxiety

(Many of these conditions are discussed in Chapter 7.)	
Skin lesions:	strawberry naevi – which take a few days to appear
	'stork' marks on the eyelids and nape of the neck (Figure 2.2)
	milia (small white skin lesions on the face) (Figure 2.3)
	urticaria neonatorum (a rash on the trunk)
	'mongolian' blue spots (on the back in Asian babies)
	epithelial 'pearls' in the mouth (gums and palate)
Sub-conjunctival haemorrhage	
Cephalhaematoma	
Positional talipes	
Tongue-tie	
Natal teeth (Figure 2.4)	
Peripheral and traumatic cyanosis	
Breast enlargement	
Oral and vulval mucosal tags	
Sacral dimple	
Eyelid oedema	
Hydrocele	
Physiological jaundice	
Skin tags and diminutive accessory digits	

Suggested scheme for routine clinical examination

The following scheme of physical examination is in common use. It is not directed at diagnosing symptomatic illness and it assumes that gross external abnormalities have been detected already. It is performed in the presence of the mother so that the doctor can explain what is being done.

Measurements

Weight, length and occipito-frontal head circumference are evaluated for gestation by reference to a centile chart.

General observation

Check that the infant exhibits the normal flexed posture and that limb movements are symmetrical. Ask yourself whether the infant's appearance is normal or whether there are dysmorphic features. Look for pallor, cyanosis, jaundice, skin rashes and birth marks.

Head

Look for abnormalities in shape of the cranium, making allowance for the moulding that occurs during birth, and assess the tension of the anterior fontanelle and the width of the sutures. The normal fontanelle varies in size considerably but if the fontanelle feels unusually full or if there is more than 1 cm of sutural separation, hydrocephalus should be suspected and a brain ultrasound scan undertaken.

Face

Look for normal facial movements and signs of facial nerve palsy.

Eyes

Asymmetry of eye size is always abnormal. It may mean that one eye is unusually small, due to congenital infection or developmental defect, or that the other eye is abnormally large, suggesting congenital glaucoma which is an emergency. The eye should be checked for signs of infection and the lenses for cataracts. There is no need to perform retinoscopy routinely.

Nose

The nose is the baby's principal airway and should be checked for signs of obstruction.

Mouth

A baby will usually open its mouth if a gentle downward pressure is applied to the chin. The palate should be inspected for clefts and palpated for submucosal clefts. The oral cavity should be checked for the presence of natal teeth, cysts or thrush (*Candida* infection – see Chapter 8).

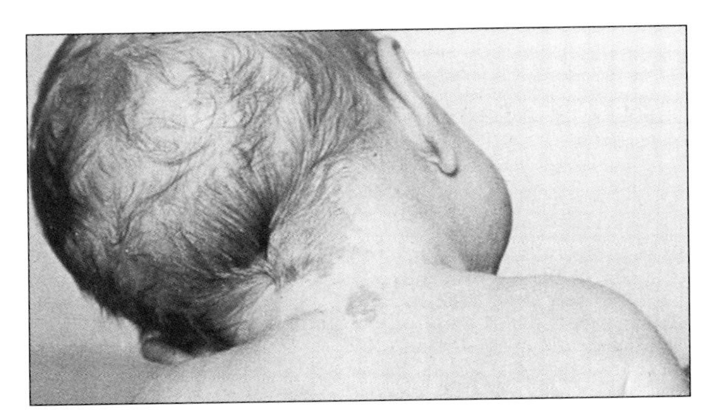

Figure 2.2

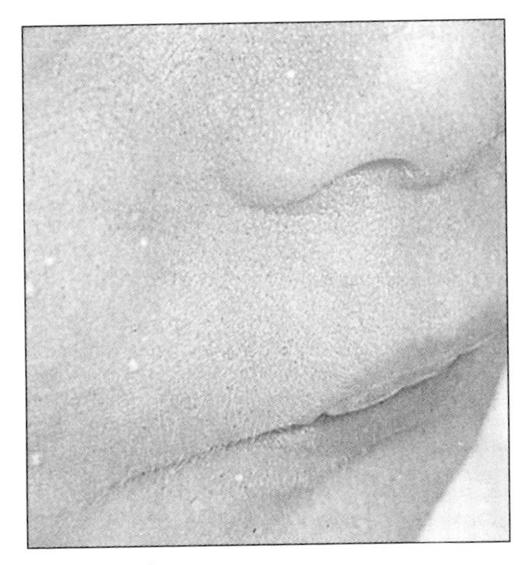

Figure 2.3

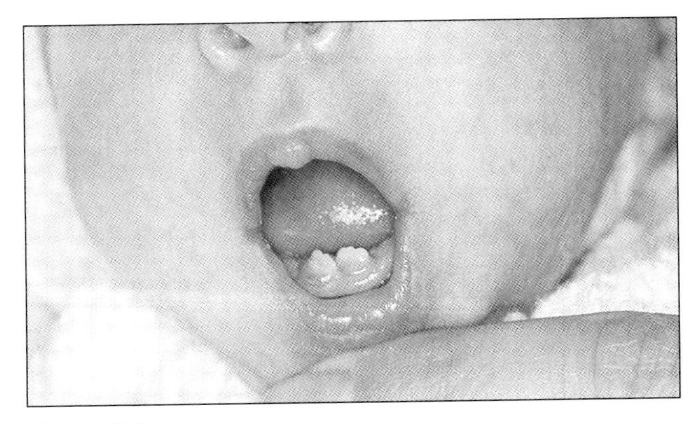

Figure 2.4

Jaw

An unusually small or recessed mandible can be a source of feeding difficulty or occasionally of respiratory obstruction.

Neck

The neck should be quickly palpated for signs of thyroid enlargement. The normal thyroid gland is impalpable. A sternomastoid tumour is not usually present at birth.

Chest

The normal respiratory rate is higher than in the adult but no healthy infant should sustain a rate of greater than 60 breaths per minute. All tachypnoeic babies merit immediate careful assessment. There is little to be gained by routinely auscultating the lungs of babies who are pink and not breathless.

Heart

Note the side of the chest on which the apex is felt, and the forcefulness of the cardiac impulse. Heart murmurs at this age are very common and relate to the transition from fetal to adult circulatory pattern. It is difficult even for experienced cardiologists to sort out clinically significant murmurs from non-significant ones. It is important, however, not to generate widespread parental anxiety by investigating and following up all babies with a heart murmur. Selection can be improved by auscultating the heart at the second examination when many transitional murmurs will have disappeared. As a rule, soft, mid or early systolic murmurs are likely to be insignificant, whereas diastolic, pan-systolic, or very loud murmurs are likely to be important.

Abdomen

The yield of positive findings from routine abdominal palpation is low. The liver edge is usually palpable about 2 cm below the right costal margin and the spleen can be tipped in at least 20% of normal babies. The lower poles of both kidneys may be palpable. It is worth checking that there is no bladder enlargement (which may indicate posterior urethral valves in male infants).

GROINS

Ensure that both femoral pulses can be felt, as their absence may denote coarctation of the aorta. Check for hernias.

GENITALIA

Check that the genitalia are clearly either male of female. Virilisation of the female fetus is accompanied by cliteromegaly and fusion of the labia (Figure 2.5) Indeterminate sex is a difficult problem for parents to come to terms with and a detailed account of how the problem is to be investigated and resolved should be provided as a matter of urgency. In the male, check that the testes are in the scrotum and that the urethral meatus is where it should be. In the female, check that there is no bulging of the perineum or vulva, which may be due to imperforate hymen and remember that a little vaginal bleeding or discharge of clear mucus are both normal phenomena secondary to the influence of maternal and placental hormones.

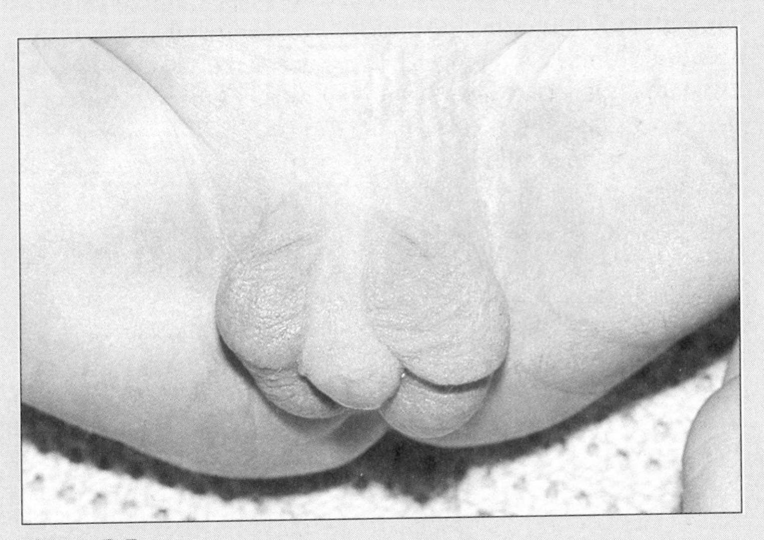

Figure 2.5

ANUS

Ask if the baby has passed meconium and check that the anus is present and normally located. There is no need for routine rectal examination.

Spine

Turn the baby prone and look for scoliosis. The entire dorsal midline should be inspected for lumps, naevi, hairy patches, pits or sinuses, each of which may be a surface indicator of spinal cord abnormality

Hips

Examination of the hips is aimed at detecting either dislocated or dislocatable joints. The value of diagnosis at this stage is that immediate treatment with splinting always brings about an excellent long-term result whereas later treatment does not. Testing the hips is best left to the end of the routine examination as it may upset the baby.

To test for dislocation, the hips and knees are flexed and the knees brought together. The hips are then abducted while the examiner feels for the femoral head flipping forward into the acetabulum. This is known as Ortolani's test (Figure 2.6).

To test for dislocatability, the opposite manoeuvre is employed. That is, the flexed hips are adducted while gentle posterior pressure is applied. The examiner feels for the femoral head slipping backwards out of the acetabulum. This is known as Barlow's test.

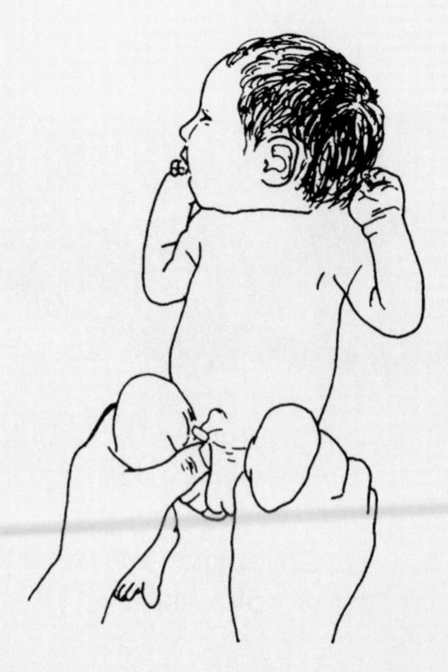

Figure 2.6

Central nervous system

A full neurological assessment of the newborn is time-consuming and demands considerable skill and experience. It is reasonable to limit the routine clinical examination to the detection of gross neurological abnormality, which can largely be excluded by observing the spontaneously moving baby while conducting the rest of the examination.

If it is concluded that follow-up is needed the parents should receive a detailed explanation.

Biochemical screening

Routine screening on dried blood-spots is carried out for phenylketonuria and hypothyroidism in all UK hospitals. Some also screen for cystic fibrosis and it is likely that this will become more common as treatment for the condition improves. (See Chapter 11.)

3 The preterm infant

Since the early 1970s the prognosis for the preterm infant has improved dramatically, while the rate of preterm delivery has increased only marginally. Relatively small in number, this group now constitutes an enormously important population in perinatal medicine. Considerable amounts of research and clinical time have been brought to bear upon the outcome. The improved prognosis has brought with it the responsibility for a parallel increase in the efforts invested in their care. The ultimate answer is the abolition of preterm delivery. In the meantime perinatal medicine must continue to focus upon the prevention of preterm delivery, the optimal management of inevitable delivery and care of the preterm infant.

Definition and incidence

The exact incidence of preterm delivery in England and Wales is not known, as gestation is not routinely recorded. Around 700 000 babies are born in England and Wales each year. Of these, 7% are low birthweight (<2.5 kg) and 1% are very low birthweight (<1.5 kg). Less than 0.5% are born under 1 kg. An estimated 6% are born preterm (<37 completed weeks' gestation). Figures from Scotland, where gestation is recorded, show that 0.3% are born between 20 and 27 weeks' gestation. Of the total NHS budget for England and Wales (£2.2 billion), approximately 0.05% (£116 m) is currently spent on the care of infants of less than 31 weeks' gestation.

Difficulties with definition have been compounded by the changes in the prognosis of the immature infant. The survival of infants of less than 28 weeks made this gestation untenable as a limit of viability and it has been changed to 24 weeks. Survival of infants under 500 g is unusual, but no longer exceptional. Currently, infants born with any signs of life are recorded as neonatal deaths. Those born without signs of life with a birthweight of 500 g or more are stillborn, and those with a birthweight of less than 500 g are recorded as abortions. It has now become apparent in the collection of health statistics that definitions based on gestation are necessary, but these have not yet evolved.

The revolution in infertility treatment has brought great happiness to many couples. Although the rate of high-order multiples is low, their impact upon neonatal medicine has been clear. Triplets, for example, with a constant rate of 1 in 10 000 since records began, have more than trebled in incidence since 1985 (Figure 3.1). Multiples are clearly more likely to deliver preterm and as a result have a high perinatal mortality rate (27 per 1000 for twins) compared with naturally conceived singletons. Happily the most recent advances in infertility management allow successful treatment with a lower incidence of multiples.

Aetiology

The cause of most preterm delivery remains unknown. It is, however, now possible to define a high-risk population. Most forms of social and or socio-economic disadvantage predispose towards preterm delivery. The mechanism of this is poorly understood but

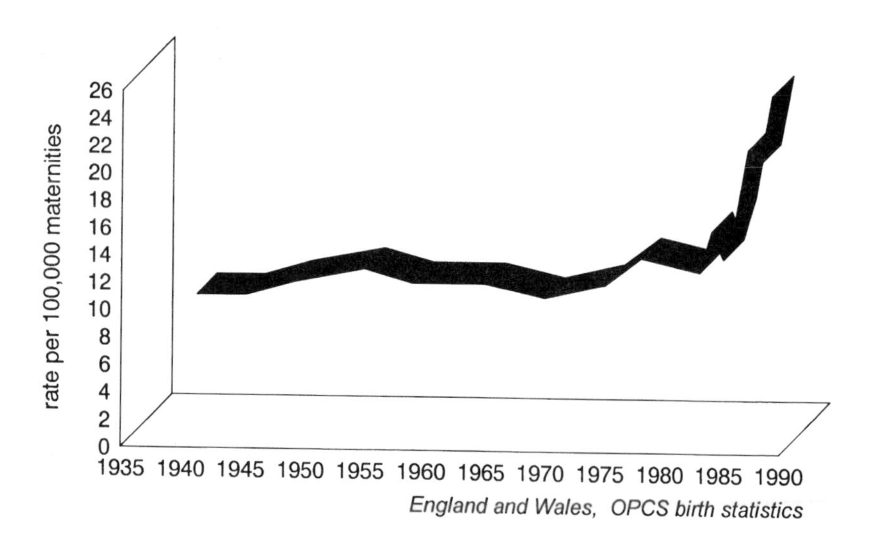

Figure 3.1 Rate of maternities resulting in triplet or higher order birth

well established across national and ethnic boundaries. A mother's personal or family history of preterm delivery is important and pregnancy in the very young or older mother is at increased risk of early delivery. Vaginal bleeding in early pregnancy and smoking are associated factors.

More specific maternal causes include pre-eclampsia. This may lead to induction of preterm labour, as pre-eclampsia is only curable by delivery and this is also true of other major adverse events during pregnancy. Cervical incompetence, uterine abnormalities, maternal infection and amnionitis may all result in preterm delivery. Fetal causes include multiple pregnancy, intrauterine hypoxia, and fetal abnormality.

Management around the time of delivery

Increasingly our knowledge of the fetus and mother allows anticipation of preterm delivery. When this is so there are a number of important considerations. Following spontaneous onset of preterm labour, it may be possible to delay delivery and tocolysis should be considered. Once preterm delivery is thought likely or inevitable, joint discussions between obstetric and neonatal staff are imperative. Delivery should be conducted in a hospital capable of providing the full level of intensive care which it is anticipated will be necessary. Transfer of a fetus *in utero* to a neonatal intensive care centre, providing this is safe for mother and baby, is infinitely preferable to postnatal transfer of the baby with all its incumbent difficulties and risks. There is no longer any doubt concerning the benefit of antenatal steroids before preterm delivery. Debate continues as to whether they should be used in the extremely preterm fetus and in the fetus who is only a few weeks preterm, but in most dexamethasone should be given. Greatest benefit will accrue when the dexamethasone course is started between 48 hours and seven days before delivery. Other antenatal treatments aimed at induction of lung maturation are not yet widely used, and in the future may include the use of thyroid-releasing hormone.

The preterm infant should be delivered in a pre-warmed room with adequate resuscitation equipment. At gestations less than 32 weeks, two paediatricians may wish to attend and as much notice as possible will earn considerable gratitude.

The essentials of management on the delivery suite are the same as those for the term infant (see Chapter 2). Hypoxia should be avoided and, of crucial importance in the preterm, hypothermia avoided. Heat loss in the preterm infant is rapid and even if advanced resuscitation is required, time should be taken to dry and wrap the newborn infant in warm towels. Hypothermia precipitates acidosis and both will act to reduce surfactant activity. After resuscitation the preterm infant should promptly be transferred to an appropriate level of care, for close observation and monitoring.

Problems of prematurity

Around 60% of very low birthweight infants require neonatal intensive care and assisted ventilation. Their management is complex and challenging and discussed at length in many worthy tomes. Problems of the preterm infant arise as a result of organ immaturity and in all but the most immature infant this is functional rather than structural immaturity. Our aim is to give a brief discussion of some of the more common problems.

Poor thermoregulation

Hypothermia should be avoided. The preterm infant may lose heat more rapidly by a number of mechanisms. Thin, poorly keratinsed skin allows high evaporative losses of water and heat, and also high losses through radiation. The infant's ability to adapt to changes in temperature is less good and reserves of energy and brown fat are low. A warm environment may be provided by an overhead heater or an incubator. Humidity allows better control of temperature and reduction of losses. The aim is a thermo-neutral environment, one where energy is neither expended in cooling nor keeping warm. The more immature and the lower the birthweight the higher the environmental temperature in the thermo-neutral range.

Feeding problems

At the lower limits of preterm survival the gut is extremely immature. Functional maturity equivalent to the term infant, including the ability to suck and swallow is not achieved until around 34 weeks' gestation. A discussion of the nutritional requirement is presented in the chapter on nutrition (see Chapter 5).

Jaundice

See Chapter 6.

Respiratory distress syndrome

Respiratory distress syndrome (RDS) is used synonymously with hyaline membrane disease. In this condition functional immaturity of the lungs has profound effects upon respiratory mechanics. An important component of this is a lack of surfactant. Endogenous surfactants are composed of a number of phospholipids and small amounts of protein. Surfactant is distributed in a thin layer of the alveolar surface and acts to reduce surface tension, allowing good compliance and ease of expansion of the lung. During expiration surfactant acts to splint open the alveoli and prevent their collapse. The absence of this therefore results in low compliance, with stiff lungs and a tendency towards atelectasis, with uniform shadowing and air bronchograms on the radiograph (Figure 3.2). Avoidance of hypoxia, hypothermia, severe stress, and antenatal administration of steroids are all important preventive measures.

The natural history of surfactant deficient RDS is of deterioration over the first day, followed by recovery as surfactant is produced naturally with consequent improvement in lung compliance. The most important principle of management during this period therefore is the maintenance of homeostasis. Ventilatory support is often needed, aiming to maintain tight control of gas exchange. Arterial

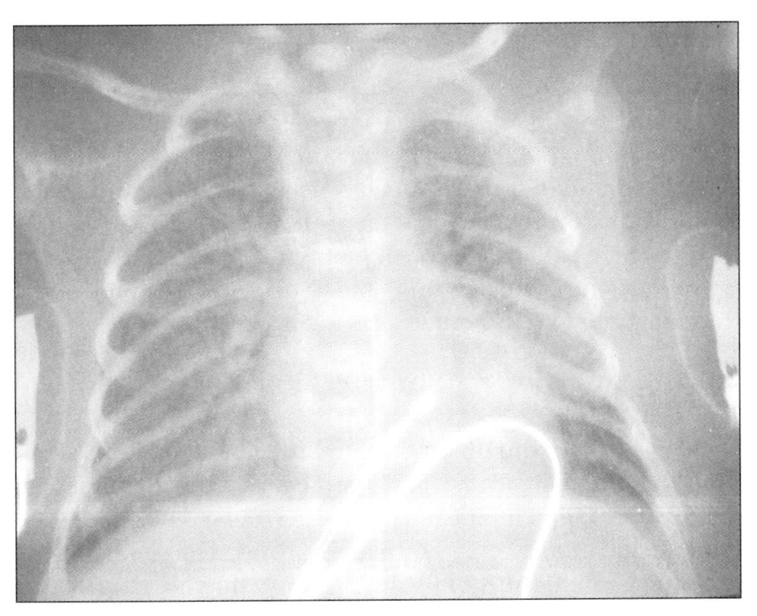

Figure 3.2

oxygen, for example, should be monitored continuously, and hypoxia and hyperoxia avoided assiduously. Equally important during this phase is careful attention to many other factors, including other blood gases, blood pressure, fluid and electrolytes, haemoglobin and so on.

Recent years have brought major advances in many features of management of RDS. Surfactant may now be administered. This has been shown in large multicentre randomised trials to reduce neonatal mortality by 40%. Surfactant is given through an endotracheal tube soon after birth and during the first 24 hours. There are a number of different preparations.

Bronchopulmonary dysplasia

Bronchopulmonary dysplasia or chronic pulmonary insufficiency of prematurity is the consequence of preterm delivery and artificial ventilation. In this condition scarring and patchy atelectasis in the lung may lead to a long-term oxygen requirement, for a number of weeks, or even months. These infants are predisposed towards later chest infection and to asthma-like problems. Much attention in neonatal intensive care is currently being directed towards reduction of this problem.

Infection

(See also Chapter 8.)

All preterm infants have immaturity of immune function. Some of the passive immunity from maternal antibodies is not achieved and cell-mediated immunity is less good. Infections are common particularly in the infant receiving prolonged intensive care. The commonest offending organism is the skin commensal *Staphylococcus epidermidis*. Invasive procedures such as intubation and central venous cannulation are important predisposing factors.

Apnoea

Immaturity of the respiratory centre in the preterm infant produces a periodic pattern of breathing. In the more immature infant periods of shallow breathing or apnoea may produce hypoxia or bradycardia. These apnoeic attacks may be frequent. Most commonly they are simply due to immaturity but the onset of apnoeic attacks in any newborn infant may be a marker of acute illness, and this should be considered. Occasionally airway obstruction, seizures and gastro-oesophageal reflux may mimic apnoeic attacks. Apnoea due to immaturity responds well to stimulation of the respiratory centre through the administration of xanthines. The safest and most effective one of these is caffeine but aminophylline and theophylline may be used.

Intracranial infarction/haemorrhage

Lack of auto-regulation of cerebral blood flow results in failure to maintain brain perfusion during hypotension. This predisposes the immature infant to hypoxic/ischaemic brain damage. The commonest pathology seen here is periventricular leucomalacia (Figure 3.3). In this condition cystic lesions appear on cranial ultrasound in the areas adjacent to the lateral ventricles. Intracranial haemorrhage is more common. Small bleeds in the subependymal area, the situation of the germinal matrix, occur commonly in the more immature infant and are usually benign. Larger bleeds into the ventricles may produce acute illness or be followed by hydrocephalus (Figure 3.4). Bleeds into the brain substance, periventricular bleeding, are more likely to carry an adverse neurological prognosis. The ability of cranial ultrasound to define the extent and nature of these events is now considerable. Experience allows prognostication, and rational decision making regarding the merits of intensive care.

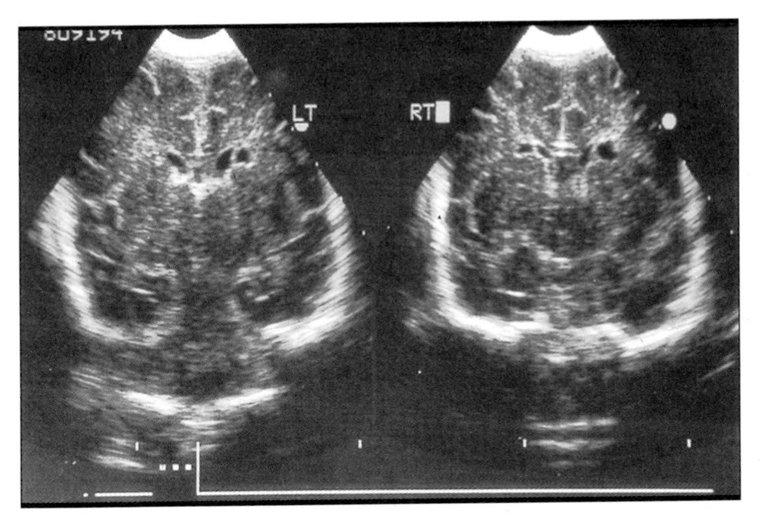

Figure 3.3

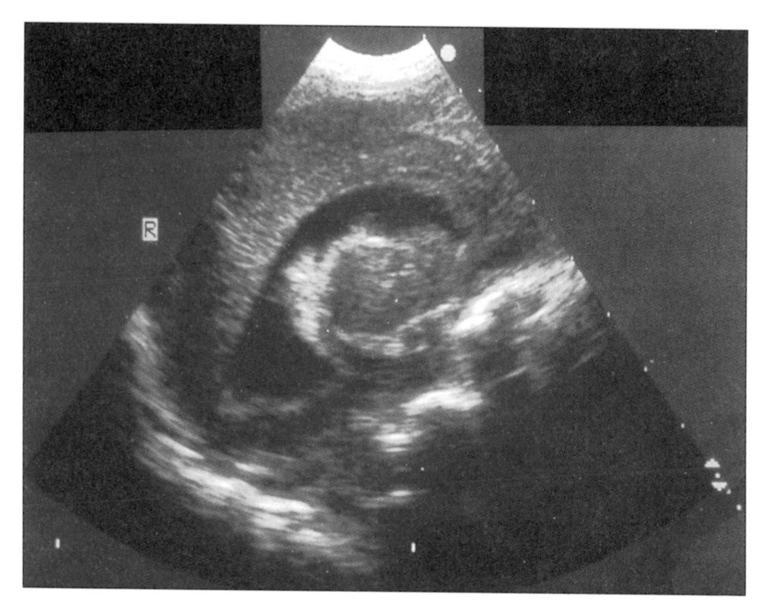

Figure 3.4

Patent ductus arteriosus

Persistent patency of the ductus arteriosus (see Chapter 1) occurs commonly in the infant below 32 weeks' gestation who is receiving intensive care. Symptoms may result from the need for increased cardiac output and consequent heart failure or from poor organ perfusion due to circulatory changes. The patent ductus may be closed by the administration of indomethacin in the first two weeks. If the ductus remains patent it will often close spontaneously in time; alternatively surgery may be required when the ductus arteriosus is contributing to ventilatory requirements.

Necrotising enterocolitis

Necrotising enterocolitis (NEC) is an ischaemic condition of the gut with secondary infection. Presentation may be non-specific but classical signs include abdominal distension, and blood and mucus in the stool. Plain abdominal X-ray will show gaseous distension, thickened loops of bowel and the presence of gas bubbles in the wall of the bowel – pneumotosis intestinalis (Figure 3.5). Complications include perforation, peritonitis and collapse. Management includes with-

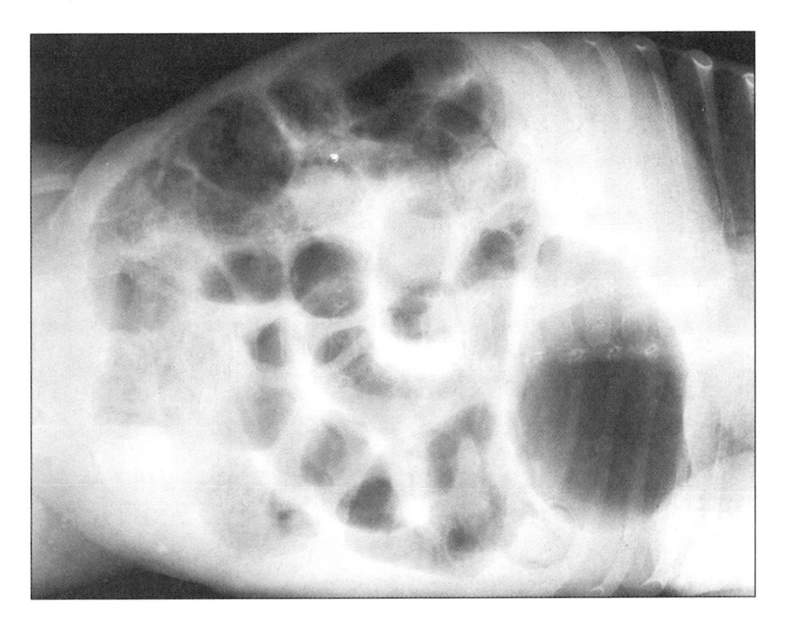

Figure 3.5

drawal of milk feeds if these have been used, antibiotics including metronidazole to treat sepsis, and supportive management with adequate volume expansion, and close monitoring. The presence of ischaemic bowel or complications requires surgery and gut resection. The condition is almost completely limited to the very low birthweight infant.

Retinopathy of prematurity

Retinopathy of prematurity (ROP), previously known as retrolental fibroplasia, occurs in infants less than 32 weeks' gestation, who require intensive care. Oxygen toxicity is well recognised as an important factor, but it is now clear that this condition may occur in infants where there is no evidence of hyperoxia. Management involves screening of all very low birthweight infants. Early phases of ROP will resolve spontaneously. As the disease advances, neovascularisation occurs on the periphery of the retinae with risk of vitreous haemorrhage and/ or retinal detachment. The management then is of cryosurgery or retinal laser treatment of the affected areas. Blindness secondary to ROP is now very rare, and around 1–3% of very low birthweight infants require active treatment.

Metabolic problems

Renal immaturity, high water losses, poor glucose homeostasis, and intensive care all conspire to produce a wide variety of problems. Close monitoring and anticipation of problems is essential. The commonest metabolic condition of long-term consequence is metabolic bone disease. This condition, previously thought to be due to vitamin D deficiency, is now recognised to be the consequence of inadequate mineral supply. During fetal life calcium and phosphate are actively transported to the fetus across the placenta in quantities which are not possible to attain in postnatal life. The result is poor skeletal mineralisation. This problem may be reduced by the use of appropriate supplements of phosphate and calcium (see Chapter 5).

Prognosis

Survival rates for the term infant have improved slowly during this century. In England and Wales the overall perinatal mortality rate is now around 8 per 1000. In term infants, free of congenital abnormality, this falls to 2–3 per 1000. Since the mid-1970s there has been a radical change in the outcome of the preterm infant. Neonatal survival rate for infants between 1.5 and 2.5 kg are now only marginally lower than those of normal birthweight infants. For infants between 1.0 and 1.5 kg rates have risen from 40% to figures in excess of 80% in most centres reporting their results (Figure 3.6). The change in outlook for the infant between 500 g and 1000 g is still more dramatic. Here survival was rare before the 1980s and currently exceeds 60% in major centres. The principal determinant of survival is gestation. Female sex carries advantage.

With improved mortality attention is now focusing on morbidity. Infants between 1.5 and 2.5 kg seldom have long-term problems as a consequence of their preterm delivery, but this becomes a far greater issue in the very low birthweight infant. The principal concerns are neurological sequelae and chronic lung problems. Retinopathy has been discussed previously. Figures for these outcomes, and in particular neurodevelopmental outcome are difficult to produce and hard to interpret. Since it is only possible to judge a child's neurological outcome after a minimum of two and possibly five years, such figures cannot reflect current neonatal practice. Improved high-quality intensive care together with the selective use of treatment for infants with a recognised poor prognosis means that in surviving very low birthweight infants, severe handicap is low at around 2–3%. Overall

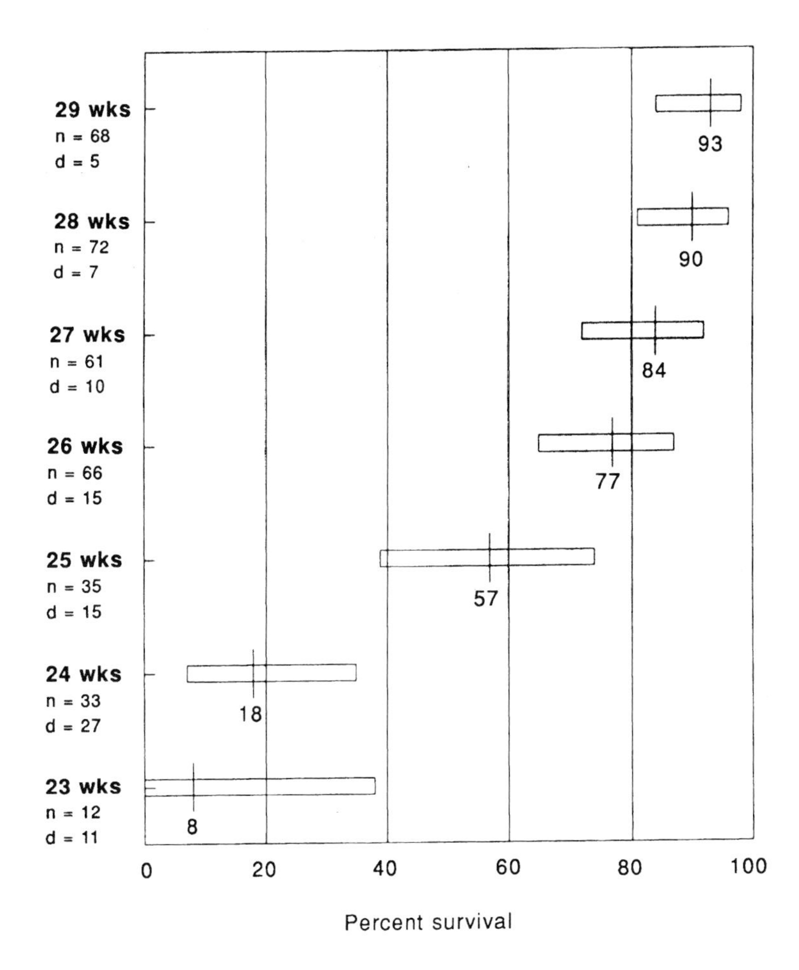

Figure 3.6 Probability of survival <30 weeks' gestation. Graph shows means and 95% confidence intervals

most series report an incidence, in this group, of any significant neurological problem of 8–12%. The commonest disorders are hearing problems and disorders of motor development, notably spastic cerebral palsy. Follow-up studies in older graduates of intensive care have suggested that a further group may suffer learning disabilities and have a distribution of intellect shifted to the left compared with the average population. Interpretation of these data is compounded by the predisposition towards preterm delivery brought by social disadvantage, making selection of appropriate controls difficult.

Recent attention has focused upon the infant of 25 weeks' gestation and less. Here the outcome currently reflects the figures previously seen for the infant of 28 weeks' gestation. It is, however, the general view that further strides into earlier gestation are unlikely. Severe handicap may occur in 15–20% of the infants born in this group, although in excess of 50% of survivors may be adversely affected. The ethical problem presented to us in perinatal medicine is clear.

4 Intrauterine growth retardation

> *'He could have been put inside a quart pot,' his mother is supposed to have said, and for a few days Isaac was so delicate he was not expected to live.*
>
> Patrick Moore, *Isaac Newton* (1957)

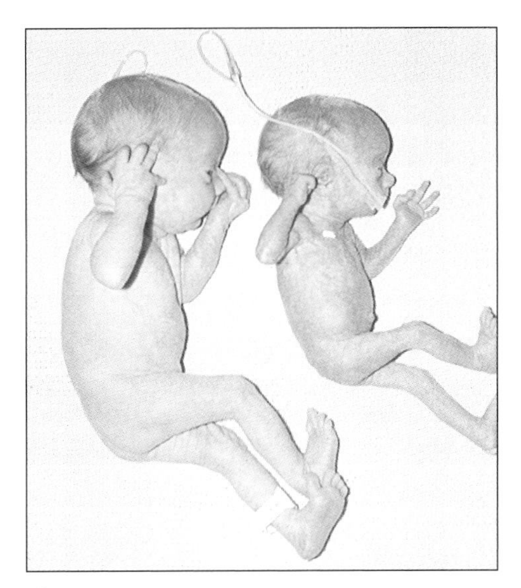

Figure 4.1

In fetal medicine and paediatrics, the measurement of growth is integral to the assessment of the child before or after birth. The essential components of this are an accurate and reproducible method of measurement, a set of validated reference data appropriate to the population being studied, and an understanding of the normal pattern of growth. Modern ultrasound allows a high degree of accuracy in fetal measurement, although this may be confounded by problems such as fetal position or oligohydramnios, which should be borne in mind when interpreting the results.

The term 'intrauterine growth retardation' (IUGR) is often a misnomer. It implies a knowledge of the genetic growth potential of any single fetus, and serial growth data demonstrating a fall across the growth centiles. Nevertheless the term is used here to imply fetal growth measurements at or below the lower end of the normal range. 'Small for dates' or 'small for gestational age' (SGA) are terms used to describe newborn infants. There is no universal accepted definition. A weight below the 10th centile or more than two standard deviations below the median for the gestation is commonly used. Accurate incidence figures are not available. Of 700 000 deliveries each year in England and Wales, a steady 7% of infants are low birthweight (>2.5 kg), and up to a third of these are SGA. These infants form a group of considerable interest in fetal and neonatal medicine.

Aetiology

Any problem with the fetus, placenta or maternal health (Figure 4.2) may predispose to IUGR. In a substantial proportion of infants who are SGA, no clear explanation is found.

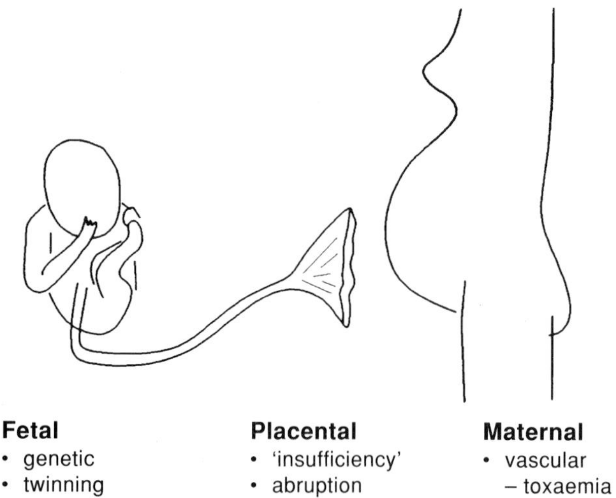

Figure 4.2

The fetus

An important determinant here is the genetic component and the stature of the parents. In some centres the presence of poor growth, particularly if there are any detectable abnormalities, is an indication for fetal chromosome studies, although, in the singleton infant, fetal abnormalities have been found in less than 10% of those with a birthweight more than two standard deviations below the median. Multiple pregnancies may have a profound effect upon fetal growth, through problems of placentation. Any other insults to the infant may be responsible and may include intrauterine infection (see Chapter 8) and irradiation.

The placenta

The diagnosis of placental insufficiency may be supported by the presence of gross or microscopic changes in the placenta, in terms of small size, infarction or abnormalities in placental vasculature. Placental abruption, malformations, and rare disorders of placental metabolism may also be implicated.

Maternal health

Pre-eclampsia, or other types of hypertensive disease, are present in between a third and a half of pregnancies with IUGR. The effect of smoking upon the placental vasculature is well established, and is reflected in a 10% reduction in median birthweight seen in mothers who smoke at least ten cigarettes a day. Some aspects of general maternal health may affect fetal growth. Severe chronic illness may have an effect *per se* or may affect the baby through a nutritional effect on the mother. Generally, however, maternal nutrition must be very poor to produce problems in fetal growth. In the Dutch famine during World War Two an effect upon fetal growth was seen only when intake was reduced below 1500 calories per day. Drugs, given therapeutically, or drugs of abuse may adversely affect fetal growth. Mothers from the extremes of maternal age or from lower social economic classes are more likely to have growth retarded infants.

Perinatal assessment

The decisions surrounding mode and timing of delivery are exquisitely difficult and require full discussion between obstetric and paediatric specialists. *In utero* the infant runs a risk of cerebral hypoxia (see Chapter 1), poor brain growth, and intrauterine death. Frequently this decision must be balanced against the known consequences of preterm delivery (see Chapter 3). Serial ultrasound measurements of head and abdominal circumference are often helpful. Increasingly the monitoring of fetal movements and cardiotocograph is being enhanced by the assessment of the fetal biophysical profile. Doppler blood velocities may be helpful, and assessment of liquor volume is important. The threshold for delivery falls as gestation advances.

Choice of mode of delivery may be influenced by awareness of the lack of fetal and placental reserve. Hypoxia during labour is more common in the SGA infant. Continuous monitoring for fetal distress is justified. Meconium staining of the liquor is common in this group, but the meconium aspiration syndrome (see Chapter 1) is much less common than in the post-mature AGA infant. There is some evidence that the preterm infant who is SGA is less likely to have severe surfactant deficient lung disease. No opportunity, however, should be missed to give the preterm infant steroids before delivery.

Assessment at birth

Accurate measurements of weight and length are possible shortly after birth. Early measurement of head circumference may be inaccurate due to moulding and it should be reassessed later in the first week. Growth retardation may have uneven effects on different organs. The majority of SGA babies have a pattern of asymmetric growth retardation, with relative preservation of brain weight and body length whilst body weight and the weight of internal organs such as the liver are more markedly reduced (Figure 4.3). Characteristically this results from fetal undernutrition later in pregnancy, and the ultimate growth prognosis is better than that seen with the symmetric pattern. In symmetrical growth retardation all organs are similarly affected. A proportion of these infants are normal, genetically small individuals, whilst some may be congenitally abnormal and may have any one of a large number of syndromic or chromosomal abnormalities (see Chapter 7) associated with IUGR. Alternatively symmetrical intrauterine growth retardation may occur when fetal nutrition is more severely affected from earlier on in pregnancy. The prognosis here is clearly dependent upon the underlying pathophysiology.

There is no clear or accepted definition of symmetry and asymmetry. The ponderal index (weight/length^3 x 100) may be used, or simpler measurements such as mid-arm circumference related to head circumference. These measurements are of considerable importance in research studies, but are not routinely performed in clinical practice.

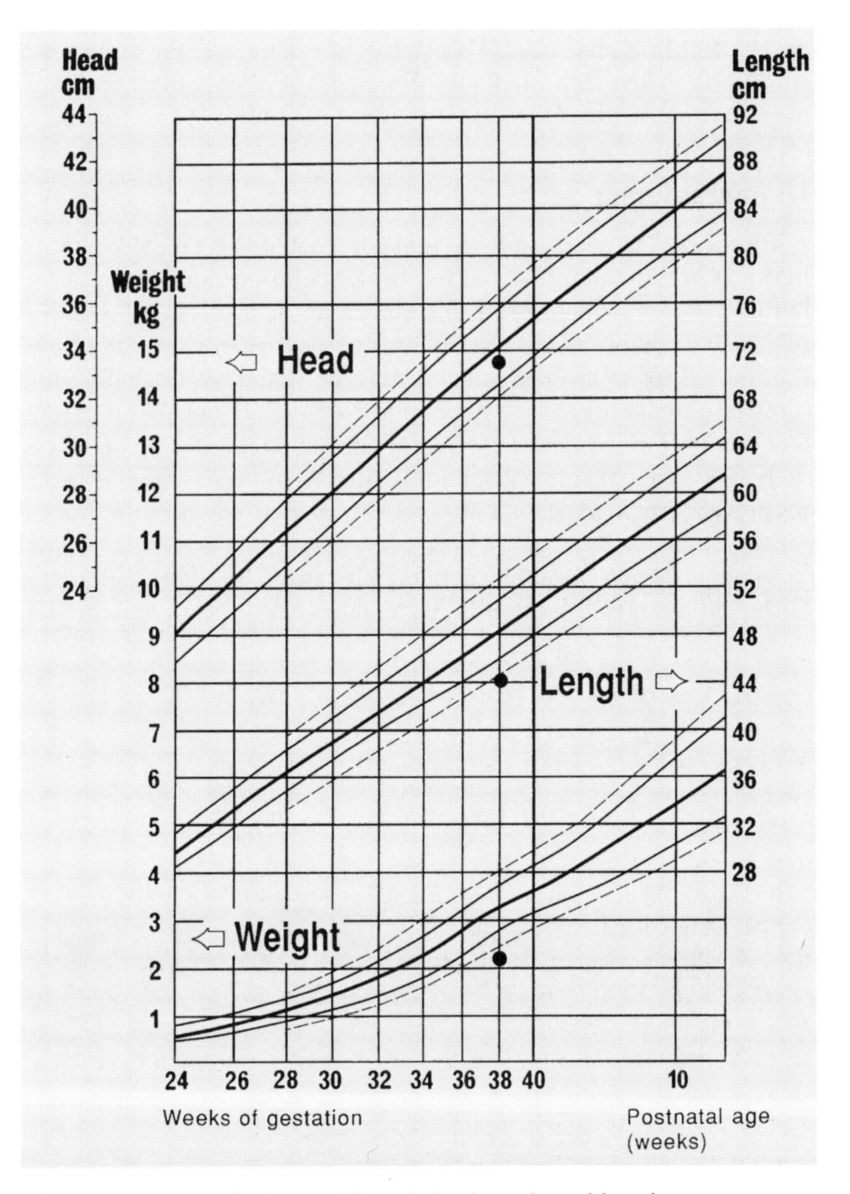

Figure 4.3 Growth chart with weight, length and head circumference from an infant with asymmetric IUGR

The neonatal consequences of fetal malnutrition

Cerebral hypoxia

As discussed previously, the SGA infant is at increased risk of brain hypoxia in the antenatal and perinatal periods. The clinical management of this is discussed elsewhere (see Chapter 1). Follow-up studies have demonstrated a poorer neurodevelopmental outcome even in those without clinical evidence of hypoxia.

Hypoglycaemia

A number of factors conspire to make hypoglycaemia more common in the SGA baby (Figure 4.4). Liver weight and stores of glycogen are reduced. Basal metabolic rate and substrate use is increased with the relatively large brain and red cell mass. These infants may also have limited ability to oxidise fat and may be hyperinsulinaemic with reduced gluconeogenesis. Symptomatic hypoglycaemia is dangerous and there is now evidence of adverse neurological outcome in infants with a blood sugar below 2.5 mmol/l. Steps therefore should be taken to prevent hypoglycaemia in this group and to monitor for its presence.

Hypoglycaemia should be actively prevented in infants below the 10th centile for their gestation. Hypoglycaemia is best prevented by

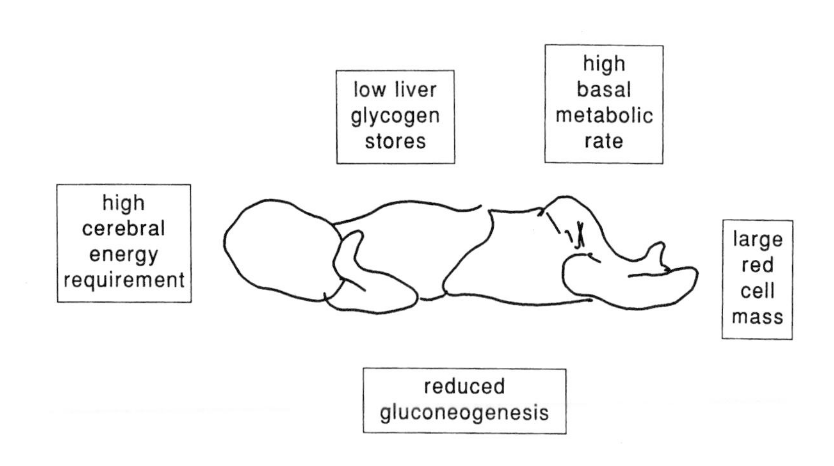

Figure 4.4 Factors leading to hypoglycaemia in the SGA infant

early and regular feeding. The first feed should be given within two hours of delivery. This is, therefore, one of the few indications for supplementing the baby whose mother wishes to breastfeed. Standard formula feed at 60–90 ml/kg/day given three hourly will prevent most hypoglycaemia. Low birthweight formula (see Chapter 5) may be used in infants under 2.5 kg and has a greater carbohydrate content. In infants whose mothers wish to avoid exposure to cow's milk protein, dextrose water may be used but is much less satisfactory. Blood sugar should be monitored frequently using a stix test before each feed over the first 48 hours, or until the problem has resolved. Problems with hypoglycaemia are most common in the first 48–72 hours, and thereafter most SGA infants may be fed following a normal regime.

Symptoms of hypoglycaemia are very variable. Infants may appear cold, sweaty, may be 'jittery', or may have subtle neurobehavioural changes. Any change in behaviour in a growth-retarded infant should be assumed to be hypoglycaemia until proven otherwise. Hypoglycaemia, a blood glucose less than 2.7 mmol/l, may result in severe neuroglycopenia and seizures. All symptomatic hypoglycaemia requires urgent management. Intravenous dextrose may be required, but care should be taken with bolus doses which may result in rebound hyperinsulinaemia and make problems worse. In symptomatic hypoglycaemia 5 ml/kg of 10% dextrose (0.5 g/kg/glucose) may be given, followed by a 10% dextrose infusion at 90 ml/kg/day, providing 6 mg/kg/min of glucose. If higher concentrations of dextrose are required central venous access may be necessary, and if more than 12 mg/kg/min of glucose is required, hyperinsulinism, primary or secondary, should be considered. Here glucagon, hydrocortisone, diazoxide, somatostatin, or growth hormone may be used, and other rare causes of neonatal hypoglycaemia should be considered.

Poor thermoregulation

Hypothermia may occur as a consequence of the large surface area, increased basal metabolic rate, and diminished energy reserves. The infant is also less able to withstand the metabolic consequences of hypothermia. Care should be taken to avoid it.

Polycythaemia

In response to the relatively hypoxic intrauterine environment the

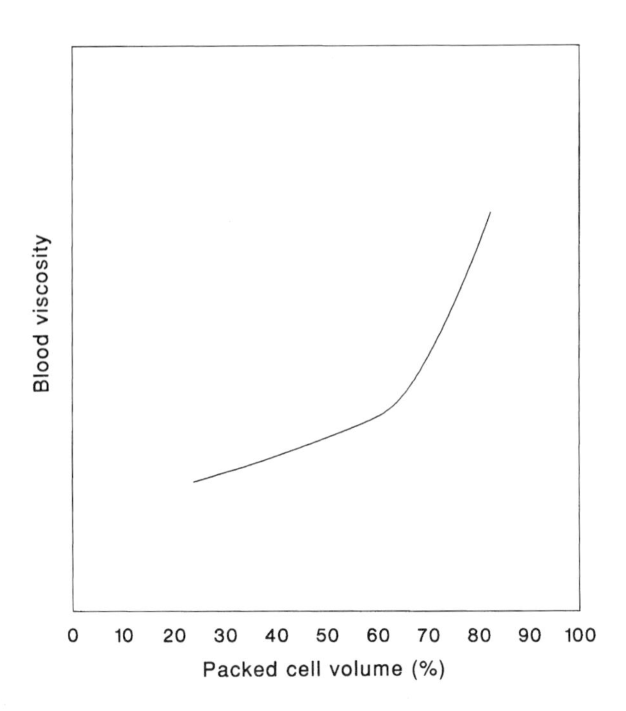

Figure 4.5 Relationship between blood viscosity and packed cell volume

SGA infant may increase his red cell mass. Whilst this may confer advantage in uterine life, postnatally this may cause problems (see also Chapter 9). Hypoglycaemia may be aggravated as mentioned above. Blood viscosity increases markedly as the packed cell volume (PCV) rises between 0.6 and 0.8 in a venous specimen (Figure 4.5). Compounded by decreased red cell deformability, local capillary stasis may occur and may lead to tissue infarction. The brain and gut are at particular risk. Central nervous system depression, fits, cortical venous thrombosis, heart failure, respiratory distress, persistent pulmonary hypertension, jaundice, hypoglycaeamia and necrotising enterocolitis are all possible. If the PCV is over 0.75 or in the presence of symptoms a reduction exchange transfusion is performed, replacing whole blood with plasma. In less severe polycythaemia temporary improvement may be produced with dextran.

Thrombocytopenia is also seen in association with polycythaemia and in infants with IUGR. Aetiology is unclear.

Cardiopulmonary problems

Persistent fetal circulation, the name given to the clinical picture in which pulmonary hypertension (see also Chapter 1) is maintained after delivery, resulting in intrapulmonary or intra-cardiac right to left shunting and persistent hypoxia, is more common in IUGR. This may be aggravated by the raised PCV. Occasionally the growth retarded infant coming from a chronically hypoxic environment may have diminished myocardial contractility. There may be a degree of cardiomegaly and right ventricular hypertrophy with tricuspid regurgitation and heart failure may be seen. Rarely acute left ventricular failure occurs almost exclusively in the infant who is ventilated as massive pulmonary haemorrhage. It presents with the appearance of bright red blood-stained pulmonary oedema welling up the endotracheal tube, and is managed with high pressure ventilation, cardiac support, and correction of any coagulation disorder.

Nutrition

The immediate nutritional problems of the growth retarded fetus are discussed above. In more marked retardation, Doppler studies of blood flow velocity in the fetus have shown re-distribution of cardiac output towards preferential perfusion of the brain and placenta. This results in relative deprivation of blood supply to the fetal gut. These infants then have a high rate of feeding problems, poor tolerance of milk feeds, and necrotising enterocolitis (see Chapter 3). There is evidence that this is more likely in severe IUGR, associated with oligohydramnios and fetal echogenic gut.

Long-term outcome

Even in the absence of overt neurological symptoms or other illness in the neonatal period, there is good evidence to suggest that these infants do not enjoy the same prognosis as their AGA counterparts. Asymmetrical IUGR carries a better prognosis for ultimate growth and neurodevelopment. Amongst symmetric IUGR some infants will have an underlying primary diagnosis and some will be normal healthy small infants. The prognosis for eventual growth in the SGA infant is variable, but complete catch-up postnatally occurs in the minority. The ability on fetal assessment to predict and prevent long-term growth or neurodevelopmental adverse outcome, is an area of considerable interest and future research.

5 Nutrition and infant feeding

There is no finer investment for any community than putting milk into babies.
Winston Churchill (1943)

A nutritional regime comprises, principally, water, energy from carbohydrate and fats, proteins, minerals, trace elements and vitamins. Adequate nutrition is essential to achieve normal growth, neurodevelopment, and health. The whole bewilderingly complex task is achieved with consummate ease by successful breastfeeding in the term infant.

The importance of nutrition cannot be overstated and in special groups, notably the preterm infants, it becomes a major challenge. Inadequacy of early nutrition may clearly affect growth, but also adversely influences long-term neurodevelopment and intelligence, and may be an important factor for later cardiovascular disease. Once established on milk the term infant requires 110 kcal/kg/day provided by 150–180 ml/kg/day of milk.

Breastfeeding

To breastfeed, women need motivation, education, leisure, privacy, freedom from pressure, and moral support, an approving public opinion, confidence in their female role, a husband that backs them up, and some help in the house. No wonder so few succeed in a culture that puts almost everything else first.
Professor John A. Davis

For almost all infants breastfeeding remains the gold standard.

Physiology

Preparation of the breast for production of milk occurs early in pregnancy through oestrogenic disinhibition of prolactin activity and increased prolactin production. After birth, breast-milk production is maintained by the frequent suckling, allowing contact and emptying the breast of milk. Ejection of milk from the breast is promoted by the 'let down' reflex. This is stimulated through the attachment of the baby to the breast or even through sight or sound of the baby, and mediated through the release of oxytocin, acting upon myoepithelial cells within the breast (Figure 5.1).

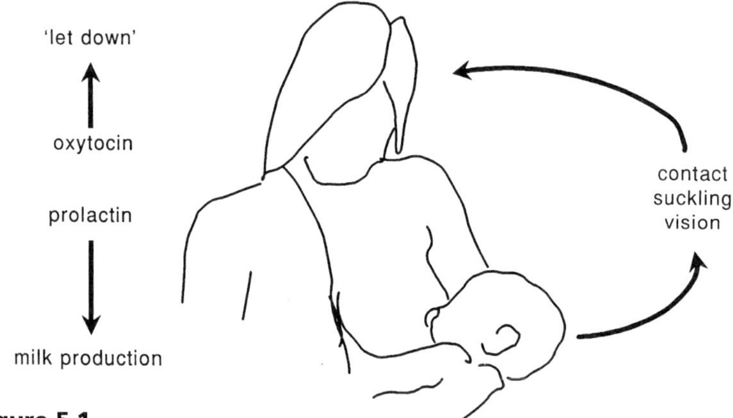

Figure 5.1

Breastfeeding is not an innate ability. Current rates of breastfeeding vary considerably around the United Kingdom but remain disappointingly low in some areas. A recent report from Scotland showed rates below 50% at one week. The repeated message from all research in this area is that the problem lies in education, our society's approach to breastfeeding and the paucity of practical and emotional support for the mother who wishes to breastfeed. Forceful and aggressive promotion of breastfeeding to the individual mother on the postnatal ward is not the answer. Improved provision and support for the mother who wishes to breastfeed and a continued drive towards general education remain the best hope.

Composition of breast milk

Breast milk provides adequate calories (110 kcal/kg/day) and protein (2.5 g/kg/day) in 150–180 ml/kg/day. It therefore contains around

70 kcal/100 ml. Calories are principally provided by carbohydrate and fat. Almost all carbohydrate (7 g/100 ml) is lactose. This disaccharide of glucose and galactose requires lactase for absorption. Lactase activity may be inadequate in the extremely preterm infants with recognised gut problems, and in the exquisitely rare condition, primary alactasia. Average fat content is 4 g/100 ml. Human breast milk contains relatively large amounts of unsaturated fatty acids and the essential fatty acids. Protein content of breast milk is considerably lower than cow's milk and a little lower than artificial formula. In breast milk, however, the biological availability of proteins is high, as whey proteins which are more soluble are dominant and casein, which precipitates from milk into a curd in an alkaline pH, is low (30%). Breast milk also contains minerals, vitamins and micro and trace elements. The amounts of iron in breast milk are extremely small, though, in a form that is readily absorbed and are adequate for a child up to the normal age of weaning onto solids. Breast milk contains and provides negligible amounts of vitamin K.

The non-nutritional components of breast milk have various functions. Several factors reduce the incidence of infection. Colostrum, the green-yellow fluid from the breast in the first few days, contains massive amounts of IgA, providing an 'immunological lining' for the gut. Lactoferrin binds iron, inhibiting the growth of coliforms in the gut and lysozyme and other non-antibody immune factors are also present. Breast milk contains growth factors, like epidermal growth factor and other biologically active messengers which promote gut motility. It is, indeed, 'a very messy pharmacological preparation'.

There is considerable variability in samples of breast milk. After colostrum early milk contains a relatively high calorie and protein content. 'Foremilk' at the beginning of the feed has a higher water content, whilst 'hindmilk' at the end of a feed, has a higher fat and calorie content. Mechanisms underlying these differences and their significance are not fully understood.

Common problems

Most problems with breastfeeding may be overcome by skilled support, help and direction. The incidence of sore or cracked nipples can be reduced by appropriate positioning of the infant, ensuring that the whole, or large amount, of the areola is within the infant's mouth and avoiding traction during separation of the infant from the breast. There is no reason to limit the length or frequency of the feeds. Some mothers find the use of a nipple shield or cream helpful.

Engorgement is common around seven days and may require removal of milk by manual expression or pump. Mastitis is most commonly not due to infection and breastfeeding may continue. Care should be taken to determine whether there is infection present, most commonly associated with damage to the nipple and in the case of true breast abscess, breastfeeding should cease.

In the infant, congenital abnormalities of the face or mouth may make breastfeeding more difficult. It is, however, amazing in the absence of neurological problems, how often infants with conditions such as bilateral cleft lip and palate may breastfeed successfully.

Advantages of breastfeeding

Breastfeeding provides a sterile, nutritionally ideal and readily available supply of milk for the baby, and once established is usually enjoyed by mother and baby. The health benefits over careful artificial formula feeding, in developed countries, are now being demon-

Table 5.1 Beneficial effects of breast milk

Advantage	*Current evidence*
Promotion of gut motility	Better tolerance of milk feeds in the preterm infant
Protection from necrotising enterocolitis	Partial or complete feeding with expressed breast milk makes NEC less likely in infants of birth weight <1850 g
Prevention of infection	Complete or partial breastfeeding for three months reduces subsequent likelihood of gastrointestinal and respiratory infection
Protection from allergy	Atopic symptoms are less likely over the first two–three years in infants with a family history of atopy
Intellectual benefit	Neurodevelopmental advantage and better intellectual outcome, even after allowance for socio-economic variables
Prevention of adult disease	Breastfeeding reduces likelihood of diabetes mellitus and ulcerative colitis

strated with greater scientific certainty (Table 5.1). Throughout the under-developed world, however, breastfeeding becomes an essential part of infant care and should continue until the age of two. In these countries, the artificially fed infant is 14 times more likely to die from diarrhoeal disease, and four times more likely to die from pneumonia.

Contraindications to breastfeeding

(See Table 5.2.)

The *British National Formulary* contains up-to-date recommendations for each individual drug. The number of drugs which are an absolute contraindication of breastfeeding is small. Examples include high-dose steroids, immuno-suppressants such as cyclosporin, radiopharmaceuticals, and cytotoxics. In some cases the drug may be avoided while in others the mother must be advised not to breastfeed. Some drugs (e.g. bromocriptine, calcitonin, high-dose thiazides) may inhibit lactation. Occasionally uncommon conditions may preclude use of certain agents (e.g. septrin in G6PD deficiency). Other contraindications to breastfeeding include untreated tuberculosis and established HIV. Occasionally in the presence of chronic maternal illness the energy demands of breastfeeding may be considered excessive.

Artificial formula feeding

The principal constituents of breast milk have been used as a model for the design of artificial formula milks. The major characteristics of formula milk are, therefore, very similar to breast milk, and most infants can satisfactorily be fed with an artificial formula. The formulae are based on cow's milk and highly modified.

Each of the four milk companies make two standard milks for the newborn infant so that should the mother wish to change the milk she can continue to buy from the same company. The two milks differ in protein content. Cow & Gate, for example, make Premium, a whey-dominant formula more similar to breast milk, and Plus which is a casein-dominant milk. Blinded controlled trials have failed to substantiate any difference in the infant appreciation of the two sorts of milk, and whey-dominant formulae are generally recommended from birth.

Artificial formula is sold as a powder and, with each tin, a scoop specifically designed for that formula. One scoop, gently filled with

Table 5.2 Drug contraindications to breastfeeding

Class	*Example*	*Advice*	*Comment*
Alcohol	All	Avoid excess	Sedation
Analgesics	*Opiates*		
	Morphine and methadone	Use with care	Minimum therapeutic dose unlikely to affect infant. Use low doses and monitor the infant
	Salicylates		
	Aspirin	Avoid	Theoretical risk of Reye's syndrome
Antiarrhythmics	Amiodarone	Avoid	Contains iodine, theoretical risk of hypothyroidism, goitre
Antibiotics (generally most may be used safely)	Chloramphenicol	Avoid	Marrow toxicity
	Ciprofloxacin	Avoid	May be used if absolutely necessary, but is concentrated in milk
	Metronidazole	Use with care	Avoid in high dose, milk may be bitter. Doses of 200–400 mg t.d.s. are thought to be safe
	Tetracycline	Avoid	Causes tooth discoloration. Use in short courses only if absolutely necessary
	Cotrimoxazole	Use in low doses only	Avoid in baby <2 weeks and in G6PD deficiency
Anticoagulants	Pheninidione	Avoid	
	Warfarin	May be used safely	Monitor mother
Anticonvulsants	Phenobarbitone	Avoid unless absolutely necessary	Drowsiness. Monitor infant
	Others	Generally safe	Check drug data sheet for newer agents
Antidepressants	*Serotonin uptake inhibitors*		
	e.g. Fluoxetine	Avoid	Insufficient information available
	MAO inhibitors	Avoid	Insufficient information available
	Tricyclics	May generally be used safely, except Doxepin	Short-term use, in normal doses. Imipramine preferred since less sedating
	Doxepin	Avoid	Sedation
Antihypertensives	Beta-blockers	Use with care	Avoid atenolol and sotolol. Propranolol, metoprolol and labetalol preferred
Anti-inflammatories	*Gold salts*		
	Auranofin	Use with great care	Theoretical possibility of rashes and idiosyncratic reactions. Manufacturers recommend avoid
	NSAIDs	May be used with care, except indomethacin	Ibuprofen preferred

Anti-inflammatories (contd)	Indomethacin *Salicylates*	Avoid Avoid	Theoretical risk of Reye's syndrome
Antimigraine drugs	Ergotamine	Avoid	
Antineoplastics	All cytotoxics	Avoid	
Antipsychotics	Lithium Phenothiazines	Avoid unless absolutely necessary Avoid unless absolutely necessary	It is essential to monitor both mother and infant if used. Manufacturers recommend avoid
Benzodiazepines	Diazepam	Avoid regular use	Sedation
Contraceptives (oral)	Combined pill and the morning after pill (PC4) Progesterone only	Use with care Used safely	Possible inhibition of lactation Does not affect lactation
Corticosteroids	Prednisolone High doses Low doses	 Avoid Used safely	Monitor the infant carefully if mother is receiving continuous treatment with doses in excess of 50 mg or an equivalent dose of another steroid
Diuretics	*Loop diuretics* Frusemide	Use with care	May cause dehydration resulting in suppressed lactation
Herbal	Ginseng	Avoid	High doses may cause androgenisation in neonate
Immuno-suppressants	Azathioprine Cyclosporin	Avoid	
Laxatives	*Anthraquinones* Senna	Use with care	Gastrointestinal disturbance. May be used safely in standard doses. Avoid in high doses
Stimulants	Amphetamines Caffeine	Avoid Avoid in excess	
Thyroid drugs	Iodine/radioiodine Carbamizole	Avoid Use with care	Concentrated in milk – risk of hypothyroidism, goitre Theoretical risk of idiosyncratic blood dyscrasias. Risk of masking hypothyroidism. Monitor infant carefully

This table is not comprehensive, and advice may change. The reader is referred to the current edition of the *British National Formulary* (BNF) or the local Hospital Drug Information Centre.

Drugs referred to may not be licensed for use in breastfeeding. Please check the current data sheet to confirm status.

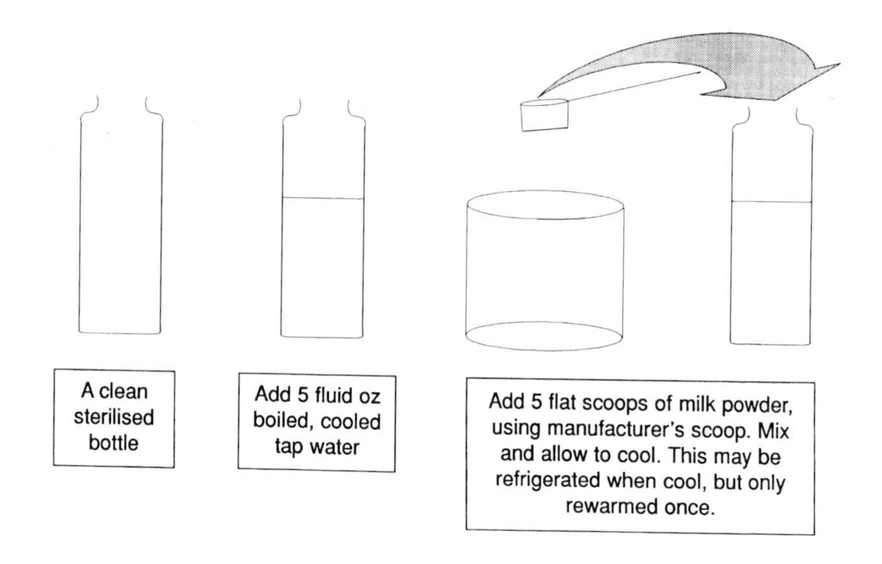

Figure 5.2 Making a 5 oz / 142 ml feed with infant formula milk powder

powder from the tin then scraped flat with a knife, is added to each ounce of previously boiled water in a sterilised bottle (Figure 5.2). Artificial formula has the obvious disadvantage of inconvenience and cost, and smells a good deal less pleasant when regurgitated over one's shoulder. The most obvious advantage is that the food can be prepared and given by someone other than the mother.

Problems with artificial formula feeding are most commonly not directly related to the composition of the milk and frequently reflect technique. Supported guidance is again needed and mothers should be dissuaded from ceaselessly changing between different formulae in the face of problems which require simple help or reassurance.

Specialised artificial formula

There is a bewildering number of different, highly modified specialised milks available, some designed specifically for rare conditions. A current trend to use a soya-based formula to prevent allergic symptoms is ill-advised and ineffective. A number of conditions in the newborn infant require particular attention to nutritional demands.

1 Preterm infant

(See also Chapter 3.)

The adequate and optimal nutrition of the preterm infant is a subject of great importance, considerable controversy and much research. The preterm infant, born with poor calorie reserves, has an urgent need for nutrition, and failure to meet these requirements results in short-term growth failure and longer term may have an adverse effect on neurodevelopmental outcome. The preterm infant has a high calorie requirement at around 135 kcal/kg/day (equivalent to over 9000 kcal/day in the adult!) and if intrauterine growth rates are to be maintained, will need 2–2.5 g/kg/day of protein. Mineral losses through the immature kidney are high and sodium requirements are approximately double those of the term infant. Calcium and phosphate requirements are higher and failure to meet results in metabolic bone disease of prematurity. The very low birthweight infant misses most of the phase of rapid somatic growth in the third trimester and, as a consequence, is also born without the equivalent reserves of iron, folate and other vitamins. These high nutritional demands must be met in the face of severe illness, intensive care and gut immaturity. The challenge is obvious.

In the very low birthweight infant choice of milk is difficult. The infant's own mother's breast milk will contain more sodium and protein content than the 'term mother'. This is generally well tolerated but may be inadequate for the infant's nutritional demands. This can be overcome by supplementing the milk with a breast-milk fortifier. Alternatively, a low birthweight formula specifically designed with the needs of these infants in mind may be used. If immaturity, illness or gut problems preclude milk feeding, parenteral nutrition is indicated.

Milk is given through a nasogastric tube as frequent, small-volume feeds or by continuous flow. As the infant matures feeds may be given less frequently and at around 34 weeks post menstrual age (gestation at birth plus postnatal age in weeks), the infant will be able to suck and swallow breast or bottle feeds. Routinely, very low birthweight infants are given supplements of vitamins (multi-vitamin preparation such as Abidec plus folate) and iron. These continue following discharge.

2 Small for gestation age infant

(See Chapter 4.)

3 Neonatal illness

In the infant who is unable to tolerate milk because of illness, nutrition should not be forgotten. Newborn infants are the single largest group receiving parenteral nutrition and this should be introduced early when it is not possible to give milk.

4 Gastrointestinal problems

(See also section below.) Infants with recognised congenital problems of the gut, those who have had neonatal surgery, infants recovering from necrotisisng enterocolitis and those with rare congenital defects of absorption require expert attention. Most commonly these infants receive a highly modified formula containing hydrolysed protein, a modified fat content and no disaccharides.

5 Inborn errors of metabolism

(See Chapter 11.)

Gastrointestinal problems in the term infant

Common problems related to feeding

Failure to take feeds well may be a symptom of almost any neonatal illness. Any infant who has been previously feeding well and ceases to do so should be carefully assessed and will often require admission to the neonatal unit. Causes include infection, heart failure, anaemia and a wide variety of other conditions. In infants with less acute symptoms, growth and weight gain should be asssessed. Most infants born at term weigh between 2.9 and 4.2 kg, and weight loss in the first days is normal and birthweight should be regained by ten days. At four months the infant's weight has doubled and by one year his weight has tripled. The average weight gain, therefore, over the first three months is 200 g per week – or 1 ounce per day and a day off on Sunday, in old money!

Vomiting is infrequent while posseting is common. Posseting, the effortless regurgitation of small amounts of milk after a feed, is normal. If an infant is gaining weight reassurance may be provided. Vomiting may be a symptom of most neonatal illnesses. If the vomitus contains bile, obstruction of the gut due to congenital anomalies or ileus should be suspected (see below). Blood in the vomit over the first day is most commonly due to the irritant effect of swallowed maternal blood from the time of delivery. This may be established by sending blood to the laboratory, to examine red cell fragility and differentiate between fetal and adult haemoglobin. If fresh or changed blood is vomited later a bleeding diathesis, notably vitamin K dependent haemorrhagic disease, should be considered (see Chapter 2). Any persistence of this symptom clearly merits detailed investigation by the paediatrician.

Eighty-five per cent of infants pass meconium during the first 24 hours and 96% during the first 48 hours. Failure to pass meconium by the end of the second day should lead to examination and assessment of the infant. The commonest problem is meconium plug. In this condition a plug of hardened meconium in the distal colon is passed after a delay and, thereafter, the problem resolves. Abdominal distension may indicate gut obstruction (see below) in Hirschsprung's disease. Rectal bleeding may represent local bleeding from a perianal fissure, a lesion higher in the gut, or a bleeding diathesis, and merits referral for investigation (see Chapter 9).

The passage of loose stools several times per day is normal and is more common in the breast-fed infant. The infant should remain well, hydrated and should gain weight. Watery diarrhoea is unusual and merits referral for investigation and prevention of dehydration.

Congenital gut anomaly and intestinal obstruction

Most congenital gut anomalies are rare with an incidence of 1 in 3–5000. Many are associated with a high risk of other congenital abnormalities. The diagnosis may be made antenatally, and indeed oesophageal and duodenal atresia should be excluded in all infants born to women with polyhydramnios. In the newborn infant who vomits, a high index of suspicion should be maintained. Vomiting that is bile-stained, or failure to pass meconium associated with abdominal distension, should be considered as obstruction until proven otherwise.

Obstruction high in the gastrointestinal tract presents either antenatally with polyhydramnios or soon after birth. **Oesophageal atresia** is most commonly associated with **tracheo-oesophageal fistula** (TOF). If any milk feed is given to an infant with a TOF, pulmonary aspiration is likely and choking will occur with feeding. To avoid this a tube should be passed into the stomach in all infants if there is a history of polyhydramnios, or in whom saliva bubbles at the lips after birth, before they are fed. A wide nasogastric tube (FG 10), that will not curl up in the pharynx, should be used. Fifty per cent of infants with TOF have associated abnormalities. **Duodenal obstruction** is most commonly an atresia, vomiting is not bile-stained, and there is a well-recognised association with Down's syndrome. Incomplete obstruction, small bowel atresias and malrotation have variable time of presentation, usually with bilious vomiting and abdominal distension. There is a high rate of associated anomalies. In **meconium ileus**, the mode of presentation of 30% of children with cystic fibrosis, distension may be marked, and may have been present antenatally with ascites.

In **Hirschsprung's disease** an aganglionic segment of bowel extends from the anus up into the colon or even small intestine. The timing and mode of presentation depend on the length of affected bowel. It should be suspected following delayed passage of meconium, in early onset constipation especially when associated with abdominal distension or failure to thrive. Diagnosis is through rectal biopsy. There is an association with Down's syndrome.

Imperforate anus (1 in 2–3000) can be diagnosed simply by inspection. The underlying anatomy varies considerably, and there is a high rate of associated congential anomaly of gut, heart and genitourinary system. In **exomphalos** the abdominal contents herniate through the umbilical ring into a sac. The sac may rupture and not be apparent. Exomphalos is most commonly diagnosed antenatally. A majority of infants with this condition have other anomalies, and there is an association with triploidy.

Gastroschisis (Figure 5.3), herniation of the abdominal contents through a para-umbilical defect, is less common, but is usually an

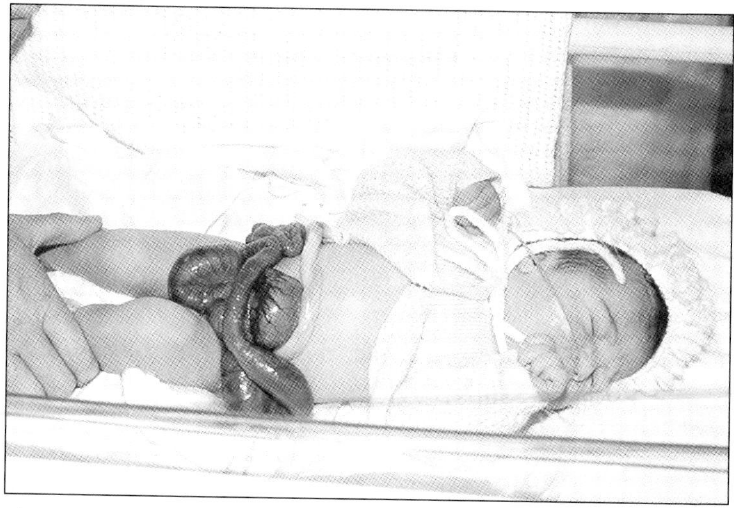

Figure 5.3

isolated defect. In exomphalos and gastroschisis herniated gut is exposed, and immediate management includes wrapping the gut in a waterproof membrane (clingfilm) to reduce plasma losses, intravenous volume replacement, nasogastric drainage, and transfer to a neonatal surgical unit. In most circumstances, infants recognised antenatally to have such problems should be transferred to a unit with surgical facilities for delivery.

6 Jaundice

Jaundice in the newborn infant is common and its nature peculiar to the neonatal period. The importance of its recognition and management lie not only in the aetiology of the jaundice, but also in the possible effects of the raised unconjugated bilirubin itself. This chapter aims to indicate when intervention is required and cover the principles of investigation and management.

Physiological jaundice

In the first week, 50% of newborn infants have some level of detectable jaundice. It is important to recognise infants who do not need investigation or intervention Most term infants will follow the 'golden rules':

1 Jaundice not apparent in the first 24 hours.
2 The infant remains well.
3 The serum bilirubin does not reach the treatment level.
4 The jaundice has faded by 14 days.

The child who obeys all these rules can be assumed to have physiological jaundice, and requires only the measurement of total bilirubin as dictated by clinical judgement.

A complex knowledge of physiology is not required to understand jaundice (Figure 6.1). The breakdown of red cells results in the production of fat-soluble bilirubin, in the unconjugated form, bound to serum albumin in the circulation. The unconjugated bilirubin is taken up by the hepatocyte, conjugated by a complex cascade of enzymes including glucuronyl transferase. Then, as the water-soluble conjugated form, bilirubin is excreted in the bile into the gut, pigmenting the stools.

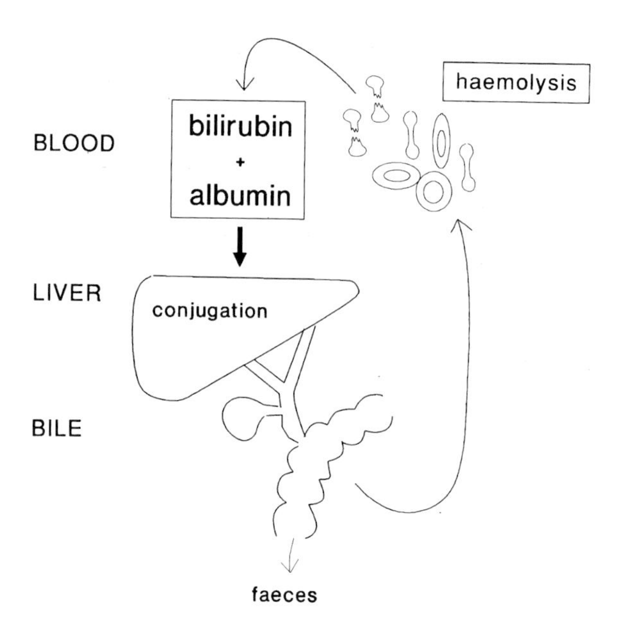

Figure 6.1 Biochemistry for clinicians!

Aetiology

We have defined physiological jaundice by the 'golden rules'. How does the breaking of each golden rule relate to the underlying pathology (Table 6.1)? Infants with early jaundice require immediate assessment, those with 'physiological plus' may require management of the raised bilirubin, and finally the child with prolonged jaundice presents the most difficult diagnostic challenges, and demands an immediacy of action which may not be obvious from the child's clinical well-being.

Early jaundice

The infant who has jaundice within 24 hours has haemolysis (see Chapter 9), until proven otherwise. Jaundice exacerbated by infection may also present this early. Haemolysis *in utero* or postnatally causes anaemia and, in the infant with relative immaturity of conjugating enzymes, lysis of only a small proportion of the red cell mass, results in a rapid rise in bilirubin. Any infant who appears even slightly jaundiced in the first 24 hours needs immediate investigation:

Mother: antenatal antibodies, blood group.
Infant: haemoglobin, total bilirubin, blood group, direct Coomb's test.

Table 6.1 Aetiology of neonatal jaundice

1 Physiological

2 Haemolytic
(a) ABO imcompatibility
(b) rhesus isoimmunisation
(c) other isoimmunisation (e.g. Kell, c, C, E)
(d) spherocytosis
(e) red cell fragility / enzyme defects (G6PD deficiency, pyruvate kinase)

3 Physiological PLUS
(a) prematurity
(b) bruising
(c) polycythaemia
(d) dehydration
(e) sepsis
(f) congenital infection
(g) gut obstruction

4 Prolonged
(a) physiological
(b) breastmilk jaundice
(c) congenital hypothyroidism
(d) neonatal hepatitis
(e) galactosaemia
(f) biliary atresia
(g) cystic fibrosis
(h) choledochal cyst
(i) congenital infection
(j) genetic, inborn errors of metabolism

Anaemia, a haemoglobin <12 g/dl, suggests severe disease, and may be an indication for immediate exchange transfusion. The Coomb's test indicates the presence of an antibody on the red cell. This is strongly positive in rhesus disease and most isoimmunisation, and may be mildly positive in ABO incompatibility. ABO incompatibility is the commonest cause of haemolysis. Unlike rhesus disease, ABO incompatibility can occur in a primigravid woman and does not require prior immunisation of the mother (see below). In ABO incompatibility the baby must have one of the A or B groups which the mother does not possess. The commonest combination is the group O mother with a group A baby. Rhesus disease is now uncommon and other blood group isoimmunisations have become relatively more important (see below). Non-isoimmune causes of haemolysis are rare (see Table 6.1) and may be indicated by family history. They differ in frequency between racial groups, and seldom cause the same severity of immediate haemolysis as rhesus disease.

If the immediate investigations confirm a raised bilirubin at less than 24 hours, phototherapy should be started and the bilirubin rechecked after four hours. Management of the rapidly rising bilirubin includes phototherapy, adequate fluids, supportive therapy and may require exchange transfusion (see below). Exchange is rarely needed in ABO incompatibility. It should be remembered that any infant with neonatal haemolysis remains at risk of anaemia over the first two months.

`Physiological plus' jaundice

The causes of exaggerated physiological jaundice (see Table 6.1) should be sought. Haemolytic jaundice may present after the first day, and this should be borne in mind. Most infants with 'physiological plus' jaundice are otherwise well and only phototherapy is needed. In the child who is jaundiced and unwell, infection should be considered first and foremost.

Toxicity of the raised bilirubin

Unconjugated bilirubin is fat soluble and can therefore cross the blood—brain barrier. Kernicterus is a clinical syndrome, associated with bilirubin staining of the brain, which produces an acute encephalopathy with seizures, and carries a prognosis of athetoid cerebral palsy and high-tone deafness. It is exquisitely rare in the term infant. Infants who are unwell, preterm or compromised in other ways, are at greater risk of an immediate or later effect upon the brain.

Assessment of the raised bilirubin

A jaundiced baby should be examined to assess the level of jaundice clinically. Classically this is done by depressing the tip of the nose or the forehead in order to blanche the capillary circulation. The sclera may also be observed. When appreciable jaundice occurs the serum total bilirubin is checked. The vast majority of this bilirubin is unconjugated. The level of total bilirubin and the child's age is used as a guide to the need for intervention.

MANAGEMENT OF THE RAISED BILIRUBIN

Phototherapy, arguably the finest thing to come out of Essex, alters the shape of the bilirubin molecule in the exposed skin, rendering it more water soluble and allowing its excretion. In recent years the threshold for phototherapy in the healthy term infant with exaggerated physiological jaundice has been raised (Figure 6.2). A lower threshold should be used in low birthweight or pre-term infants.

Phototherapy may make an infant irritable, is associated with loose stools, and requires separation of the infant from his mother. The bright light is uncomfortable and the infant's eyes should be shielded. The light should be turned off during sampling for serum bilirubin. Phototherapy should continue while the child's total bilirubin lies above the phototherapy line. Total bilirubin is checked daily, and on the day after phototherapy is stopped, to look for

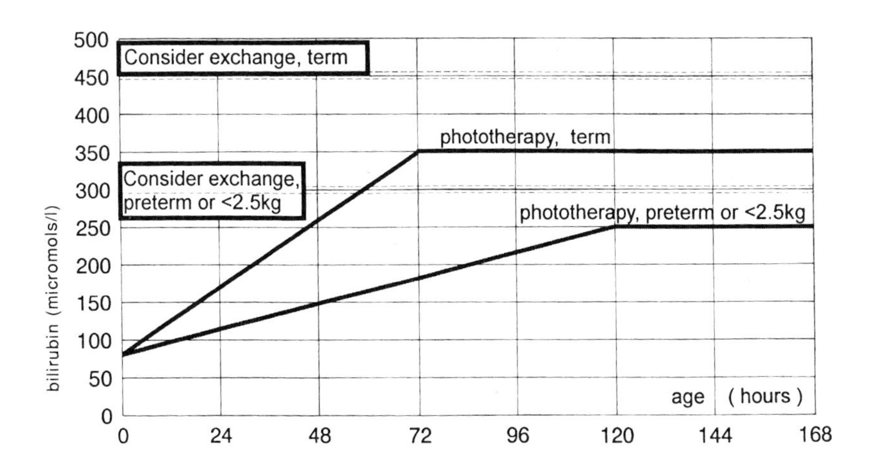

- Jaundice in the first 24 hours suggests haemolysis and requires investigation.
- Marked jaundice at any age requires investigation and early treatment.
- Persistent jaundice, at 14 days, merits investigation.

- For pre-term infants on the neonatal unit different guidelines should be used:
  exchange level = gestation x 10 micromols/l
  phototherapy level = exchange level minus 100 micromols/l

Figure 6.2 The treatment of non-haemolytic jaundice in the healthy infant

rebound hyperbilirubinaemia. Attention to hydration and adequate nutrition is important and may help control the level of hyperbilirubinaemia.

Exchange transfusion is an important therapeutic tool, but is not without risk of serious adverse effects and attention should be given to other measures including intensive phototherapy and adequate hydration before it is employed. It should be considered when the total bilirubin exceeds the baby's gestation in weeks multiplied by 10. Most commonly it is required in haemolytic jaundice with the advantage that it corrects anaemia, removes the Coomb's positive red-cell mass, reduces the total bilirubin, removes antibody, and provides albumen which is not bound to bilirubin. It is rarely needed in ABO incompatibility and 'physiological plus' jaundice.

Prolonged jaundice

The frequency of jaundice at 14 days is not known, but by 21 days only 1% of all infants and 2% of breast-fed infants remain clinically jaundiced. These infants require investigation. There are many causes of prolonged jaundice. The two commonest causes are physiological jaundice, in an infant who has not read the textbooks, and breastmilk jaundice. The mechanism behind breastmilk jaundice is not known. Inhibition of glucuronyl transferase or increased absorption of bilirubin from the gut may play a part. In breastmilk jaundice the infant remains well and requires no intervention. Central to the problem of prolonged jaundice, however, is the fact that the infant with pathological prolonged jaundice will not appear ill at presentation.

Infants with biliary atresia (1 in 10 000) who are diagnosed and treated surgically before six weeks of age, have a survival rate of 80% at 10 years. In those where the diagnosis is delayed beyond this time this rate falls, without liver transplantation, to 10% (Figure 6.3). The possibility of this diagnosis makes investigation of all infants who are jaundiced between two and three weeks of age mandatory. Stools should be examined for pallor, the urine for the presence of bilirubin, and a conjugated bilirubin measured (abnormal when conjugated bilirubin exceeds 25% of the total bilirubin). When any of these is abnormal the child should be referred for immediate investigation by a paediatrician.

Age at operation (days)	Survival rate at 10 years
1 –60	73%
61 – 70	35%
71 – 90	23%
91+	11%

Figure 6.3 Survival without need for liver transplantation following the Kesai procedure for biliary atresia: the effect of age at operation

Isoimmunisation

The introduction of universal anti-D treatment in 1979 has made rhesus disease rare. The rhesus-negative mother may become immunised at any event associated with feto–maternal bleeding. This includes delivery, abortion and amniocentesis or other invasive prenatal diagnostic techniques. No opportunity should be missed to prevent immunisation of the rhesus-negative mother. Recent interest has focused on the routine administration of anti-D to rhesus-negative mothers during pregnancy, but it is not yet known whether this is justifiable.

As rhesus disease has become less common, the importance of other causes of isoimmunisation has become more apparent. The Kell antigen, where immunisation most commonly occurs following blood transfusion, the other rhesus antigens, the Duffy factor, and rarer blood group antigens can all result in isoimmune antibodies and produce haemolysis in the fetus. Decision making based on the mother's serology is difficult. One thing is clear: all antibodies may be significant and the absolute level of the antibody titre does not clearly relate to the severity of disease in the fetus. Expert advice should be sought whenever abnormal serology is found in a mother.

The management of fetal haemolytic disease has changed considerably in the last 10 years. It may be necessary to give consideration to early plasmapheresis to remove the antibody from the maternal circulation. Amniocentesis allows measurement of bilirubin in the liquor, and fetal intervention, while cordocentesis permits diagnostic investigation and intrauterine blood transfusion. Decisions over intrauterine intervention and the optimal timing of delivery require a careful multidisciplinary approach from obstetrician, paediatrician and laboratory.

7 Common congenital abnormalities

As many as one in 15 newborn babies has some defect of morphogenesis and about a third of these will exert a significant effect on the individual's health or chance of survival. Approximately one in every 250 babies dies during the first year of life as a direct result of some congenital defect of morphogenesis. Table 7.1 gives an idea of the frequency of some kinds of malformation.

Congenital defects of morphogenesis can be subclassified into **malformations**, in which tissues form abnormally, **deformations**, which are the result of unusual forces acting on normal tissue and

Table 7.1 Incidence of some common, major malformations

Anencephaly	1:2500
Spina bifida (see Figure 7.1)	1:1750
Hydrocephalus	1:2600
Cleft palate	1:1850
Cleft lip and palate (see Figure 7.2)	1:1250
Oesophageal atresia	1:3000
Anorectoral atresia	1:2500
Renal agenesis/dysgenesis	1:2800
Polydactyly	1:1000
Syndactyly	1:2000
Reduction deformity of the limbs (see Figure 7.3)	1:1300
Club foot (see Figure 7.5)	1:700
Exomphalos/ gastroschisis	1:2800
Diaphragmatic hernia	1:3500
Down's syndrome	1:600
Skeletal dysplasia	1:4000

disruptions, which are the result of the breakdown of normal tissue. These distinctions are helpful in understanding the origin of morphogenetic defects.

Although our understanding of the aetiology of morphogenetic defects is gradually increasing we can still only account for a minority of them in precise causal terms. Single gene defects and chromosome anomalies account for between 10 and 20% of the total. A small number are attributable to intrauterine infection (e.g. rubella, cytomegalovirus), fewer to known teratogens and even fewer to chemical toxins and ionising radiation. It is thought that most morphogenetic defects are the end result of an interplay between multiple genetic and environmental factors. Advances in the primary prevention of such defects will have to await a better understanding of the mechanisms involved.

Prenatal diagnosis

As the fetus has become more accessible to study, as a result of techniques such as ultrasound and blood sampling, many defects of morphogenesis are now diagnosed prenatally. This development has

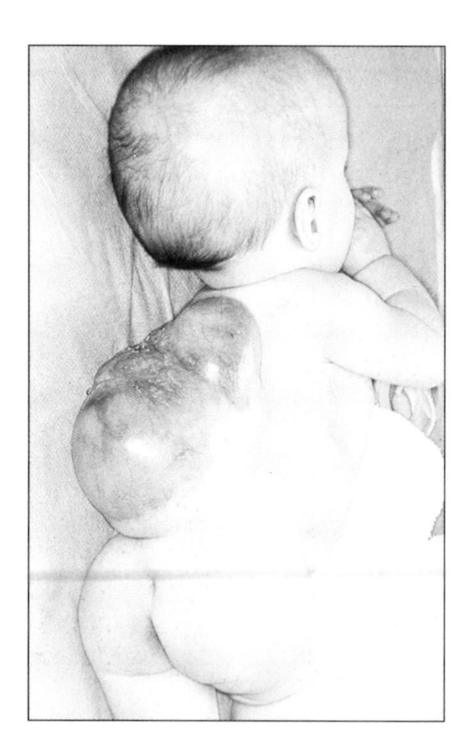

Figure 7.1

major implications for potential parents, obstetricians and paediatricians. The implications for potential parents are too obvious to require discussion here. The implications for the obstetrician include the need to acquire up-to-date knowledge about the whole spectrum of prenatally diagnosable conditions, and to brush up on probability theory and the techniques of non-directive counselling. The paediatrician also has to adjust, both to seeing less pathology as a result of termination of pregnancy and to the need to grapple with some conditions which would either not present at all or else present much later in life. The situation is one in which there is a pressing need for close collaboration between obstetrician, paediatrician and paediatric surgeon in order that the correct decisions are made and that parents are given accurate information on which to base decisions.

The options available for the management of prenatally diagnosed defects of morphogenesis are currently few. They amount to termination for serious and untreatable ones, fetal therapy for a few and making sure that the child is born in a unit capable of managing the problem for the rest.

Malformation syndromes

A malformation syndrome is said to exist when there are several discrete defects of morphogenesis which have occurred significantly frequently in association with one another to qualify for the designation 'syndrome' rather than merely a chance association. Most of these disorders have a genetic basis although in many cases this

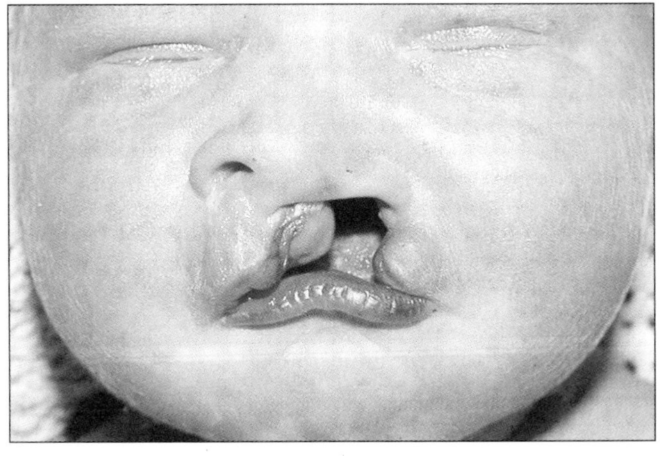

Figure 7.2

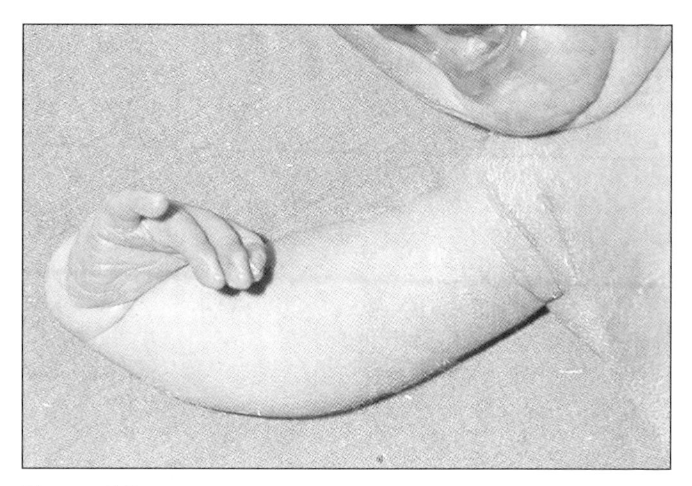

Figure 7.3

follows no clear pattern of mendelian inheritance and shows no currently identifiable abnormality of chromosome morphology.

Many syndromes are associated with prenatal growth failure, although, unless they are associated with detectable chromosome abnormalities or with specific features accessible to detection by ultrasound, most of them remain undiagnosed until birth. Many syndromes are associated with facial and other external abnormalities and are relatively amenable to diagnosis postnatally, with the help of illustrated dysmorphology textbooks and computerised databases. Accurate diagnosis is essential for prognosis and for estimating recurrence risks and the possibilities of prenatal diagnosis. The early involvement of a clinical geneticist is invaluable both for diagnosis and counselling.

Some prenatally diagnosed conditions

Renal abnormalities

Prenatal diagnosis by ultrasound has made a large impact here. Important conditions like urethral valves may now be diagnosed, in the hope of avoiding renal damage (see Figure 7.4). The effects of prenatal diagnosis range from elective termination, through experimental (but largely futile) attempts at fetal therapy, to the generation of needless anxiety over minor deviations from the normal. Somewhere in the middle are infants in whom prenatal diagnosis has had a powerfully beneficial effect on long-term outcome.

Cardiac abnormalities

The major impact here has been to provide the family and the paediatrician with an opportunity to discuss and plan investigation and therapy. It is important to realise that the standard four-chamber view of the fetal heart will miss a number of important defects.

Gastrointestinal tract abnormalities

Oesophageal and duodenal atresia, diaphragmatic hernia, exomphalos, gastroschisis and intestinal perforation are often diagnosed prenatally. This allows anticipation of the defect at delivery, which should take place in a centre with the necessary experience and resources to manage it effectively (see also Chapter 5).

Skeletal abnormalities

The differential diagnosis of prenatally diagnosed skeletal abnormalities can be difficult at times. Apart from the opportunity to terminate the pregnancy in cases with a very poor prognosis, and to discuss the problem with parents, prenatal diagnosis offers little advantage.

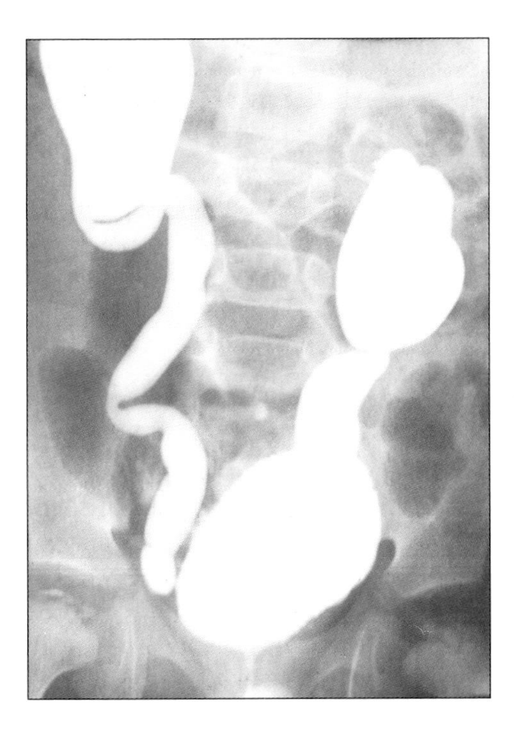

Figure 7.4

Common minor abnormalities

Some 2% of newborn infants are afflicted by abnormalities which will have little or no adverse effect on their health and which by and large do not require medical intervention. Such problems may, nevertheless, be a source of considerable anxiety to parents. The best way to deal with this anxiety is to give prompt and accurate information about the significance and the natural history of the defect concerned. This should be well within the capacity of the practising obstetrician.

Skin lesions

STORK MARK (NAEVUS FLAMMEUS)

This is a flat, pinkish capillary haemangioma commonly found at the nape of the neck, in the middle of the forehead or over the upper eyelids. Those at the nape of the neck persist throughout life but those on the face gradually fade during the first two or three years, although they may become visible again when the child cries. These lesions require no treatment.

STRAWBERRY NAEVUS

This is a soft, raised, bright red capillary haemangioma often containing or overlying a bluish cavernous haemangioma. Although a few of these lesions are apparent at birth the vast majority develop during the first few days or weeks of life and then gradually increase in size during the first six months. They may then remain static for a few months before they start to involute. Typically, involution of a strawberry naevus begins with the development of grey fibrotic plaques on the surface. The vast majority of strawberry naevi have disappeared more or less completely by the age of three and there is usually little residual cosmetic defect. Exceptionally, if a naevus interferes with important function, or is very large, direct intervention with steroids, interferon or surgery is indicated.

PORT WINE STAIN

This is a form of flat capillary haemangioma which does not fade but rather darkens as time goes by, to form a flat purple patch of skin which is disfiguring. These can now be treated with laser therapy and their appearance improved considerably. Port wine stains affecting the area of skin innervated by the ophthalmic division of the trigeminal nerve may be associated with an intracranial haemangioma. This is known as the Sturge-Weber syndrome and affected children may have trouble with convulsions, neurological abnormalites, mental handicap or glaucoma.

Mongolian blue spots

These are large, slate-grey or blue-black macules, which look rather like bruises. They are found in infants of oriental, Asian or Negro origin. They are most commonly found over the buttocks and lower back but sometimes there are more extensive lesions involving the lower limbs, back, flanks and shoulders. They represent collections of spindle-shaped melanocytes located deep within the dermis. They gradually fade and are rarely visible beyond the age of five years. They are of no medical significance.

Urticaria neonatorum (erythema toxicum)

This erythematous rash can be seen in almost 50% of term infants at some time during the first week of life. It is rare among preterm infants. The characteristic lesion is a small, pale papule which commonly evolves into a vesicle containing eosinophils. Each papule is surrounded by an area of intensely bright erythema. Some infants have just a few of these lesions but in others the rash is widespread and may affect any area of the body. Individual lesions tend to come and go over a few hours but the condition usually lasts for a few days before disappearing spontaneously.

To this day, the cause of neonatal urticaria is not known but we do know that it is completely benign. Its medical importance lies in the anxiety which it might provoke in parents. The most important differential diagnosis is staphylococcal skin infection which is a potentially serious condition generally requiring antibiotic therapy (see Chapter 8).

Subcutaneous fat necrosis

These lesions are sharply circumscribed, hard nodules of a dusky purple hue. They are mostly found over the buttocks, back, arms and thighs and vary considerably in size.

The cause of subcutaneous fat necrosis is not properly understood. It is usually described in association with obstetric trauma, birth asphyxia and hypothermia. Most infants with subcutaneous fat necrosis are well but some exhibit signs of a systemic illness with pyrexia and malaise. The lesions almost invariably resolve over the course of a few months and no treatment is usually necessary.

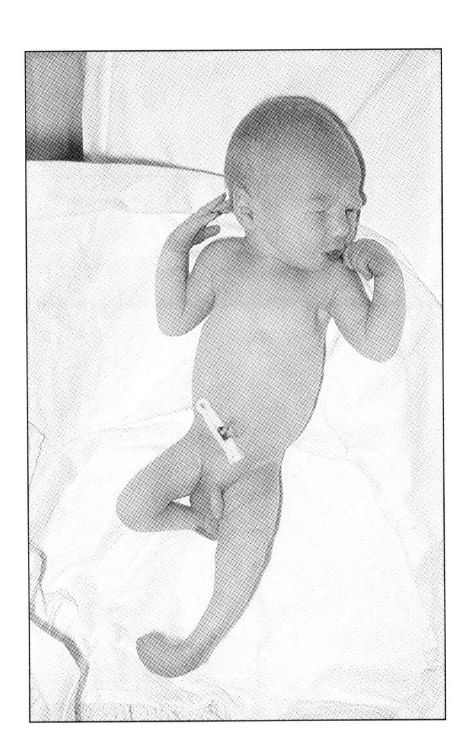

Figure 7.5

POSITIONAL TALIPES

Minor degrees of talipes are common and result from mechanical pressures *in utero*. The commonest form is that in which there is plantar flexion (equinus) and foot adduction (varus) at the mid tarsal joint. If the foot with talipes equino-varus can be fully dorsi-flexed and everted so that the little toe touches the outside of the leg without undue force it will correct spontaneously. If the position cannot be overcorrected as described orthopaedic referral is essential. The other form of talipes, talipes calcaneo-valgus rarely requires orthopaedic intervention and can usually be easily corrected with simple exercises.

SACRAL DIMPLE

Many babies have a dimple over the lower part of the sacrum, at the upper end of the natal cleft. These are not associated with underlying spinal abnormalities and are harmless. Any sinus, naevus or other superficial lesion higher up on the spine, however, may be associated with an underlying defect of communication with the central nervous system and requires careful evaluation and follow-up.

8 Infection of the fetus and newborn

Fetal and neonatal infection continues to be an important cause of morbidity and mortality, although significantly less so in the developed than in the developing world. In terms of opportunities for intervention it is useful to classify infections into those acquired by the transplacental passage of micro-organisms, those acquired following rupture of the membranes or during delivery and those acquired from the environment after birth.

Transplacental infection

Whenever the maternal bloodstream is invaded by micro-organisms there is a risk of placental and/or fetal infection. Fortunately, maternal immune defences and the defence mechanisms in the placenta, which include the villous trophoblast, placental macrophages and the local production of immune factors, mean that relatively few maternal infections result in invasion of the fetus. Certain micro-organisms are more likely than others to cross the placenta and the most important fetal pathogens are listed in Table 8.1.

The effects of transplacental infection range from resorption of the embryo, abortion, stillbirth, congenital malformation, intrauterine growth retardation, preterm birth and tissue and organ damage caused by chronic postnatal infection. A detailed account of all transplacental infections is beyond the scope of this book but it is important for the obstetrician to have a good knowledge of the likely effect on the fetus of maternal infections acquired during pregnancy so that appropriate counselling and management can be undertaken. A limited amount of congenital rubella and congenital HIV infection will be seen by obstetricians, especially those practising in large metropolitan centres.

Table 8.1 Some well-recognised causes of transplacental fetal infection

Viruses:	Bacteria:
• rubella	• *Treponema pallidum*
• cytomegalovirus	• *Mycobacterium tuberculosis*
• herpes simplex	• *Listeria monocytogenes*
• varicella-zoster	• *Salmonella*
• mumps	• *Campylobacter*
• Coxsackie B	
• echovirus	**Protozoa:**
• poliovirus	• *Toxoplasma gondii*
• hepatitis B and C	• plasmodia
• HIV	
• parvovirus	

Congenital rubella

The rubella virus has a unique ability to cause malformations compatible with life, notably congenital heart defects, cataracts and other ocular defects, sensorineural deafness and microcephaly with mental retardation. Additionally, in common with cytomegalovirus (CMV) and toxoplasmosis, an infected baby may be born with evidence of active viraemia as shown by jaundice, hepato-

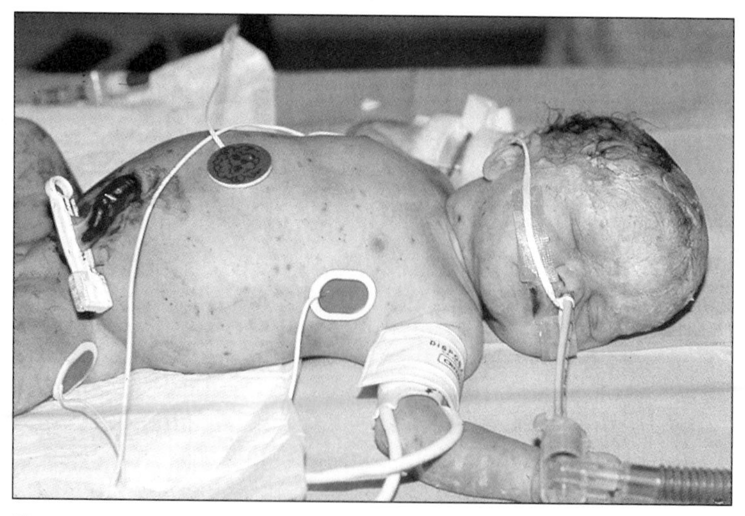

Figure 8.1

splenomegaly, thrombocytopenic purpura (Figure 8.1) and signs of inflammation in many organs and tissues including the eye, lung, central nervous system and bone. The risk of malformation in congenital rubella depends on the gestation at the time of infection. The risk of damage in sero-positive infants is 85% if fetal infection occurs in the first trimester and approximately 35% after infection during weeks 13–16. Hopefully, the introduction of the mumps, measles, rubella immunisation in early childhood will do more for reducing the risk of congenital rubella than the previous programme of immunising girls only in late childhood. Until such time as congenital rubella is eliminated by the immunisation programme, serological screening of pregnant women must be continued. The opportunity should be taken to vaccinate all rubella sero-negative women in the postpartum period.

Congenital HIV infection

Anonymous screening showed one in 580 pregnant women in London in 1994 to be HIV positive. Vertical transmission of HIV can occur transplacentally, during parturition or postnatally via breast-feeding. The overall rate of perinatal vertical transmission is currently about 25% although this varies from one report to another and is likely to fall with better ascertainment of maternal HIV status. Transmission via breastmilk is possible and, in the developed world at least, infected women should be counselled not to breastfeed their infants. In the developing world the benefits of breastfeeding may outweigh the risk of HIV transmission. In a recent UK study 23% of infected children developed AIDS in the first year of life, but in certain parts of the world this figure is much higher. Few children with congenital HIV infection will reach their fifth birthday. The prognosis would seem quite bad enough to justify termination of pregnancy but this is by no means a universally chosen option. The very few studies into the use of zidovudine in the treatment of vertically infected children have shown a degree of clinical improvement in some but the effects on the immunological and virological status of the children has been only transient.

Infection acquired intrapartum

Very occasionally, micro-organisms penetrate intact membranes to cause fetal infection but it is usually not until the membranes rupture that the fetus is exposed to the vaginal flora. Thereafter, the probability of contamination of the fetus increases and, of course, during vaginal delivery contamination inevitably occurs. Babies born by Caesarean section with intact membranes avoid the vaginal flora but are soon contaminated by environmental organisms. In the vast majority of cases this initial contact with micro-organisms results in harmless colonisation of the infant but there is a delicate balance between colonisation and infection. All newborn babies are relatively immunocompromised as outlined in Table 8.2. This table also includes some particular predisposing factors relevant to particular cases.

As a result of the newborn infant's immunocompromised state even organisms of relatively low pathogenicity can cause serious infection. However, certain organisms are notorious neonatal pathogens. These are listed in Table 8.3.

Clinical presentation of infection in the newborn

The intrinsic susceptibility of the newborn to infection means that an aggressive approach to diagnosis and therapy is necessary to reduce mortality and morbidity. When there are particular risk factors, as shown in Table 8.2, the threshold for investigation and intervention should be even lower. Any baby exhibiting one or more of the signs listed in Table 8.4 should come under suspicion for infection, unless there is a clear alternative explanation, and should be carefully

Table 8.2 Factors predisposing to neonatal infection

Factors common to all infants:
- Diminished neutrophil pool and poor chemotaxis, phagocytosis and killing ability
- Diminished complement activity and poor ability to opsonise certain organisms
- Diminished antibody response, related to intrinsic immaturity of B cells and diminished T-cell help for antibody production
- Impaired T-cell activity

Particular predisposing factors:
- Prematurity
- Intrauterine growth retardation
- Particularly heavy colonisation
- High pathogenicity of organisms

Table 8.3 Micro-organisms commonly implicated in neonatal sepsis

Bacteria:
- Group B streptococcus
- *Staphylococcus aureus*
- *Staphylococcus epidermidis* (in preterm infants or intravascular lines)
- *Listeria monocytogenes*
- *Haemophilus influenzae*
- *E. coli*
- *Chlamydia trachomatis*
- *Neisseria gonorrhoea*

Viruses:
- herpes simplex
- Coxsackie
- echovirus

Fungi:
- *Candida albicans*
- rhizopus species

Table 8.4 Clinical signs of neonatal infection

- lethargy and hypotonia
- poor feeding, abdominal distension or vomiting
- loose stools
- pallor and mottling of the skin
- prolonged jaundice
- disturbed temperature regulation
- tachypnoea / apnoeic episodes

Table 8.5 The neonatal infection screen

- Blood culture
- Full blood count, including differential white count and white cell morphology
- Microscopy and culture of urine
- Lumbar puncture (discretionary, but indicated if the baby is obviously ill or exhibits any neurological abnormality)
- Swabs from any infected lesions
- Chest X-ray
- C-reactive protein – or other non-specific indicator of infection

assessed and investigated according to the protocol outlined in Table 8.5.

If infection is suspected on clinical grounds, broad spectrum antibiotic therapy should be started at once. A combination of ampicillin and gentamicin remains a very suitable starting therapy in the absence of any clue as to the offending organism. If particular organisms are suspected, for example as the result of a high vaginal swab taken from the mother, then the antibiotic therapy should be tailored to cover those. The antibiotics should always be given intravenously and the baby carefully observed. If the baby's condition improves rapidly, the white count and C-reactive protein (CRP) are normal and the blood cultures are negative at 48 hours, antibiotic therapy can usually be safely stopped. Otherwise treatment is generally continued for five days, although longer in particular circumstances – see below.

Some common infections

Cutaneous infections

Bacterial infection of the skin or umbilicus is usually due to *Staphylococcus aureus*. This is a very dangerous organism for the newborn and the threshold for starting therapy with flucloxacillin should be low. Oral therapy is satisfactory if the baby shows no signs of illness, otherwise intravenous therapy is indicated.

Conjunctivitis

Sticky, but non-inflamed eyes are common in the newborn and all that is required in most cases is bathing with warm, sterile saline for a few days. When there is inflammation, a swab should be sent to the microbiology laboratory and therapy started with either neomycin or chloramphenicol eye drops.

The commonest causal organisms are staphylococci, streptococci, *E. coli*, *Haemophilus*, chlamydia and neisseria, including *N. gonorrhoeae*. The last two warrant particular mention because they can both rapidly cause corneal scarring.

Chlamydial conjunctivitis

Between 3% and 10% of women attending antenatal clinics in the UK harbour chlamydia. One in three exposed infants will develop conjunctivitis, which usually presents between five and 12 days of age. Diagnosis is by either culture or antigen detection. The rapid monoclonal antibody-based test is more reliable in the diagnosis of conjunctivitis than it is in the diagnosis of genital infection. In practice chlamydia is often diagnosed after an eye infection has failed to resolve with conventional antibiotic therapy. Treatment is with tetracycline eye drops, which represents the only legitimate use of tetracycline in the newborn. Oral erythromycin should also be given for five days to eradicate chlamydia from the nasopharynx, to prevent subsequent pneumonia.

Gonococcal conjunctivitis

Relatively rare in the UK but still an important cause of blindness world-wide, because of corneal scarring. Gonococcal conjunctivitis usually presents within the first five days of life and is often rapidly progressive, so that the lids swell to close the eye, which oozes pus (see Figure 8.2). Any suspicion of gonococcal ophthalmia warrants discussion with the microbiology laboratory over the best approach to diagnosis and immediate treatment with local and systemic penicillin. To begin with, eye drops are administered half-hourly. With early diagnosis and treatment the prognosis is very good.

Oral and perineal candida

Oral thrush is a common problem. It presents as white plaques on the oral mucosa and can cause feeding difficulties. Treatment is with either nystatin oral suspension or miconazole gel, which should be

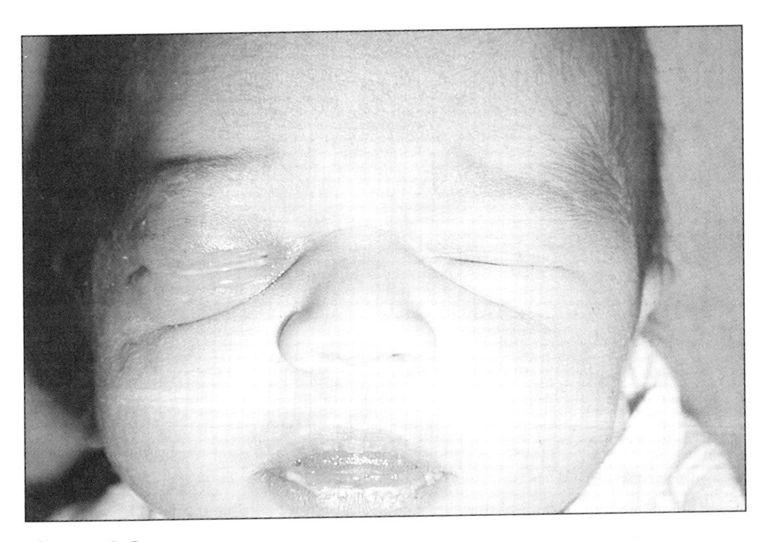

Figure 8.2

continued for about a week after the lesions have disappeared. Feeding bottles and teats should be meticulously sterilised while treatment is under way.

Candida nappy rash is typified by satellite lesions around a central inflamed area. Treatment with nystatin or miconazole cream is effective.

Congenital pneumonia

This usually follows invasion of the uterine cavity following membrane rupture although infection during delivery or transplacental infection are possible. Prolonged rupture of the membranes is the most important predisposing factor. Group B streptococci are the most notorious cause of congenital pneumonia but many other pathogens may be involved, including *Listeria, Chlamydia* and *Haemophilus.*

If consolidation is widespread at birth resuscitation may be difficult or impossible. More commonly, signs of respiratory distress develop soon after birth and rapidly worsen, although some congenital pneumonias may present more insidiously at any time during the neonatal period. In severe cases, respiratory failure is soon followed by metabolic acidosis and circulatory failure. In preterm infants the early signs of congenital pneumonia cannot be distinguished from surfactant deficient respiratory distress syndrome and that is why all babies who develop signs of respiratory disease soon after birth should receive broad spectrum antibiotic therapy until infection is ruled out as the cause. A combination of ampicillin and gentamicin is suitable.

MENINGITIS

Most neonatal meningitis is due either to group B streptococci or *E. coli,* although all known neonatal pathogens can cause meningitis. The prognosis is very poor and depends crucially on the speed with which the diagnosis is suspected and investigation and therapy started. Unfortunately, the signs of meningitis in the newborn are quite non-specific in the early stages, which is when therapy must be started if a good outcome is to be achieved. Meningeal infection almost invariably follows on from septicaemia and the prevention of meningeal spread is one of the main reasons why the baby who is thought to be septic should receive urgent investigation and therapy. Ampicillin and gentamicin remain the best opening combination in the absence of knowledge of the organism, but third-generation cephalosporins have their advocates. Intraventricular therapy with gentamicin is sometimes needed.

Urinary tract infection

In contrast to the situation in older children and adults most urinary tract infections in the newborn occur in males – as indeed do infections of all kinds. Once again the presentation is non-specific and the daignosis is usually suspected on the results of a routine septic screen. Confirmation by suprapubic bladder aspiration may be required to exclude contamination from the perineum. Treatment is with ampicillin and gentamicin, given intravenously. All cases should be investigated with renal ultrasound since some 30% will have an underlying structural abnormality. Follow-up is essential and further urinary tract investigations should be undertaken if infection recurs.

9 Blood disorders

At birth, the normal term infant has a haemoglobin of about 17 g/dl, a white cell count in the range 10—30 x 10^9/l, predominantly polymorphs, and a platelet count in the range 150—300 x 10^9/l. The white cell picture has changed considerably during the first week of life with the total count falling to between 5 and 15 x 10^9/l and a predominance of lymphocytes developing. After birth, the haemoglobin concentration falls by about 1 g per week until it levels out at around 12 g/dl by six weeks of age. There are no striking changes in the platelet count after birth.

The red cells

The red cells of the newborn infant have a half life of 60–90 days. They have a much higher glycolytic rate than adult red cells and the fetal red cell mass accounts for about 15% of the total glucose consumption.

Anaemia

Anaemia at birth is due either to fetal blood loss or haemolysis and other causes, such as marrow aplasia, are far less common.

Fetal blood loss

The commonest causes of antepartum fetal blood loss are twin-twin transfusion (see Figure 9.1) and feto-maternal haemorrhage. In each case very large amounts of fetal blood can be lost either chronically or acutely. Intrapartum fetal blood loss can occur as a result of twin-twin transfusion, feto-maternal haemorrhage, placenta praevia, placental abruption, tearing of the normal or abnormal umbilical cord and bleeding into the scalp during ventouse delivery.

When the blood loss is acute, the infant presents with clinical signs

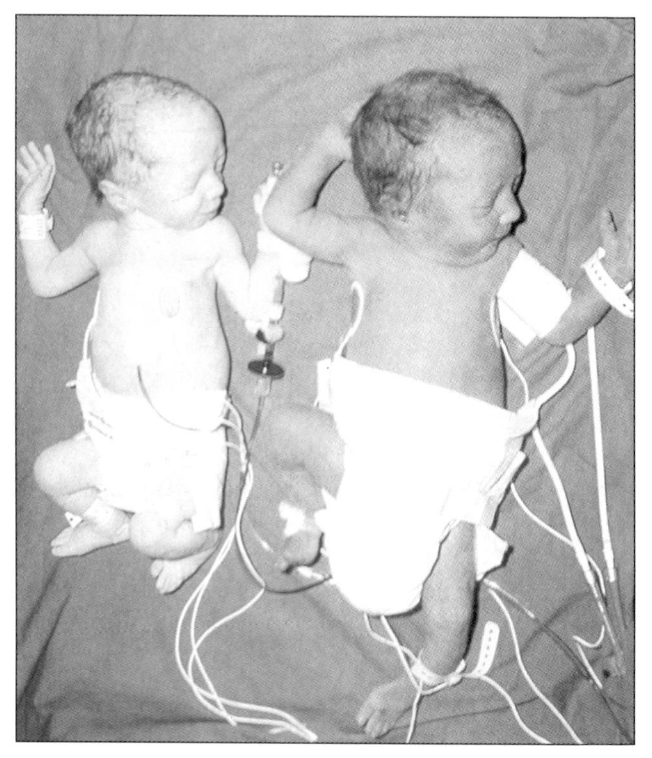

Figure 9.1

of acute asphyxia and the existence of hypovolaemia as the prime cause of the baby's condition is usually not immediately obvious. It is only after volume replacement during resuscitation that the low haemoglobin concentration becomes apparent. In the case of chronic haemorrhage, circulating volume is usually normal and the infant's symptoms range from hydrops (see Chapter 10) to mere apathy and pallor.

The treatment for anaemia due to acute blood loss is ideally by whole blood transfusion but for the reasons outlined above is more commonly volume replacement with colloid to begin with, followed by transfusion of packed cells. The treatment of chronic anaemia, with normal or increased blood volume, is either by transfusion of packed cells or else by exchange transfusion.

Haemolytic anaemia

The main causes of fetal haemolytic anaemia are shown in Table 9.1.

In clinical practice in the UK rhesus haemolytic disease remains

Table 9.1 Causes of haemolytic anaemia in the newborn

Immune:
- rhesus and ABO incompatibility
- secondary to maternal immune diseases such as auto-immune haemolytic anaemia or systemic lupus erythematosus (SLE)
- acquired red blood-cell disorders

Infection, e.g. as in cytomegalovirus or syphilis:
- disseminated intravascular coagulation

Hereditary disorders of the red blood cell:
- membrane defects such as in hereditary spherocytosis
- enzyme abnormalities such as in glucose-6-phosphate dehydrogenase (G6PD) or pyruvate kinase deficiency
- haemoglobinopathies, especially alpha thalassaemia

the commonest cause of severe haemolytic anaemia presenting at birth. The treatment of haemolytic anaemia in the newborn is dependent on cause. A very important consequence of the haemolytic process is the generation of large amounts of unconjugated bilirubin which may be more of a threat to the well-being of the infant than the anaemia itself – see Chapter 6.

Hypoplastic anaemia

The best-known congenital hypoplastic anaemia is the Diamond-Blackfan syndrome but it is extremely rare. There is also a transient hypoplastic anaemia, or even pancytopenia, which sometimes presents in the neonatal period. Emerging as one of the most common causes of neonatal hypoplastic anaemia, although still fortunately rare, is parvovirus infection. The human parvovirus B19 has a great affinity for erythroid precursors in the bone barrow (see Chapter 8).

Polycythaemia

The usual definition of neonatal polycythaemia is a venous haematocrit of greater than 60%. Capillary blood overestimates the haematocrit and can only be used to exclude polycythaemia. The main causes of neonatal polycythaemia are outlined in Table 9.2 (see also Chapter 1, Table 1.3 and Figure 1.2).

Table 9.2 Main causes of neonatal polycythaemia

- chronic intrauterine hypoxia
- maternal diabetes
- congenital hypothyroidism
- delayed clamping of the umbilical cord
- materno-fetal transfusion
- twin-twin transfusion

Most polycythaemic infants are asymptomatic but symptoms, when present, are due either to increased blood viscosity and poor tissue perfusion or to associated metabolic abnormalities such as jaundice or hypoglycaemia. The consequences of hyperviscosity can be serious and include cerebral infarction, renal failure, necrotising enterocolitis and peripheral gangrene. Hypoglycaemia is due to glucose consumption by the increased red cell mass and the jaundice is due to increased bilirubin production as the result of red cell breakdown.

The treatment of polycythaemia is by partial exchange transfusion with plasma but it is difficult to draw up very clear guidelines concerning which infants should be treated. While virtually all neonatologists would agree that babies with venous haematocrits of 65% or more who have symptoms that could be attributable to polycythaemia should be treated by dilutional exchange, it is more difficult to decide when to treat the asymptomatic polycythaemic infant. We would reserve dilutional exchange transfusion for asymptomatic infants whose venous haematocrit exceeded 70%. Maintaining good hydration is important and infusion of low molecular weight dextran offers theoretical benefits in terms of inhibiting red cell aggregation.

Neonatal bleeding disorders

The majority of neonatal bleeding disorders are due either to thrombocytopenia or to congenital or acquired deficiencies of the coagulation proteins; that is, apart from bleeding into the central nervous system of the preterm infant in which immaturity of the vasculature is implicated. Table 9.3 shows a useful practical classification of the causes of abnormal bleeding in the newborn in relation to the state of health and the results of three common tests.

Neonatal thrombocytopenia

The usual lower limit of normal for neonatal platelet count is 150 x 10^9/l. The two principal causes of neonatal thrombocytopenia are both immune-mediated.

Neonatal isoimmune thrombocytopenia

This is analogous to rhesus incompatibility, with the infant's platelets expressing an antigen that is lacking on the maternal platelets. Commonly, the maternal antibody is directed against the PLA^1 antigen. Incompatibility between mother and infant with respect to the PLA^1 antigen exists in approximately 1:50 pregnancies but the risk of neonatal isoimmune thrombocytopenia is only about 1:2500. This is because sensitisation is limited to the 10% or so of mothers who have a particular human leucocyte antigen (HLA) and diabetic retinopathy (DR) type.

Fifty per cent of cases of isoimmune thrombocytopenia occur in a first pregnancy and once the condition has occurred there is an 80% risk of recurrence in subsequent pregnancies.

Management of the newborn will depend on the severity of the thrombocytopenia and on the occurrence of clinical bleeding. If this particular cause of neonatal thrombocytopenia is suspected or diagnosed, treatment is by a transfusion of PLA^1 negative platelets, as PLA^1 positive platelets are rapidly destroyed by the antibody. Intravenous immunoglobulin is a useful alternative, or supplementary, treatment. The problem ultimately subsides at about two

Table 9.3 Coagulation disorders in the newborn

Condition	*Platelet count*	*PT*	*PTT*
1 The healthy baby			
Immune thrombocytopenia	reduced	normal	normal
Haemorrhagic disease of the newborn	normal	increased	increased
Hereditary clotting factor deficiencies	normal	normal	increased
2 The sick infant			
DIC	reduced	increased	increased
Liver disease	normal	increased	increased

months of age once maternal antibody is cleared from the baby's circulation.

Because of the high recurrence risk special precautions are required during a subsequent pregnancy. Unfortunately, antibody studies on the mother do not have much prognostic value and the only effective way of monitoring the fetus is to do platelet counts on fetal blood obtained by cordocentesis. This approach is obviously not generally available and for this reason suppression of maternal antibody synthesis by administration of intravenous immunoglobulin has been tried, with some success. Delivery by elective Caesarean section should be considered in order to reduce trauma to the potentially thrombocytopenic infant and PLA^1 negative platelets should be obtained prior to delivery for immediate transfusion. Such platelets can be obtained from the mother and processed by the haematology laboratory in order to remove antibody.

Neonatal thrombocytopenia secondary to maternal autoimmune thrombocytopenia

The fetuses of women with idiopathic thrombocytopenia may suffer thrombocytopenia as a result of transplacental passage of antibody. Generally, the severity of the fetal thrombocytopenia reflects the severity of the maternal thrombocytopenia, although mothers who have had splenectomy may have high antibody titres but a normal platelet count. The administration of intravenous immunoglobulin to pregnant women with active idiopathic thrombocytopenia has been very effective in preventing fetal thrombocytopenia. Serious neonatal haemorrhage from this cause is relatively uncommon, but infants may often have petechiae (Figure 9.2). Treatment with platelet infusion is general ineffective because of the presence of antibody directed against a public antigen but it would be normal to give platelets if serious haemorrhage developed. Intravenous immunoglobulin is indicated if the platelet count is less than 20×10^9/l, or there is significant bleeding.

Haemorrhagic disease of the newborn

The routine use of vitamin K to prevent haemorrhagic disease of the newborn has been outlined in Chapter 2. As long as an effective policy for giving prophylactic vitamin K is in place haemorrhagic disease of the newborn is not seen. A late form of haemorrhagic disease due to vitamin K deficiency is occasionally seen later during the first year of life, most commonly around 6–8 weeks of age. This

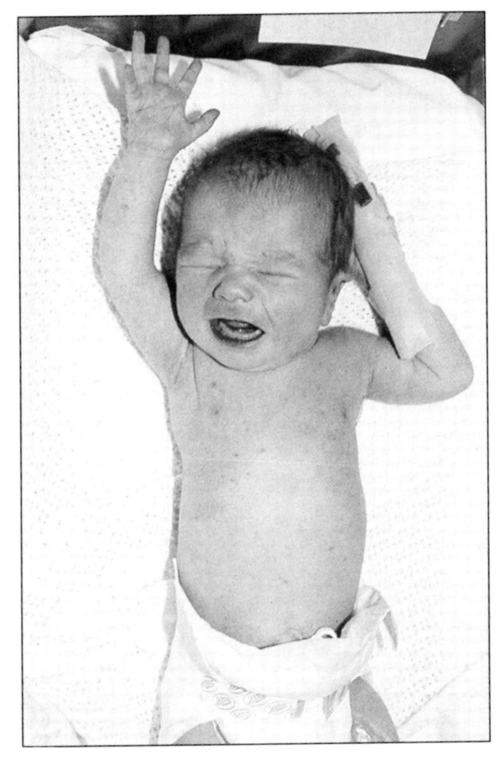

Figure 9.2

may be associated with clinical states causing impaired vitamin K absorption, such as diarrhoea and liver disease. Breast-fed infants who have received only oral vitamin K at birth are particularly vulnerable to late haemorrhagic disease and that is the rationale for supplementary doses at one and four weeks of age.

Hereditary clotting factor deficiency

Classic haemophilia (factor 8 deficiency) and Christmas disease (factor 9 deficiency) are by far the commonest hereditary clotting factor deficiencies that might present with haemorrhage in the neonatal period. Interestingly, even in classical haemophilia serious bleeding in the neonatal period is rare. It is most likely to be seen following traumatic delivery or surgery. In most cases where the fetus is suspected of having an hereditary clotting factor deficiency vaginal delivery is appropriate and the indications for birth by Caesarean section are no different than for the rest of the population.

Disseminated intravascular coagulation (DIC)

DIC may complicate neonatal sepsis, asphyxia, hypotension and the intrauterine death of a co-twin. Infants with DIC are usually very ill and the diagnosis is not difficult with the help of routinely available laboratory tests. Heparin is contraindicated in neonatal DIC, which is treated by addressing the underlying problem and by infusing fresh frozen plasma and platelets.

10 Hydrops fetalis

Hydrops fetalis is a descriptive term implying generalised widespread subcutaneous oedema, often in a fetus who also has ascites and pleural effusion and frequently associated with placental oedema and polyhydramnios. Isolated pleural effusions or ascites do not constitute hydrops fetalis. They may, however, precede it and often have a similar aetiology. Estimates of the incidence of hydrops fetalis are around 1 in 2000.

Aetiology

It is traditional to divide hydrops into two main groups. In 'immune' hydrops, oedema is secondary to anaemia due to an isoimmune antibody, classically rhesus disease. In this condition high-output cardiac failure results in oedema, occurring when the fetal haemoglobin falls below around 5 g/dl. 'Non-immune' hydrops may be secondary to any other cause and is suggested by the absence of an isoimmune antibody in the mother's blood. Cardiac causes represent almost one third of non-immune hydrops. Heart failure may be secondary to dysrhythmia, severe congenital heart disease or failure of the myocardium. The mechanisms underlying hydrops in other conditions include obstruction of venous return to the heart, mediastinal shift and heart failure and hypoproteinaemia with low oncotic pressure. In some conditions the mechanism is not understood.

A large number of congenital anomalies may be associated with hydrops, notably those with chromosomal abnormalities. In different series, 5–20% of non-immune hydrops remain without explanation.

Investigation and management of the fetus

The diagnosis of hydrops fetalis is made by ultrasound (Figure 10.1 shows an hydropic fetal hand) and the antenatal management offers

Table 10.1 Causes of hydrops fetalis

Anaemic
- immune: rhesus, ABO, Kell, etc.
- non-immune: feto-maternal bleeding, twin-twin transfusion, G6PD and thalassaemia

Cardiac
- arrhythmia: congenital heart block, SVT, congenital heart disease, cardiomyopathy

Thoracic
- chylothorax, cystic adenomatoid malformation of the lung, pulmonary lymphangiectasia

Hepatic/GI
- meconium peritonitis, atresias, hepatitis

Renal
- congenital nephrosis, renal dysplasia

Neoplasia
- neuroblastoma

Infection
- parvovirus, TORCH, syphilis

Multisystem anomalies
- chromosomal: trisomies 13,18 and 21, Turner syndrome
- non-chromosomal: lethal dwarfism, CNS malformations, arthrogryposis, neuromuscular disorders

Maternal
- diabetes, toxaemia

Placental
- venous thrombosis, chorioangioma

Idiopathic

a considerable challenge to the obstetric and paediatric teams. The full family history, including enquiry for consanguinity, should be carefully reviewed and may yield essential information. The fetus should be carefully examined on more than one occasion with high resolution imaging. In the presence of abnormalities a karyotype is performed and other tests may be suggested. The mother's serum should be checked for isoimmune antibodies, G6PD, haemoglobin electrophoresis and a Kleihauer. Serology for syphilis, TORCH and parvovirus may be helpful and should complement full assessment of the pregnancy. The fetal heart rate should be monitored carefully over a prolonged period to look for periods of very slow or fast rhythms and a detailed cardiac ultrasound performed to look for structural abnormalities. One further, poorly understood, feature of

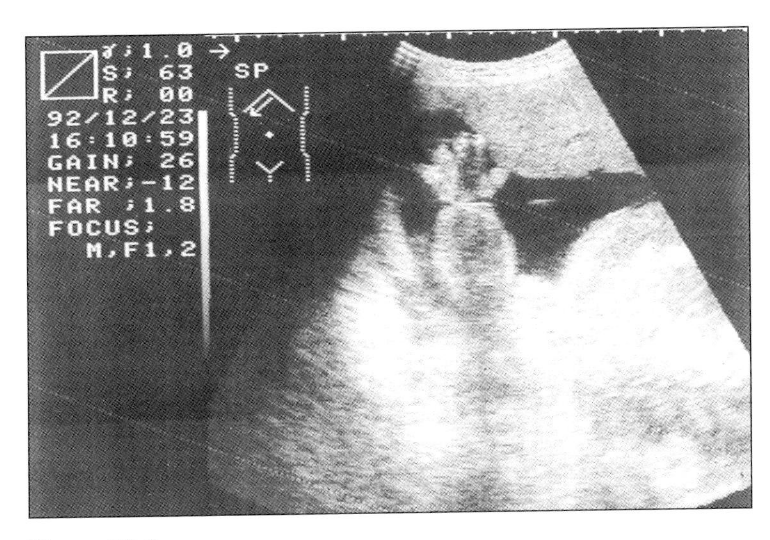

Figure 10.1

interest is the 'mirror syndrome', in which the mother also develops oedema and may go on to experience hypertension, proteinuria and even pulmonary oedema.

Cordocentesis offers direct access to the hydropic fetus. In haemolytic conditions, amniocentesis and measurement of bilirubin in the liquor may suffice. Cordocentesis, however, allows measurement of fetal haemoglobin, group, and Coomb's test and in the presence of anaemia, blood transfusion may be administered through the same needle. In non-immune hydrops cordocentesis also allows rapid chromosome analysis, measurement of albumin, and the performance of most investigations based on serum or plasma.

When hydrops is explained by congenital heart defect, the lesion is usually severe and the prognosis poor. Bradyarrhythmia is usually due to complete heart block, and may be associated with maternal auto-antibodies, as in SLE. Complete heart block seldom leads to hydrops, but when this occurs, intrauterine intervention has not been successful, and delivery for postnatal pacing may be considered. Tachyarrhythmia, usually supraventricular tachycardia, carries the best prognosis of the cardiac conditions associated with hydrops. Sinus rhythm may be restored in the fetus by digitalising the mother or by the use of other antiarrhythmics such as flecainide.

The timing of delivery of the hydropic infant is a difficult decision for the obstetrician and paediatrician. Hydropic infants are ill and, if delivered preterm, are likely to have severe hyaline membrane disease. Elective preterm delivery should only be considered when absolutely necessary. Clearly, if it is possible through intrauterine intervention to bring about resolution of the hydrops prior to delivery, this is preferable.

Immediate management of the newborn infant

If a lethal abnormality has been found antenatally intervention is not justified. Otherwise attempts should be made to resuscitate the hydropic infant in order to allow time for assessment and investigation. The paediatrician will welcome advance notice and will need time to ensure that at least two paediatricians are present for the delivery. In general, these infants will require intubation and IPPV from delivery (see Figure 10.2). Pleural effusions or ascites may embarrass ventilation and it may be necessary to tap these on the resuscitaire (see Chapter 1). After physical examination, rapid assessment is needed of the infant's haematology and biochemistry. In the hydropic infant who is anaemic urgent exchange transfusion with uncross-matched O negative blood during full intensive care and ventilation is the main hope of success.

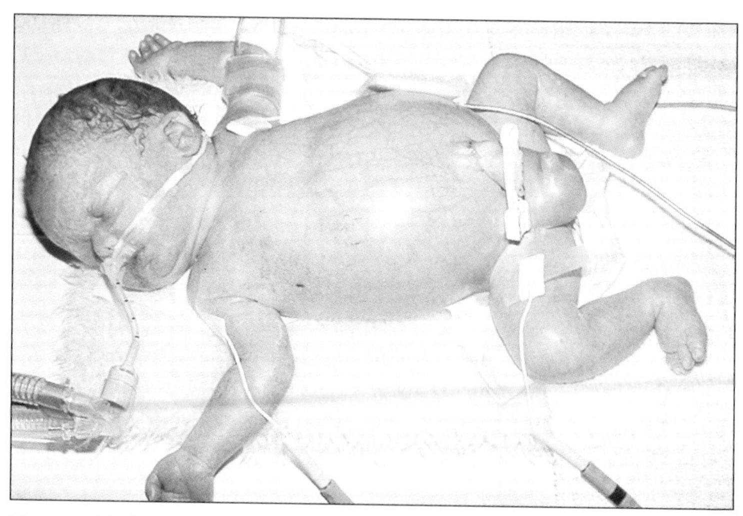

Figure 10.2

Subsequent management and prognosis

The neonatal challenge posed by these infants is considerable, often leading to a stormy period over the first day or two, even in the infant who eventually does well. General management demands adequate gas exchange, maintenance of normal acid base status and correction of other metabolic disorders. If ascites and pleural effusions are tapped, fluid should be put aside for analysis. Urine output should be closely monitored and urine saved for analysis. Peripheral subcutaneous oedema may be helped by intravenous frusemide and digitalisation may be considered.

A large number of investigations are indicated as suggested by the range of aetiology, and prognosis is clearly dependent upon primary diagnosis. Immune hydrops should no longer occur. Routine screening for isoimmune antibodies coupled with improved ultrasound techniques and the possibility of intrauterine blood transfusion make it possible to prevent this. Survival rates for anaemic hydrops before cordocentesis exceeded 90%.

Mortality in non-immune hydrops is high, ranging from 50% to 90% in various series. This is not only a reflection of the underlying causes of hydrops but also of the severity of the disorder that will induce these changes in the fetus. In this group, the infant with tachyarrhythmia and a structurally normal heart probably has the best prognosis. In general, at the present, intrauterine intervention in other groups has not been successful. Amongst hydropic infants, with their appalling prognosis, fetal surgery is currently been explored in conditions such as cystic adenomatoid malformation of the lung. It remains experimental.

11 Inborn errors of metabolism

Any recollection of the distant memory of metabolic pathways leads to the conclusion that there is room for thousands of inborn errors of metabolism. This is correct. Individually the more common ones are rare and the others very rare. Precise characterisation and diagnosis is difficult but there are some general points which may be made. A small number of conditions merit a few specific notes.

General picture

Effect of metabolic defect

The general model of an inborn error is of an enzyme deficiency at a specific point in a metabolic chain of events (Figure 11.1). The consequence is that the individual is less able to produce the products of metabolism distal to the enzyme block; there may be a build up of metabolites proximal to the critical step; and a feedback loop, sensing the absence of the missing metabolite, may drive the metabolic process harder, resulting in the increased production of intermediary metabolites or the accidental production of other substances in large amounts. The metabolic consequences of any one of these mechanisms may result in symptoms. Diagnosis is rarely through demonstration of low levels of the end product, but more often through the detection of excessive amounts of substances generated by the metabolic process prior to the enzyme block.

Genetics

The commonest genetic basis for inborn errors of metabolism is an autosomal recessive pattern of inheritance. This is true of the vast majority of inborn errors with a notable exception of ornithine transcarbamylase deficiency, an X-linked disorder the expression of

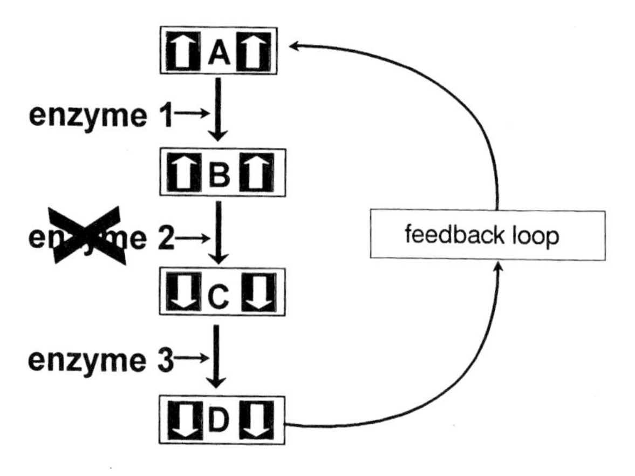

Enzyme 2 is non-functional. Low levels of D provide positive feedback driving the metabolic pathway. Clinical symptoms may result from low levels of C or D *or* the high levels of A or B. Diagnosis is usually made by measuring the high levels of A or B, or by determination of enzyme activity.

Figure 11.1 Schematic inborn error of metabolism

which in the female is dependent upon random inactivation of the X chromosome in each cell – Lyonisation.

The elucidation of a detailed family history is essential. Particular note should be taken of unexplained neonatal deaths, race, and consanguinity. The rate of inborn errors seen amongst ethnic groups with a high rate of consanguinity far exceeds that seen in the remainder of the population.

Clinical presentation

The clinical manifestations of inborn errors of metabolism are extremely varied. They may be considered in the presence of any neonatal symptom. Certain patterns, however, emerge more frequently. The commonest of these are hypoglycaemia, metabolic acidosis, unexplained collapse, neurological symptoms or seizures, or an abnormal smell to the infant or his urine. None of these features is diagnostic. In a nutshell, when symptoms such as these arise without certain explanation, particularly if there is a family history of disease or consanguinity, a high index of suspicion is needed.

Immediate management

Upon suspicion a number of simple steps should be taken. Protein intake should be stopped as in a number of these conditions protein catabolism may fuel the production of toxic metabolites. An adequate and plentiful fluid intake should be ensured together with a high calorie intake provided initially by 10% dextrose. Electrolytes and acid-base imbalance should be corrected and hypoglycaemia prevented.

Diagnostic investigation

The single most important step, following suspicion of an inborn error, is to take blood, collect urine and, in the presence of neurological symptoms, check the plasma ammonia. The next most important step is to contact a Regional Reference Laboratory for metabolic disorders. Consultation with the specialist biochemist is essential. They should be provided with the details of the history and the clinical course. Most frequently diagnosis is made from analysis of amino acids or organic acids within the urine. Specific enzymes may be measured, and on occasion final diagnosis is only reached after more complex investigation such as fibroblast culture and enzyme assay or liver biopsy.

In a small but increasing number of these conditions specific therapy is available. Diagnosis will allow early intervention where indicated. It may be possible to give a detailed prognosis to the parents, together with other information about the disorder. Without a diagnosis, clearly genetic counselling and subsequent prenatal diagnosis in future pregnancies is not possible.

Prenatal diagnosis

This is seldom possible without a definitive diagnosis in an index case. Consultation with a clinical geneticist will provide: accurate calculation of recurrence risk (avoid doing amateur genetic counselling!); information about timing and nature of investigation; and advice to the parents. Choice of technique for fetal diagnosis will depend upon a joint decision between parents, geneticist and obstetrician.

Specific conditions

Four specific conditions merit a brief mention.

1 Phenylketonuria

Phenylketonuria (PKU) is an autosomal recessive condition with an incidence of one in 5–10 000. It is due to a deficiency of L-phenylalinine hydroxylase preventing the production of tyrosine but, importantly, resulting in high levels of phenylalinine which is toxic to the brain. The natural history of this disease without intervention is one of severe mental retardation, seizures and the classic appearance of fair hair, blue eyes and eczema.

Screening for PKU is done at around the seventh day of life. A successful test requires that the infant has been fed for at least three days beforehand. In a small number of centres in the UK the assay is not possible if the child has received antibiotics. In most centres this is not relevant. A postcard-shaped piece of thick filter paper is printed to allow labelling with the child's name and date of birth (Figure 11.2). At one end small circles are printed and blood is collected at heel prick and allowed to soak into the filter paper in order to fill the circles. Small amounts of filter paper are punched out of this area and analysed for phenylalanine. A child with PKU needs a diet containing only small amounts of phenylalinine and continued careful metabolic and dietetic surveillance. The diet may be relaxed in the teenage years, but should be reintroduced, again with careful monitoring, prior to conception in young women.

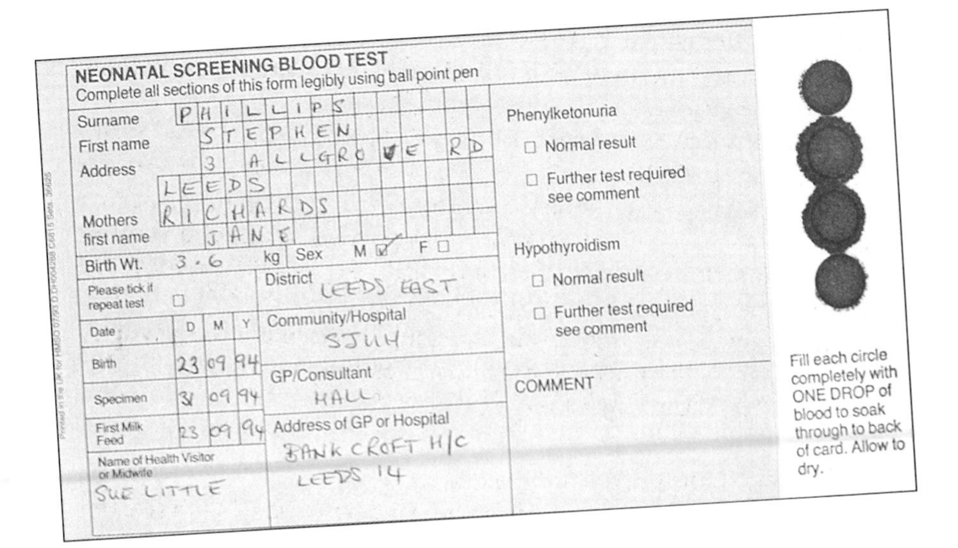

NEONATAL SCREENING BLOOD TEST
Complete all sections of this form legibly using ball point pen

Surname: PHILLIPS
First name: STEPHEN
Address: 3 ALLGROVE RD LEEDS
Mothers first name: RICHARDS JANE
Birth Wt. 3.6 kg Sex M ☑ F ☐
Please tick if repeat test ☐

Date	D	M	Y
Birth	23	09	94
Specimen	30	09	94
First Milk Feed	23	09	94

Name of Health Visitor or Midwife: SUE LITTLE
District: LEEDS EAST
Community/Hospital: SJUH
GP/Consultant: HALL
Address of GP or Hospital: BANK CROFT H/C LEEDS 14

Phenylketonuria
☐ Normal result
☐ Further test required see comment

Hypothyroidism
☐ Normal result
☐ Further test required see comment

COMMENT

Fill each circle completely with ONE DROP of blood to soak through to back of card. Allow to dry.

Figure 11.2

2 Galactosaemia

This is an autosomal recessive condition with an incidence of around 1 in 10 000. It is due to the absence of galactose-1-phosphate-uridyl transferase. The inability to metabolise galactose from milk results in its accumulation. This produces a varied clinical picture and the presence of galactose, a reducing substance, in the urine. Infants suffer from jaundice and vomiting, and become less well in the second week of life. Cataracts, hepatomegaly, fits and severe infection are characteristic. Diagnosis is difficult since the infant may recover when given clear fluids, and then again become unwell when re-fed milk. Whole blood is used to measure the enzyme. Treatment involves the long-term use of a lactose-free milk.

3 Congenital adrenal hyperplasia

This condition is autosomal recessive with an incidence of around 1 in 5000. It is most commonly due to 21 hydroxylase deficiency in the adrenal gland, resulting in failure of endogenous corticosteroid production. In fetal life feedback to the pituitary gland results in a high level of adrenocorticotropic hormone (ACTH) and which drives the adrenal gland resulting in the overproduction of androgens. The affected boy may not be noticed to be abnormal at delivery although pigmentation of the genitalia may be present. The girl on the other hand will be born with virilisation of the female genitalia, with marked hypertrophy of the clitoris and fusion of the labia. The gonads are not palpable. In this, as in any condition with abnormal genitalia, sex should not be ascribed at delivery and investigations should be commenced.

A diagnosis may be made from the third and fifth day by the measurement of plasma 17-OH progesterone, a steroid precursor which is present in increased amounts. Failure to diagnose at this stage will allow the onset of an Addisonian crisis in the second week of life, characterised by hypotension, collapse, hypoglycaemia, and possibly sudden death.

Treatment is successful through lifelong replacement therapy with glucocorticoids (hydrocortisone) and mineralocorticoids (fludrocrotisone). Genitoplasty may be required in girls.

4 Congenital hypothyroidism

This is not usually an inborn error of metabolism but has been included here because screening is done at the same time as PKU.

Congenital hypothyroidism is most commonly due to the absence of a thyroid gland, but may rarely be due to enzyme problems within the gland. Thyroid function is diminished, the infant has a low thyroid hormone, and a high level of thyroid-stimulating hormone through the feedback mechanism. Blood is collected in the identical fashion described above for PKU. The blood spot is analysed for TSH. (Very rarely hypothyroidism is secondary to hypopituitarism, and TSH will not be elevated.) Treatment is lifelong replacement of thyroid hormone. Failure to diagnose this condition results in an infant who is initially slow to feed, jaundiced and fails to gain weight, but most importantly will then go on to develop cretinism with associated mental retardation (see Figure 11.3). The prognosis with early diagnosis and management is good.

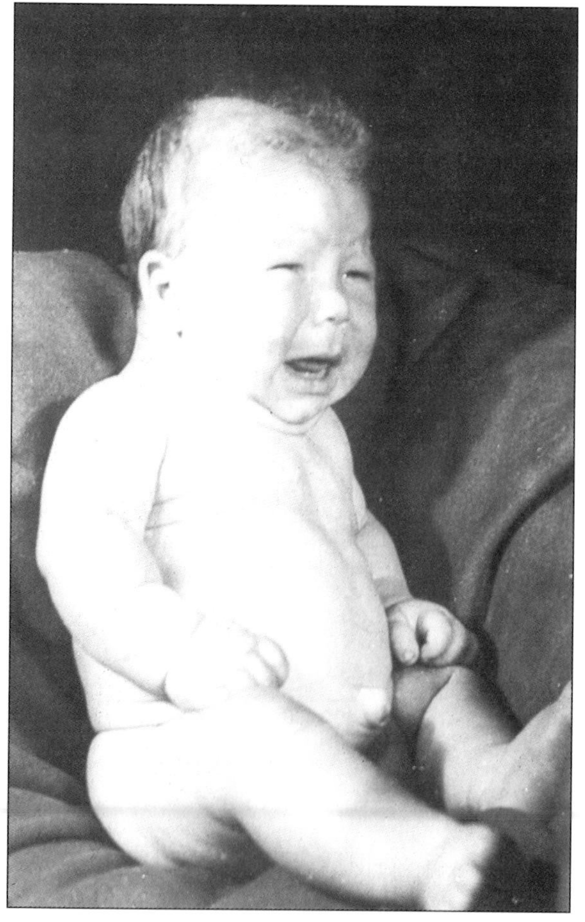

Figure 11.3

Routine screening in England and Wales

All infants are screened for PKU and hypothyroidism as described above. In many centres screening for cystic fibrosis is performed through measurement of circulating immunoreactive trypsin on a blood spot taken in exactly the same fashion. In some centres full amino-acid chromatography is performed rather than simple measurement of phenylalanine and other diagnoses may be made. Finally, limited screening in certain racial groups may be performed. The criteria and requirements of a good screening test are well recognised, but beyond the scope of this chapter, and prolonged and detailed study may be necessary before conclusions are drawn about the merits of any new screening test.

12 Neonatal effects of maternal disease

Maternal diabetes

Pathophysiology

Maternal diabetes can adversely affect the fetal environment in two ways. The commonest adverse effects are those mediated by maternal hyperglycaemia. Less common are the adverse effects of fetal hypoxia and malnutrition resulting from maternal diabetic vasculopathy.

The fetal blood-glucose concentration normally follows the pattern of the maternal blood-glucose concentration but at a slightly lower level. Maternal hyperglycaemia is associated with fetal hyperglycaemia but in response to maternal hypoglycaemia the fetus seems generally able to maintain its blood-glucose concentration from endogenous sources of glucose. The effects of fetal hyperglycaemia are numerous and are outlined in Table 12.1.

The better the control of maternal diabetes throughout pregnancy the less likely is the fetus to suffer from the adverse effects listed, including a lower risk of congenital malformation if attention is paid to maternal glucose homeostasis pre- and peri-conceptionally. Now that it is possible to achieve good control of maternal diabetes throughout the period of conception and pregnancy, the outlook for the baby should be little different from normal and the atrocious perinatal mortality rates that used to be associated with maternal diabetes in pregnancy have become a thing of the past. However, despite the best efforts of obstetrician and physician we still do see the occasional diabetic cherub and such babies often present a serious challenge to the neonatologist. As ever, it greatly helps the neonatologist to be forewarned of the impending birth of such babies.

Table 12.1 Effects of elevated maternal blood-glucose concentrations on the fetus

1 Congenital anomalies
When maternal diabetic control is not scrupulously maintained around the time of conception the incidence of congenital anomalies is about 8%. Cardiac and renal anomalies predominate but vertebral anomalies, including the cordal regression syndrome with sacral agenesis, are a more specific problem of the infant of the diabetic mother.

2 Macrosomia
Infants of poorly controlled diabetic mothers are large and have organomegaly, especially involving the liver, adrenals and heart. In some cases the cardiomegaly amounts to a hypertrophic cardiomyopathy which may cause congestive heart failure. The cardiomyopathy usually resolves completely during the weeks following birth. Interestingly, some 30% of infants of mothers with good diabetic control have weights above the 90th centile for gestation, particularly those infants whose mothers are obese or have gained weight excessively during pregnancy.

3 Respiratory distress syndrome (RDS)
The relative risk of respiratory distress syndrome is approximately five times greater than control infants matched for gestational age. Prenatal assessment of the risk of RDS in infants of diabetic mothers is tricky because the lecithin:sphingomyelin ratio is less reliable than in normal infants. The presence of phosphatidyl glycerol in amniotic fluid or an L:S ratio of greater than three would suggest that significant RDS is unlikely. This presdisposition makes avoidance of other factors which may add to the risk of RDS, such as perinatal asphyxia, more critical in these infants.

4 Hypoglycaemia
In response to hyperglycaemia during fetal life, hyperplasia of beta cells in the pancreas occurs. After birth it takes the newborn infant some time to downgrade its insulin production and in the absence of a high glucose intake hypoglycaemia often occurs. Infants of diabetic mothers also lack some of the normal compensatory responses to hypoglycaemia. Symptomatic hypoglycaemia is rare, however, among infants of diabetic mothers because in the newborn, although not in the adult, insulin enables glucose entry into the nervous system. Neonatal hypoglycaemia due to maternal diabetes usually presents within a short time of birth and often ceases to be a problem beyond about 12–24 hours of age. The exception to this rule is the infant of a diabetic mother who has also been asphyxiated and in those circumstances profound and prolonged neonatal hypoglycaemia is sometimes seen.

The effects of maternal vascular disease

Women with long-standing insulin-dependent diabetes that has progressed to the point of vascular complications may produce infants with growth impairment. Figure 12.1 shows two infants of diabetic mothers, one macrosomic and the other showing marked intrauterine growth retardation. Growth-retarded infants of diabetic mothers suffer the same adverse consequences of growth impairment from other causes (see Chapter 4).

Maternal thyroid disease

Pathophysiology

Maternal thyroxine and TSH do not cross the placenta in physiologically significant amounts. The fetal thyroid axis is therefore autonomous. Maternal disease exerts its effects through the transplacental passage of immunoglobulin G (IgG) thyroid stimulating antibodies or maternal anti-thyroid drugs. In mothers with

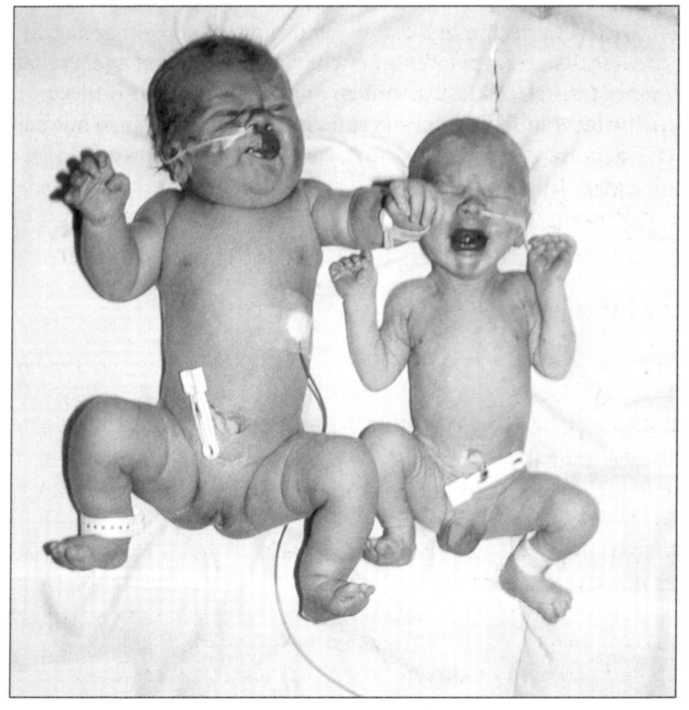

Figure 12.1

thyrotoxicosis, propylthiouracil or carbimazole are the drugs of choice; iodides should be avoided and no pregnant mother should be given radio-iodine.

Transient neonatal hypothyroidism and goitre

The most important cause of hypothyroidism in the neonatal period is thyroid agenesis or dysgenesis (see Chapter 11), conditions which are unrelated to maternal thyroid status and are permanent. Infants may, however, develop temporary hypothyroidism when the mother is receiving anti-thyroid treatment with carbimazole or propylthiouracil during pregnancy. This is an unusual effect of maternal treatment, and produces a mild form of neonatal hypothyroidism which resolves spontaneously and very rarely requires thyroxine treatment. The clinical features of prolonged gestation, feeding problems, poor temperature and tone control and prolonged jaundice are those seen in true neonatal hypothyroidism. Maternal iodide ingestion, accidental or therapeutic, may induce a goitre in an infant who is hypothyroid or euthyroid.

Maternal hyperthyroidism

This is a more important condition to the infant. In Graves disease, 1–3% of infants will have clinical hyperthyroidism secondary to the transplacental passage of thyroid stimulating antibodies. Immunoglobulin M (IgM) does not cross the placenta and therefore the significant antibodies are IgG. Principal amongst these is long-acting, thyroid stimulating (LATS) antibody, where maternal levels relate to the severity of neonatal disease. The aim of management should be detection of hyperthyroidism in the mother, and treatment with propylthiouracil or carbimazole which may both suppress antibody production in the mother and confer some protection on the infant. Occasionally transplacental thyroid stimulating antibodies may affect the fetus, producing heart failure or hydops, and in digitalisation of the mother and fetus may be helpful. Importantly, the mother who previously had Graves disease may be euthyroid but still have elevated levels of antibodies which may affect her fetus.

In the newborn infant the clinical picture varies from mild irritability and jitteryness with a tachycardia to a severe, life-threatening illness associated with extreme tachycardia and even tachyarrhythmia and intractable heart failure. The infant may have exophthalmos or any other of the features of thyrotoxicosis. Initial treatment of the symptomatic infant is propranolol and anti-thyroid drugs as used in the mother. The prognosis for the infant is usually good if complications are avoided, with resolution of the thyrotoxicosis in two or three months. There is evidence, however, to suggest that these infants later have a lower IQ and may be predisposed to craniosynostosis.

Systemic lupus erythematosis

Pathophysiology

The neonatal effects of maternal systemic lupus erythematosis (SLE) are mediated through the transplacental passage of IgG auto-antibodies. The severity of the illness in the infant is not directly related to the levels of antibody in the mother. Amongst the lupus antibodies, anti-Ro is particularly important in the aetiology of fetal cardiac problems; however, any of the maternal antibodies that may cross the placenta and indeed the infant may develop the full picture of SLE. The exact proportion of infants of affected mothers who develop symptoms is not known. For the mother, pregnancy may have a beneficial effect upon SLE with improvement in the third trimester and, not surprisingly, this is also beneficial to the affected fetus.

Fetal cardiac effects

Two important conditions occur in the fetus: complete heart block (CHB) and endocardial fibroelastosis. Lupus antibodies damage the atrioventricular conduction pathways, resulting in heart block, which in SLE is most commonly CHB, with complete atrioventricular dissociation. In association with maternal SLE the heart is most commonly structurally normal. In infants whose mothers do not have SLE, CHB is commonly associated with severe complex structural heart defects. The finding, therefore, of CHB and a structurally normal heart should prompt careful investigation of the mother.

In CHB, the fetal heart rate is usually below 100 beats per minute. Fetal and neonatal prognosis is related to the heart rate and as it drops below 60 per minute, heart failure becomes more likely. Extremely slow heart rate may be associated with hydrops in the fetus, and before this occurs, if gestation allows, delivery may be indicated. Attempts at fetal therapy through maternal administration of chronotropes, like isoprenaline, have not been universally successful.

After delivery, echocardiography should be performed as clinical examination is an unreliable indicator of complex cardiac lesions. Infants with a heart rate over 60 are unlikely to run into problems. In the presence of heart failure or more profound bradycardia, isoprenaline is given while awaiting pacing. Prognosis is related to the degree of neonatal illness and, rarely, these infants require life-long pacing.

Endocardial fibroelastosis is much less common, carries a less good prognosis and is associated with poor myocardial contractility and heart failure.

Haematological disease

A haemolytic anaemia may occur in the neonate, similar to that seen in the mother. Consequent problems are anaemia and jaundice and may be complicated by disseminated intravascular coagulation. Leucopenia is seen but is rarely severe. Thrombocytopenia is more common and again mediated through the transplacental antibodies. Treatment of the mother or baby with high-dose steroid will increase the circulating platelet count. The prognosis is good providing the infant does not have severe neonatal illness or bleeding.

Other effects of SLE

Mothers with SLE are prone to spontaneous abortion and lupus placental disease may lead to intrauterine growth retardation. A search for lupus antibodies is therefore commonly performed in investigation of unexplained abortion and IUGR. In extreme cases, in addition to any of the above features, infants may be born with the picture of lupus with any of the features seen in the adult. These include the butterfly skin rash, other skin problems and hepatitis, and are more likely in the female infant.

Myasthenia gravis

Pathophysiology

Myasthenia gravis is almost always due to an IgG antibody against the acetylcholine receptor protein. This antibody is not found in other auto-immune conditions and acts by deposition in an immune complex on the postsynaptic membrane. Disease in the mother may improve or deteriorate during pregnancy. Importantly antibodies may be present in women with no symptoms of myasthenia gravis, and may persist in those who are asymptomatic after thymectomy.

Transient neonatal myasthenia gravis

Of babies born to mothers known to have myasthenia gravis, 10–20% will develop a transient form of the disease, beginning within hours or days and usually lasting up to six weeks, but occasionally longer. The severity of the disease in the infant is not related to the severity of symptoms in the mother. The fetus is, however, more likely to be affected in the mother who has high circulating levels of the antibody.

The commonest symptoms in the infant are hypotonia and feeding problems, but may extend to poor respiratory function and even necessitate ventilatory assistance (Figure 12.2). Ptosis is less common in the infant. Diagnosis requires a high index of suspicion and is

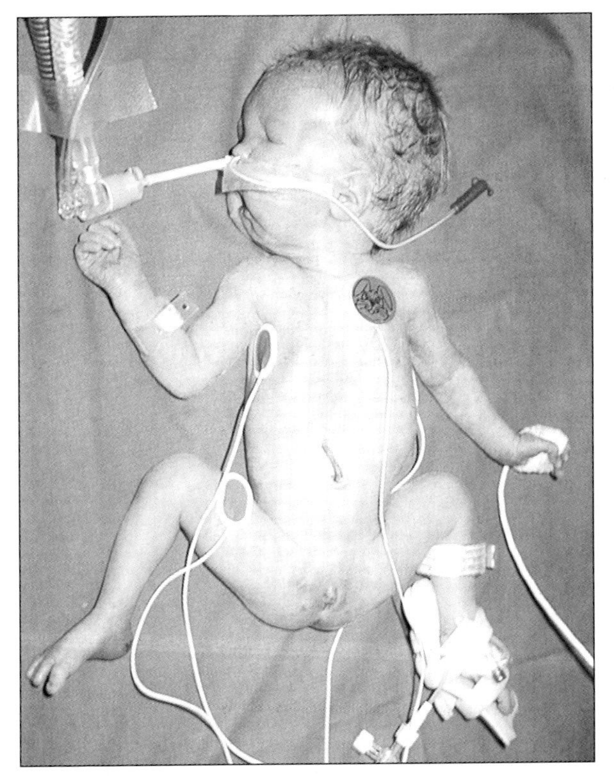

Figure 12.2

confirmed in the infant with a tensilon (edrophonium) test. Maintenance therapy is usually with neostigmine or pyridostigmine. Occasionally in severe cases, exchange transfusion has been attempted in order to remove maternal antibodies from the infant's circulation. The prognosis is excellent with spontaneous resolution, providing there are no complications in the neonatal period.

An extremely rare neonatal form of true myasthenia exists. This may be inherited and is persistent.

Other auto-immune disease

Any maternal auto-immune disease mediated through an IgG antibody may theoretically have an effect upon the fetus. Some conditions like temporal arteritis are rare in mothers of reproductive age, while others such as chronic active hepatitis may reduce fertility. Aside from SLE, thyroid disease and myasthenia gravis, the most important conditions to the fetus are idiopathic thrombocytopenic purpura and auto-immune haemolysis which are discussed elsewhere (see Chapter 9).

Inflammatory bowel disease as an example of chronic maternal illness

Maternal Crohn's disease and ulcerative colitis do not usually affect the fetus. They are, however, good examples of systemic diseases in the mother who, when pregnant, merits special consideration with regard to general maternal health and nutrition, and also the therapeutic agents employed. Inflammatory bowel disease (IBD) may be exacerbated by pregnancy. Maternal malnutrition and generalised illness results in a higher rate of spontaneous abortion and in intrauterine growth retardation. IBD should be managed aggressively in the mother, and close attention should be given to maintaining maternal nutritional status and metabolic homeostasis.

Drug therapy

Special consideration should be given to drug therapy. Aminosalicylic acid derivatives (e.g. sulphasalazine) may result in intrauterine or postnatal haemolysis in the infant. Folate supplements may be given to the mother to prevent this, and should be given to the newborn infant. High-dose corticosteroid (a dose greater than prednisolone 10 mg daily or equivalent) may produce fetal adrenal suppression.

The benefits of its use, however, usually outweigh the possible detrimental effects. Finally, immune suppressants such as azathioprine are contraindicated in pregnancy. They may result in spontaneous abortion and should be avoided as soon as pregnancy is recognised. As in any other chronic illness, however, disruption of the menstrual cycle may lead to failure of recognition of early pregnancy when amenorrhoea is noted and lead to accidental exposure, in the first trimester, to drugs which are normally avoided.

Multidisciplinary approach to serious maternal illness

IBD is used here as an example of a maternal illness which may affect the fetus but any severe or chronic maternal illness may compromise fetal health. In this area, par excellence, close collaboration between obstetrician, paediatrician and the mother's physicians and surgeons is essential. We have recently been involved in the delivery of a baby, preterm, by Caesarean section and, at the same operation, a liver transplant in the mother for chronic active hepatitis. Mother and child have done extremely well. This sort of venture can only be considered where a large multidisciplinary team can be brought to bear upon the problem.

Maternal substance abuse

All available data on the subject of the fetal implications of maternal alcohol or drug abuse must be viewed with circumspection. It is often not possible to know exactly what substance and how much each mother has taken, making it very hard to relate fetal exposure to neonatal outcome. Sadly, it is an area of increasing importance in neonatal medicine, but fortunately mothers afflicted by drug addition are becoming more aware of the possible effects upon their unborn child and more often seek earlier attention and help. This group of mothers is at high risk of human immunodeficiency virus (HIV) infection and hepatitis (see Chapter 8). The problems related to drugs are those associated with direct toxicity to the fetus and those which result from drug withdrawal after birth. Often this is against a background of maternal illness and social deprivation.

Maternal alcohol related disease

Fetal alcohol syndrome

Any intake of alcohol should be discouraged in the first trimester. Moderate drinking, not exceeding one unit per day, may be safe in the final trimester. Large amounts of alcohol, equivalent to six units per day, during the early weeks of pregnancy results in a well-recognised dysmorphic syndrome. Infants suffer intrauterine growth retardation and have an increased risk of intrauterine death. At delivery they are small for gestational age with microcephaly and go on to have mental retardation. The face is abnormal with a broad nose, a long upper lip and a small jaw, and there may be associated congenital heart disease. Prevention is the only therapeutic tool.

Neonatal alcohol withdrawal

Neonatal alcohol withdrawal may occur with a cluster of symptoms similar to those seen with opiates, as discussed below. This is more likely in a mother taking in excess of 10 units a week in the final trimester.

Maternal drug addiction

Infants conceived by mothers who are abusing drugs have an increased chance of intrauterine growth retardation, low birthweight, intrauterine death and perinatal asphyxia. Of these infants, 50% are born preterm. There is considerable advantage in encouraging mothers to come forward with honesty for help before conception or early in pregnancy. Conversion from heroin or other opiates to methadone is advantageous, allowing control of exposure, avoiding contaminants and possibly improving the prognosis for the infants.

Neonatal drug withdrawal syndrome

The most important neonatal problem with the opiates is one of withdrawal. During withdrawal the infant goes through an illness ('cold turkey') as he or she comes off opiates. This process is slower and more prolonged than in the adult, partly because the half life of opiates in the infant is much longer.

Withdrawal produces a constellation of symptoms. The infant is usually irritable and inconsolable, making nursing very difficult and often associated with feeding problems, snuffles and diarrhoea. Infants will cry incessantly and may have respiratory distress but may also have apnoeic attacks. Untreated intense irritability may precede seizures and even death. In the longer term poor weight gain is often a feature. In addition to these effects, prenatal use of cocaine, with its sympathomimetic action, produces placental vaso-constriction, and a high risk of intrauterine death, abortion and IUGR.

The withdrawal syndrome varies according to the dose and drug which the mother has been taking. The half life of the drug has an effect on the speed of withdrawal, cocaine base (Crack) and heroin being rapid and methadone slower. Onset of withdrawal may be from hours to 10 days and infants of known maternal drug abusers should be carefully observed for at least 10 days. Morphine is used to treat opiate withdrawal and this is required by approximately one third of infants born to mothers who are known to abuse opiates. The dose and frequency of morphine is very variable and while some infants will require no treatment, others may require regular morphine for a period of many weeks. In these infants the dose is slowly reduced. In some infants symptoms cannot be controlled with morphine and chlorpromazine is added, and if seizures occur anticonvulsants are indicated. These infants should not at any stage be given naxolone. In the infant of the mother abusing cocaine, chlorpromazine is the treatment of choice.

Mothers who continue to abuse drugs should not breastfeed. Discharge home into the parents' care should only be done after full and careful consideration with colleagues from social services. Child protection is clearly an important issue here and a large proportion of these infants eventually need foster care or adoption.

Cannabis has not been shown to have any deleterious effect upon the fetus.

Cigarette smoking

The evidence that smoking more than 20 cigarettes is detrimental to the fetus is compelling. All cigarette smoking should be strongly discouraged before and throughout pregnancy. Smoking is associated with intrauterine growth retardation, preterm delivery and increased perinatal mortality. There is no association with increased congenital anomalies. Recent evidence has suggested a biological programming induced by maternal smoking during pregnancy. These infants have an increased rate of sudden infant death syndrome and recent data suggest that they are more likely to suffer chronic respiratory problems in early life.

Suggested references for further reading

Major textbooks of neonatal medicine

Textbook of Neonatology (1992, 2nd ed.) edited by N. R. C. Roberton. Edinburgh: Churchill Livingstone – this is the main British reference work.

Diseases of the Newborn (1991, 6th ed.) edited by A. J. Schaffer, M. E. Avery, H. W. Taeusch and R. A. Ballard. Philadelphia: W. B. Saunders – this is the main American reference work.

Pocket sized books

A Manual of Neonatal Intensive Care (1993, 3rd ed.), by N. R. C. Roberton. London: Edward Arnold

A Neonatal Vade-Mecum (1995, 2nd ed.), edited by P. J. Fleming, B. D. Speidel, N. Marlow *et al.* London: Edward Arnold

Practical Management of the Newborn (1993, 5th ed.), edited by R. J. K. Brown, H.B. Valman and I. M. Balfour-Lynn. Oxford: Blackwell Science

Specialist reference works

Drug Therapy in Infants and Children: Pharmacologic Principles and Clinical Experience (1984) by R. J. Roberts. Philadelphia: W. B. Saunders (now out of print, but copies may be available through libraries)

Fetal and Neonatal Neurology and Neurosurgery (1995, 2nd ed.), edited by M. I. Levene *et al.* Edinburgh: Churchill Livingstone

Infectious Diseases of the Fetus and Newborn Infant (1994, 4th ed.), edited by J. S. Remington and J. O. Klein. London: W. B. Saunders

Recognizable Patterns of Human Malformation (1988, 4th ed.), edited by D. W. Smith and K. L. Jones. London: W. B. Saunders

Useful software

The Cochrane Pregnancy and Childbirth Database. Update Software – available from BMJ Publishing Group, BMA House, Tavistock Square, London WC1H 9JR

The London Dysmorphology Data Base, Oxford University Press, Walton Street, Oxford, OX2 6DP

The London Neurogenetics Database, Oxford University Press, Walton Street, Oxford, OX2 6DP

Index

A
ABO 75, 108
anaemia 74–5, 99, 109
haemolytic 74, 100
Apgar score 8
apnoea 42–3
ascites 107, 110

B
bag and mask ventilation 9
biliary atresia 78
birth asphyxia 5–8
birth injury 20
skeletal 22
soft tissue injuries 23
bleeding diathesis 69
breastfeeding 59–63
advantages 62
common problems 61
composition of breast milk 60
contraindications 63
physiology 60
bronchopulmonary dysplasia 42

C
candida 95
cardiac massage 14
cataracts 30
cephalhaematoma 23
cerebral hypoxia 54
cerebral palsy 15–17
chromosome 109
clavicle fracture 22
coagulation disorders 102
colostrum 61
complete heart block 125
congenital adrenal hyperplasia 117
congenital anomalies 69, 81–8, 107, 108
common, minor 86–8
gut anomalies 69–71, 85
incidence 81
prenatal diagnosis 82
skeletal 85
congenital arrhythmia 109
congenital dislocation of the hip
detection 34
congenital heart disease 13, 85, 107, 108
complete heart block in SLE 125
congenital HIV 91
congenital infection 107–9
congenital rubella 90
conjunctivitis 94
chlamydia 94
gonococcal 95
cordocentesis 109, 111
cystic adenomatoid malformation 108

D
dexamethasone, preterm infant 39
DIC 106
Down's syndrome 20, 28, 69–70, 81
drug withdrawal syndrome 130–31
drugs in labour 24
duodenal atresia 69–70

E
Erb's palsy 20
erythema toxicum 87
examination of the hips 34
examination of the newborn 28–35
exchange transfusion 78
exomphalos 70

F
facial nerve palsy 21, 30
fat necrosis 87
feeding 59–68
feeding problems 68

fetal alcohol syndrome 130
fetal assessment 1
fetal blood gas status 2
fetal circulation 4
fetal haemoglobin 4
fetal oxygenation. 5
fetomaternal bleeding 13, 19, 99, 108
fontanelle 30
formula feeding 63
composition of milk 63
specialised formulae 66–7

G

galactosaemia 114
gastrointestinal problems 68
gastroschisis 70
glucose 6 phosphatase deficiency (G6PD) 108

H

haemangioma, capillary 86
haemangioma, port wine stain 86
haemangioma, strawberry naevus 86
haematology
coagulation disorder 105
coagulation disorders 102
normal values 99
thrombocytopenia 103
haemophilia 105
haemorrhage, intracranial 20
haemorrhagic disease of the newborn 26, 104
Hirschsprung's disease 70
HIV 91
hydrocephalus 30
hydrops fetalis 13, 100, 107–11
hypoglycaemia 54
maternal diabetes 122
hypothermia
prevention 25
hypothryoidism
congenital 117–18
goitre 124
screening 119
transient 124

I

imperforate anus 70
inborn errors of metabolism 68, 113–19
clinical presentation 114
genetics 113
investigation 115
indeterminate sex 33
infant of a diabetic mother 121
infection 89
candida 95–6
congenital pneumonia 96
congenital, viral 89
intrapartum acquisition 19
meningitis 96
organisms responsible 93
predisposing factors in newborn 92
preterm 42
signs of neonatal infection 93
skin 94
transplacental 89
urinary tract infection 97
intestinal obstruction 69
intracranial haemorrhage 20
intracranial infarction/ haemorrhage 43
intubation during resuscitation 11–12
isoimmunisation 79, 107, 108, 111
IUGR 49–57
aetiology 50
neonatal consequences 54–7
perinatal assessment 51

J

jaundice 73–80
aetiology 74, 75
golden rules 73
management of hyperbilirubinaemia 77
physiological 73
physiological plus 76
table of aetiology 75
toxicity of bilirubin 76

K

kernicterus 76
Klumpke's palsy 20–21

L

lung liquid 2

M

maternal alcohol or drug abuse 129–31
maternal diabetes 121
benefits of improved control 121
congenital anomalies 122
effects of vascular disease 123
macrosomia 122
respiratory distress syndrome 123
maternal disease
diabetes 121

inflammatory bowel disease 128
thryotoxicosis 124
thyroid disease 123–5
meconium 69
meconium aspiration syndrome 17
meconium ileus 70
meningitis 96
mirror syndrome 108–9
mongolian blue spots 87
myasthenia gravis 126–8

N

necrotising enterocolitis 44
neonatal resuscitation 110–11
adrenaline 14
bag and mask ventilation 9
intubation 11
preterm 39
prevention of heat loss 9
problems 13
suction, stimulation, oxygen 9
nerve palsies 20–22
newborn examination 28–35
nutrition 57, 59–68
IUGR 57
preterm infant 67

O

oedema 107
opiate addiction 130
neonatal withdrawal 130
outcome
IUGR 57

P

passage of urine and meconium 37
patent ductus arteriosus 2, 44
periventricular bleeding 43
periventricular leucomalacia 43
persistent fetal circulation 18, 57
persistent pulmonary hypertension of the newborn 18, 57
phenylketonuria 116
phototherapy 77
phrenic nerve palsy 21
pneumonia 96
pneumothorax 13
polycythaemia 55–6, 101–2
polyhydramnios 107
port wine stain 86
prenatal diagnosis 84–5
preterm infant 37–48
aetiology 38
apnoea 42
incidence 37
infertility treatment 38
intracranial infarction/ haemorrhage 43
metabolic problems 46
nutrition 40, 67
prognosis 37, 46
thermoregulation 40
prolonged jaundice 78

R

respiratory distress syndrome 41
maternal diabetes 122
prevention 39–40
retinopathy of prematurity 45
rhesus disease 79
routine screening in England and Wales 35, 119
rubella 90

S

skull fracture 22
small for gestation age 67
sternomastoid tumour 24
strawberry naevus 86
sub-aponeurotic haemorrhage 24
surfactant 2
syndromes 83
systemic lupus erythematosis 125
haematology 126

T

tachypnoea 32
talipes 88
thermoregulation 55
thrombocytopenia 103
thyrotoxicosis
transient neonatal disease 124
tracheo-oesophageal fistula 69
transition to extrauterine life 1
physiology 1
twin-twin transfusion 99, 108

U

umbilical cord 27
urinary tract infection 97
urticaria neonatorum 87

V

very low birthweight 37
vitamin K 25, 61, 68–9, 104
vomiting 68

Neonatology
for the
MRCOG

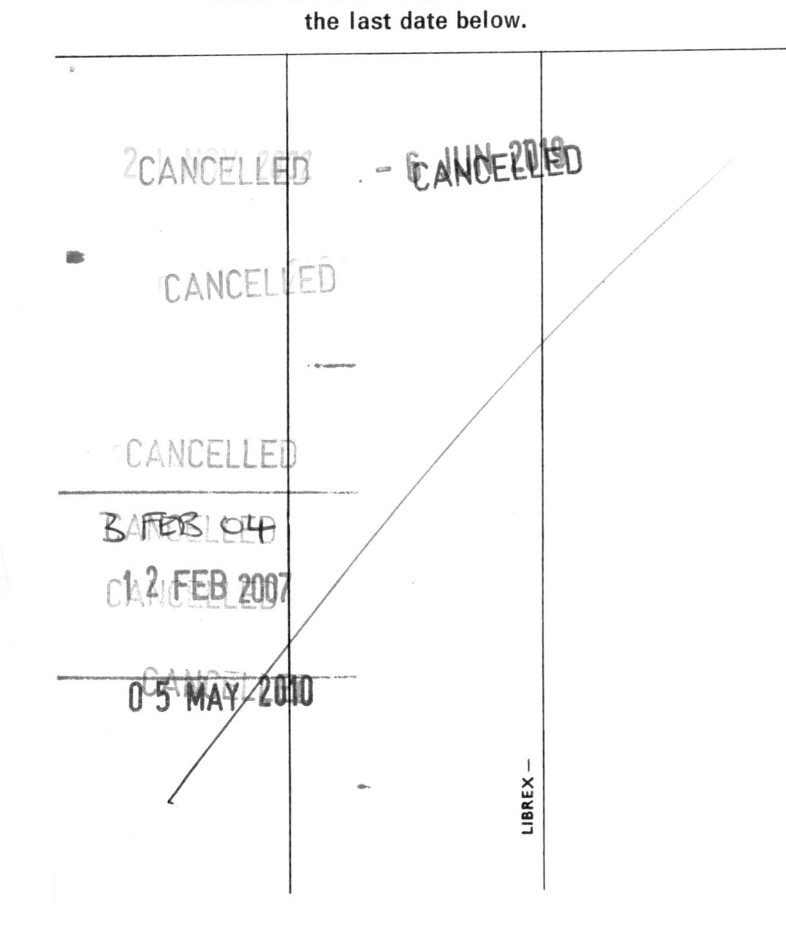

Proposed titles in the MRCOG Series

Antenatal Disorders for the MRCOG

Contraception for the MRCOG

Genetics and Fetal Medicine for the MRCOG

Gynaecological Oncology for the MRCOG

Gynaecological Pathology for the MRCOG

Gynaecological Urology for the MRCOG

Infertility for the MRCOG

Intrapartum Care for the MRCOG

Menstrual Problems for the MRCOG

Neonatology for the MRCOG

Reproductive Endocrinology for the MRCOG

The MRCOG: A Guide to the Examination

ART ESSENTIALS

KUNST BETRACHTEN

ART ESSENTIALS

KUNST BETRACHTEN

JANETTA
REBOLD BENTON

MIDAS

INHALT

6 EINFÜHRUNG

8 WAS IST KUNST?

36 KUNST ERLEBEN, ANALYSIEREN UND WERTSCHÄTZEN

66 MATERIALIEN UND TECHNIKEN

98 ABER WAS BEDEUTET DAS?

130 SECHS BESONDERE KÜNSTLERINNEN UND KÜNSTLER

166 Glossar
171 Literaturempfehlungen
172 Index
174 Bildnachweise

EINFÜHRUNG

Pablo Picasso, der vielleicht einflussreichste Künstler des 20. Jahrhunderts, äußerte die Idee, Kunst wäre dazu da, uns vom Staub des täglichen Lebens zu befreien. Die bildenden Künste regen uns zum Nachdenken an und bereichern unser Leben in vielerlei Hinsicht. Sie liefern innovative Ideen, ermöglichen uns den Genuss von Schönheit und wecken vielfältige Emotionen – und sie verwirren uns zuweilen. *Kunst betrachten* liefert einen klaren und strukturierten Überblick über die Grundlagen, die allen visuellen Kunstformen gleich sind. Es hilft uns, Kunst umsichtig, neugierig und letztlich kritisch zu hinterfragen. Indem wir unseren Blick für die Kunst schärfen, verstehen wir auch ihre Konzepte deutlich besser.

Die Fülle an Informationen und die Vorschläge in diesem Buch, wie Sie sich der Kunst nähern können, intensivieren Ihr Kunsterlebnis, denn sie liefern eine solide Grundlage für den einfachen Genuss wie auch für ein tiefergehendes Verständnis. Um über ein »Ich verstehe nicht viel von Kunst, aber ich weiß, was mir gefällt« hinauszukommen, muss man verstehen, warum man Kunst mag. Genau das ist das Ziel dieses Buches.

Dieses Buch nähert sich dem Thema »Kunst betrachten«, indem es eine Reihe von Fragen stellt und einige der großen Debatten der Kunstgeschichte vorstellt. Es werden mutige Versuche unternommen, den ungenauen, aber häufig verwendeten Begriff »Kunst« zu definieren. Wie Sie Kunst erleben, analysieren und schätzen, ist bedingt durch das Verständnis der grundlegenden Elemente, einschließlich ästhetischer Prinzipien und Stile. Ein Verständnis der von Künstlern verwendeten »Materialien und Techniken« ermöglicht es, zu beurteilen, was in bestimmten Medien möglich ist (und was nicht).

Haben Sie sich schon einmal gefragt: »Und was bedeutet das nun?« In diesem Abschnitt sehen wir uns Beispiele an, die helfen, die Botschaften in der Kunst zu enträtseln. Der Kontext ist der Schlüssel zum Verständnis eines bestimmten Symbols. Das letzte Kapitel untersucht das Leben und die Arbeit von »Sechs besonderen Künstlerinnen und Künstlern«: Leonardo da Vinci, Rembrandt van Rijn, Vincent van Gogh, Frida Kahlo, Pablo Picasso und Andy Warhol. Aus verschiedenen Ländern und Epochen stammend, nimmt jeder von ihnen eine Schlüsselstellung in der Kunstgeschichte ein.

WAS IST KUNST?

-

Schönheit ist Wahrheit, Wahr ist Schön! – Nicht viel,
Nur dies weißt du – und brauchst nicht mehr zu wissen.

-

John Keats
1819

Norman Rockwell
Boys Playing Leapfrog, veröffentlicht auf dem Cover der *Saturday Evening Post*, 28. Juni 1919
Öl auf Leinwand, Abmessungen des Originals unbekannt
Norman Rockwell Museum, Stockbridge, MA

Der Amerikaner Rockwell schuf während seiner Laufbahn mehr als 4.000 Werke, meist für Zeitschriften. Sollte Rockwell eher als Illustrator denn als Künstler gelten, weil seine Arbeiten vor allem für die massenhafte Verbreitung in Zeitschriften gedacht waren? Wie sehr unterscheidet sich Rockwells Werk von dem des hochgelobten niederländischen Künstlers Pieter Bruegel des Älteren aus dem 16. Jahrhundert (gegenüber unten)?

In diesem Buch dreht sich alles um die Art und Weise, wie Sie sich den bildenden Künsten, vor allem der Malerei und Bildhauerei, nähern können. Sie erhalten Anregungen, wie Sie mit Kunst umgehen können. Ich möchte Ihnen Hilfsmittel und Erkenntnisse an die Hand geben, mit deren Hilfe Sie Ihr Verständnis und Ihre Wertschätzung für die Kunst steigern sowie Ihre Beobachtungsgabe verbessern können.

STANDPUNKT UND PERSÖNLICHE VORLIEBEN

Die Antwort jedes Einzelnen auf die Fragen »Was ist Kunst?« und »Was ist gute Kunst?« hängt von seinen persönlichen Vorlieben ab. Was glauben *Sie*? Gefällt es *Ihnen*? Es hat Vorteile, empfänglich für ein breites Spektrum an Kunstformen zu sein und diese unvoreingenommen und vorurteilsfrei zu beurteilen. Natürlich lässt es sich kaum vermeiden, die Ideen, ästhetischen Vorlieben und Ansichten des 21. Jahrhunderts auf Kunstwerke früherer Epochen anzuwenden, vor allem, wenn sie aus völlig anderen Kulturen stammen. Seien Sie dennoch flexibel und verzichten Sie auf Positionen wie »Ich mag keine zeitgenössische Kunst« oder »Metallskulpturen interessieren mich nicht«.

Vermutlich wird dieses Buch Ihre Vorlieben nicht ändern. Wahrscheinlich sind es nach der Lektüre immer noch dieselben. Allerdings sollten Sie dann einen Bezugsrahmen erworben haben, mithilfe dessen Sie leichter verstehen, *warum* Sie ein Kunstwerk nicht mögen, und intelligent analysieren und eloquent erklären können, *weshalb* Ihnen fast alles lieber ist als zeitgenössische Metallskulpturen.

Fürchten Sie sich nicht vor Kunstmuseen. Fühlen Sie sich nicht genötigt, die sogenannten »alten Meister« zu lobpreisen. Sie müssen keine Schuld verspüren, wenn Ihnen ein Kunstwerk im Louvre oder in der Eremitage nicht gefällt. Ich habe einmal im Bostoner Museum of Fine Arts gehört, wie ein kleiner Junge seinen Vater fragte, ob sie in einer Kirche seien. Das zeigt, welch eine selbstgerechte Atmosphäre oft in Museen herrscht.

ZUR DEFINITION VON »KUNST«

Es gibt keine exakte Definition von »Kunst«. Wenn Sie Google fragen »Was ist Kunst?«, erhalten Sie viele Millionen Ergebnisse. Eine Kurzfassung vieler umfangreicher Definitionen besagt, dass Kunst aus Werken von Schönheit oder emotionaler Stärke besteht, die mittels Fantasie und Können geschaffen wurden. Selbst Funk & Wagnalls *Standard Dictionary of the English Language* muss nach einem längeren Diskurs eingestehen, dass »Kunst kein Synonym hat«. Und tatsächlich ist Kunst nichts Absolutes. Es gibt keine Formeln oder Regeln, um die Frage zu beantworten: »Was ist Kunst?« Es existiert nicht einmal ein quasi-wissenschaftliches Bewertungssystem (wenn 51 Prozent mit »Ja« antworten, muss es Kunst sein). Je nachdem, wie breit, inklusiv oder großzügig Ihre persönliche Definition von Kunst ist, werden Sie fast immer irgendeine Form von Kunst um sich herum finden.

Pieter Bruegel der Ältere
Die Kinderspiele
(Detail), 1560
Öl auf Holztafel,
116,4 x 160,3 cm
Kunsthistorisches
Museum, Wien

Bruegel der Ältere, ein gefeierter Künstler, führte Genre-Themen in die niederländische Kunst des 16. Jahrhunderts ein. Wenn die Unterscheidung zwischen Illustration und schöner Kunst nicht anhand des Motivs oder der Zeit und des Ortes der Veröffentlichung erfolgen kann, wie dann?

Was kann als »schöne Kunst« bezeichnet werden? Als »Kunst«? Als »Kunsthandwerk«? Sind solche Unterscheidungen überhaupt nötig? Viele Menschen nennen sich selbst Künstler (oder würden es gern). Das dürfen sie, da es anders als bei Ingenieuren, Ärzten oder Rechtsanwälten keine Ausbildungsanforderungen, Prüfungen oder rechtlichen Kontrollen dafür gibt. Der amerikanische Pop-Art-Künstler Andy Warhol sagte: »Ein Künstler ist jemand, der Dinge herstellt, die die Menschen nicht haben müssen.« Er definierte Kunst als »was man sich erlauben kann«.

Pablo Picasso
Stierkopf, 1942
Mit einem Metalllenker verschweißter Lederfahrradsitz, 33,5 x 43,5 x 19 cm
Musée Picasso, Paris

Picasso, geboren in Spanien, aber in Frankreich tätig, war einer der berühmtesten und kreativsten Künstler des 20. Jahrhunderts. Er zeigt uns mit dieser genialen Nutzung von Fahrradteilen, dass man Kunst auch in den einfachsten Dingen finden kann. Doch ist sein *Stierkopf* in einem Museum, weil er Kunst ist, weil er genial ist oder weil er von Picasso ist?

-

Sollten wir zu dem Schluss kommen, dass etwas eher als schöne Kunst bezeichnet wird, je älter es ist?

-

Wenn die kluge Sozialkritik die Gemälde und Drucke des englischen Künstlers William Hogarth aus dem 18. Jahrhundert und die politischen Karikaturen des französischen Künstlers Honoré Daumier aus dem 19. Jahrhundert als Kunst betrachtet, was ist dann mit den heutigen Cartoons? Wenn heutige Cartoons nicht als schöne Kunst gelten, die Cartoons früherer Zeiten dagegen schon, sollten wir dann zu dem Schluss kommen, dass etwas eher als schöne Kunst bezeichnet wird, je älter es ist?

Dürfen wir etwas wie die aus bereits vorhandenen Gegenständen zusammengesetzten »Readymades« Kunst nennen? Pablo Picassos *Stierkopf* (1942; gegenüber) besteht aus dem Lenker und dem Sitz eines Fahrrads, die er zusammengeschweißt hat. Sicher waren dafür Fantasie und Einsicht nötig, Fähigkeiten, die man meist mit Kunst assoziiert. Schließlich sah Picasso etwas in den gewöhnlichen Fahrradteilen, das andere nicht sahen, und setzte diese Objekte neu zusammen. Angesichts der heutigen Versuche, unsere Umwelt zu schonen, würde ich dies »Recycelte Fahrradkunst« nennen. Picasso verwendete auch in anderen Werken einfache Gegenstände, etwa in *Pavian mit Jungem* (1951; Museum of Modern Art, New York), bei dem der Kopf der Pavianmutter aus zwei in Bronze gegossenen Spielzeugautos seines Sohnes Claude besteht.

-

Liebe ist ein gleichermaßen ungenauer Begriff und die Antwort hängt davon ab, wen Sie fragen.

-

Vielleicht ist die Frage »Was ist Kunst« vergleichbar mit »Was ist Liebe?«, da Liebe ein gleichermaßen ungenauer Begriff ist und die Ant-

wort davon abhängt, wen Sie fragen. Es gibt verschiedene Arten von Liebe – die der Eltern für ihr Kind oder des Kindes für seine Eltern ist anders als die romantische Leidenschaft oder die patriotische Liebe. Der Grad der Emotionen variiert von leichter Zuneigung bis zur intensiven und allumfassenden Liebe, für die Menschen ihr Leben gegeben haben. Liebe kann flüchtig sein oder auch ein Leben lang anhalten. Ist also das fragliche Kunstwerk eines, das Sie nur kurz bewundern, oder ruft es Gedanken hervor, die Sie tief bewegen? Werden Sie es nach einer Stunde vergessen haben oder möchten Sie es jeden Morgen bewundern, wenn Sie erwachen?

Die Antwort auf die Frage »Was ist Kunst?« wurde mit der Zeit immer facettenreicher und umfassender, was auch an der Einführung neuer Techniken und Materialien liegt. Für viele Menschen steht die

Delphine Diallo
Hybrid 8, 2011
Chromogener Druck
aus einer Auflage von 15,
114,3 x 76,2 cm
Kopfschmuck von Joanne
Petit-Frère,
Privatsammlung

Die senegalesisch-französische Fotografin Diallo und die amerikanische Haarkünstlerin Petit-Frère erkunden das künstlerische Potenzial eines ungewöhnlichen Mediums. Skulpturen aus kunstvoll geflochtenen menschlichen Haaren könnte man als tragbare, erneuerbare Kunst betrachten.

Fotografie heute gleichberechtigt neben der Malerei. Der künstlerische Status der Computergrafik muss erst noch etabliert werden. Unsere zunehmende Bereitschaft, eine Vielzahl an visuellen Ausdrucksmöglichkeiten zu akzeptieren, führte dazu, dass darunter auch Kunstformen sind, die früher als »primitiv« oder »Außenseiterkunst« marginalisiert oder gar verpönt wurden, wie die sogenannte »Graffiti-Kunst«, ein Begriff, der einst als Widerspruch in sich aufgefasst worden wäre.

Kreativität und der Reiz des Neuen treffen in den Fotografien der senegalesisch-französischen Delphine Diallo aufeinander. Ihre Porträts konzentrieren sich auf das von ihr »Göttlich Weiblich« genannte, die innere Schönheit und Energie von Frauen. In *Hybrid 8* (2011; gegenüber) ist das Modell sowohl maskiert als auch unmaskiert, verborgen hinter seinem Haar, das seine ethnische Kultur enthüllt. Diallo arbeitet mit der Amerikanerin Joanne Petit-Frère zusammen, die Haar als künstlerisches Medium nutzt, um mithilfe traditioneller Flechttechniken skulpturartige Formen zu erschaffen, die sonst aus konventionellen Materialien entstehen. Die Natur ist für Petit-Frère die größte Inspirationsquelle und die von ihr geschaffenen Formen vermitteln eine organische Anmutung.

-

Kunst und Musik vermitteln gewissermaßen die gleichen Emotionen.

-

Es gibt viele Verbindungen zwischen den verschiedenen Kunstformen und Künstler arbeiten oft in mehr als einer kreativen Disziplin. Die ästhetischen Konzepte, die in den Analysen von Malerei und Bildhauerei zu finden sind und in diesem Buch dargestellt werden, gelten auch für andere Kunstformen – vor allem für Musik, Tanz und Theater. Oft ist das Vokabular in diesen Disziplinen sehr ähnlich. So können etwa Adjektive wie laut, weich, hart oder sanft sowohl Farben als auch Töne beschreiben. Gemälde, in denen der Künstler kurze, schnelle Pinselstriche auf die Leinwand bringt, lassen sich mit einem Stakkato vergleichen, bei dem die Töne kurz, aber akzentuiert gespielt werden. Kunst und Musik vermitteln gewissermaßen die gleichen Emotionen.

WIESO ERSCHAFFT MAN KUNST?

Kunst wurde in allen Teilen der Welt, zu allen Zeiten, in allen Gesellschaften geschaffen: Der Wunsch nach Kreativität ist universell. Die Gründe dafür sind aber ganz verschieden. Denken Sie beim Betrachten eines Kunstwerks über dessen Funktion und die Absicht des Künstlers nach. Es könnte die abgebildete Person verewigen oder das Ansehen eines Gönners erhöhen. Vielleicht erzählt es eine Geschichte oder zeichnet ein wichtiges historisches Ereignis nach. Oder es demonstriert die Fertigkeiten eines jungen Künstlers. Vielleicht bewahrt das Gemälde die natürliche Schönheit einer Landschaft oder eines Blumenarrangements. Jede dieser Möglichkeiten könnte der Anstoß für ein Kunstwerk sein – oder auch etwas völlig anderes. Die folgenden Beispiele zeigen, wie viele Zwecke Kunst erfüllen kann.

Der altägyptische *Sitzende Schreiber* (unten) stammt aus einem Grab in Sakkara, war also niemals für die Augen der Lebenden bestimmt. Es gibt zahlreiche ähnliche Skulpturen ägyptischer Schreiber; sie sollten dem Pharao in der nächsten Welt ebenso dienen wie ein lebender Schreiber in diesem Leben. Die Kunst ersetzt eine lebende Person aus Fleisch und Blut durch eine unbelebte aus Stein und Farbe.

Die Absicht hinter neueren Kunstwerken ist manchmal schwerer zu erkennen. 2002 schablonierte der geheimnisumwitterte britische Künstler Banksy das Bild eines kleinen Mädchens, das einen herzförmigen Luftballon fliegen lässt, neben die Worte »There is Always

Unbekannter Künstler
Sitzender Schreiber,
aus Sakkara, Ägypten,
ca. 2600–2350 v. Chr.,
4. oder 5. Dynastie
Bemalter Kalkstein,
Augen aus Bergkristall in Kupfer,
53,7 x 44 x 35 cm
Musée du Louvre, Paris

Die Pharaos erwarteten von ihren Dienern, die in Statuen, Reliefs oder Gemälden dargestellt wurden, dass diese sie in das Nachleben begleiten und ihnen bis in alle Ewigkeit dienen. Diese idealen Angestellten, die niemals zu spät zur Arbeit kamen, waren immer aufmerksam und bereit, zu Diensten zu stehen.

Banksy
Girl with Balloon, 2006
Direkt nach der Auktion bei Sotheby's 2018 geschreddert, umbenannt in *Love Is in the Bin*
Sprühfarbe, Acrylfarbe, Leinwand, Holz, Schreddermechanismus,,
101 x 78 x 18 cm
Staatsgalerie, Stuttgart

Banksy, der anonyme britische Street/ Graffiti-Künstler, dessen Identität bisher ungeklärt ist, schafft genial schablonierte Bilder, die oft satirische Botschaften über aktuelle soziale und politische Fragen vermitteln.

Hope« auf die Waterloo Bridge in London. Der Ballon verkörpert vielleicht die Liebe und Hoffnung, die die kindliche Unschuld begleitet, und die nun außer Reichweite schweben. Eine Leinwand dieses Bildes wurde 2018 auf einer Auktion bei Sotheby's in London für £1.042.000 verkauft. Als der Hammer des Auktionators fiel, wurde im Rahmen von *Girl with Balloon* – sehr zum Erstaunen der anwesenden Zuschauer – ein Schredder aktiviert! Der Schredder zerstörte das Bild zur Hälfte (oben). Banksy benannte das Werk um in *Love Is in the Bin (Die Liebe ist im Eimer)*. Welche Absicht verfolgte Banksy? Wollte er den Kunstsammlern bei Sotheby's sagen, dass der

Wert der Kunst ebenso flüchtig ist wie die Unschuld? War es eine Art von »Performance-Kunst«? Ein Publicity-Coup? Zumindest erregte Banksy weltweite Aufmerksamkeit und der Wert des zerstörten Werks – und vielleicht auch seiner anderen Werke – stieg weiter.

Manchmal muss man bestehende Annahmen über den Zweck eines Kunstwerks revidieren. Wollte der niederländische Künstler Jan van Eyck mit dem 1434 gemalten Bild *Die Arnolfini-Hochzeit* (gegenüber) die Hochzeit von Giovanni Arnolfini und Jeanne Cenami dokumentieren, wie man lange vermutete? An der Wand über dem Spiegel steht »Jan van Eyck war hier«, der Künstler war also Zeuge des Ereignisses. Ein weiterer Beweis für seine Anwesenheit ist seine Reflexion in dem Spiegel, der das Paar von hinten zeigt. Allerdings lässt die spätere Entdeckung, dass Cenami Arnolfinis zweite Frau war und ihre Ehe erst 1447 geschlossen wurde (obwohl der Künstler bereits 1441 verstarb), an der Identität der Figuren zweifeln. Kunsthistoriker fragen sich, ob das Gemälde als Hochzeits- oder als Verlobungsdokument, als Erinnerungsporträt einer ersten Ehefrau, die vielleicht im Kindbett gestorben war, oder als etwas anderes gedacht war, das möglicherweise erst durch den Fund eines Dokuments aus dem 15. Jahrhundert enthüllt wird.

Jan van Eyck
Die Arnolfini-Hochzeit, 1434
Öl auf Eichentafel, 82,2 x 60 cm
National Gallery, London

Für eine lange Zeit hielt man die Personen, die der niederländische Künstler Jan van Eyck hier abbildete, für Giovanni Arnolfini und Jeanne Cenami. Die Entdeckung, dass Arnolfini und Cenami erst nach dem Tod des Künstlers heirateten, lässt nun allerdings Zweifel aufkommen – sowohl über die Namen des Paares als auch über den Zweck dieses Gemäldes.

KUNST ALS AUFZEICHNUNG DER GESCHICHTE

Als visuelle Berichte liefern Kunstwerke manchmal Einblicke in die Kultur, in der sie entstanden sind: Glaubensvorstellungen, Grad des Wohlstands, Politik, Religion, Sitten, Kleidung und mehr. Jan van Eyck malte nicht nur das Innere eines gehobenen Haushalts in den Niederlanden des 15. Jahrhunderts, sondern auch eine Lebensart. Heutige Betrachter würden beim Blick auf den Bauch der Frau vermuten, dass die Verlobung oder Hochzeit gerade noch rechtzeitig stattfindet. Dabei war ihr vorgewölbter Bauch eine zeitgenössische Mode, die auch von denen sorgfältig gepflegt wurde, die normalerweise nicht so aussahen. Der Schnitt des Gewandes und ein gepolsterter Beutel unter dem Kleid sowie die Haltung der Trägerin sorgten für das gewünschte »schwangere« Erscheinungsbild. Ebenso modern in dieser Zeit war die gehörnte Frisur, für die man das Haar um Drahtkegel wickelte, die an den Schläfen befestigt wurden.

Nicht nur Bilder, sondern auch die Umstände ihrer Entstehung liefern historische Informationen.

Unbekannter Künstler
Initiation des Kublai Khan und Übergabe Tibets an Phagpa im Jahre 1264,
Tibet,
ca. 16.–17. Jahrhundert
Pigment auf Stoff,
64,5 x 41,6 cm
Rubin Museum of Art,
New York

Kunst als historisches Narrativ gibt es auf der ganzen Welt. Hier dokumentierte der tibetische Künstler die Übertragung von Macht und Autorität, womit er unwiderlegbar beweist, dass in jeder Sprache gilt: »Ein Bild sagt mehr als tausend Worte.«

Kunst kann wichtige Ereignisse in der religiösen und politischen Geschichte, manchmal in beiden, dokumentieren. Das Bild oben zeigt den inthronisierten Guru Phagpa (1235–80), den Anführer der Sakya-Schule des tibetischen Buddhismus, wie er 1264 die Macht des Mongolenherrschers Kublai Khan (1215–94) anerkennt. Kublai Khan wiederum verlieh Phagpa die Macht über Teile Tibets. Um in diesem tibetischen Gemälde Phagpas größere Bedeutung zu zeigen, stellte ihn der Künstler viel größer dar als Kublai Khan, der zum Zeichen des Respekts seine Handflächen aneinanderlegt. Kublai Khan gründete 1271 die Yuan-Dynastie in China.

Nicht nur Bilder, sondern auch die Umstände ihrer Entstehung liefern historische Informationen. Bei einer Auftragsarbeit müssen Sie die Beziehung zwischen Künstler, Kunden und fertigem Werk betrachten. Wie viel lässt sich auf die kreativen Ideen des Künstlers zurückführen – statt auf die Anforderungen des Auftraggebers? Dieser (oder seine Organisation) spielte wahrscheinlich eine wichtige Rolle bei der Festlegung des Resultats.

Duccio di Buoninsegna
Maestà, Vorderseite eines Hochaltars, 1308–11
Eitempera und Gold auf Holztafel, 2,13 x 3,96 m
Museo dell'Opera Metropolitana del Duomo, Siena

Informationen über das Leben von Duccio, dem führenden sienesischen Künstler des frühen 14. Jahrhunderts, helfen uns, sein Werk zu verstehen. Neben dem Vertrag für die *Maestà* und Dokumente über andere Aufträge gibt es in den Stadtarchiven Aufzeichnungen über seine vielen Weinrechnungen und die Geldbußen für schlechtes Betragen!

Vor dem 19. Jahrhundert arbeiteten Künstler im Westen fast ausschließlich auf Bestellung.

Die Vorstellung, dass der Künstler Motive malt oder formt, die ihm persönlich etwas bedeuten, und die Werke dann später über einen Agenten, eine Galerie oder eine Ausstellung verkauft, wurde erst im 19. Jahrhundert zur Normalität. Vorher arbeitete man fast ausschließlich auf Bestellung. Der Kunde gab möglicherweise das Motiv vor, vielleicht auch die Bildsprache, um dessen Sinn zu vermitteln, die Größe des Werkes und die Menge an bestimmten Materialien, vor allem bei teuren Pigmenten oder Metallen. Kunde und Künstler vereinbarten manchmal auch, welche Freiheiten sich der Künstler nehmen konnte, etwa, ob er Assistenten beschäftigen oder gleichzeitig andere Aufträge annehmen durfte.

Ein seltenes überliefertes Beispiel für einen Vertrag zwischen den Domherren von Siena und dem italienischen Künstler Duccio behandelt sein Altarbild *Maestà* (1308–11; unten). Dieser Vertrag,

der im Staatsarchiv von Siena liegt, besagt, dass Duccio keine Helfer beschäftigen durfte, die ganze Arbeit selbst ausführen musste und erst andere Gemälde beginnen durfte, nachdem er die *Maestà* abgeschlossen hatte, was 1311 geschah.

KUNST UND FUNKTIONALITÄT

Ist ein Kunstwerk, das einem praktischen Zweck dient, weniger »Kunst«, als wenn es eine rein ästhetische Funktion hat? Die Frage von Kunst versus Handwerk hat einige außerordentlich feine Facetten. Besitzt etwa ein reich bestickter Stoff, der als Wandbehang dient, einen höheren künstlerischen Wert als ein ebenso verzierter Stoff, der als Kleidungsstück getragen wird? Wenn ein Künstler ein Bild sowohl auf eine Leinwand als auch auf eine Schüssel malt, die anschließend für die Massenproduktion und den häuslichen Gebrauch gedacht ist, rangiert dann die Schüssel in der künstlerischen Hierarchie unter der Leinwand?

Der italienische Manierist Benvenuto Cellini schuf für den französischen König Franz I. prächtige allegorische Figuren von Neptun und der Erde (1540–43; unten) aus Gold und Emaille. Sinkt ihr Status, weil es eigentlich Salz- und Pfeffergefäße sind? Die Einstellung zu dieser

Frage hat sich im Laufe der Jahre gewandelt. Cellini lebte im 16. Jahrhundert, lange bevor die Europäer im 18. Jahrhundert das Konzept der schönen Künste definierten. Die schönen Künste, die für hohe ästhetische Qualität stehen, wurden von den angewandten Künsten unterschieden, bei denen es um die Herstellung und Verzierung funktionaler Objekte geht, wie kunstvoll sie auch sein mögen. Manche behaupten, diese Unterscheidung solle hohe künstlerische Standards bewahren, während andere sie für Elitedenken halten.

Müssen Museumskuratoren diese Frage beantworten? In Kunstmuseen sind heutzutage alle möglichen Objekte zu sehen. Im Metropolitan Museum of Art in New York stehen Rüstungen und Waffen, manche von berühmten Künstlern entworfen, neben den traditionellen schönen Künsten. Sollten Rüstungen also als schöne Kunst gelten? Das Musée d'Orsay in Paris stellt neben den Gemälden und Skulpturen der französischen Impressionisten Möbel aus. Noch extremer: Arthur Youngs Hubschrauber Bell-47D1 von 1945 hängt an der Decke des Museum of Modern Art in New York. Was halten Sie von der Ausstellung »Art of the Motorcycle« am Guggenheim Museum in New York von 1998, die anschließend auch in Chicago, Bilbao und Las Vegas zu sehen war? Wäre den Ingenieuren, die diese Motorräder für den Massenmarkt entwickelt hatten, in den Sinn gekommen, dass ihre Produkte in berühmten Kunstmuseen ausgestellt werden könnten? Kann ein Objekt von Kuratoren und Kritikern zu Kunst erklärt werden, auch wenn seine Schöpfer das früher nie in Betracht gezogen hätten?

Benvenuto Cellini
Neptun und Erde, Salz- und Pfeffergefäße, 1540–43
Gold, Emaille, Ebenholz und Elfenbein, 26,3 x 28,5 x 21,5 cm
Kunsthistorisches Museum, Wien

Cellini, Bildhauer der wichtigsten Mäzene in Frankreich und Italien, rühmte sich in seiner Autobiografie seiner Fähigkeiten als Künstler (und Liebhaber). Dieses außergewöhnliche Gefäß für Gewürze mit seiner komplexen Ikonografie (Salz kommt aus dem Meer des Neptun und Pfeffer aus der Erde) bringt schöne Kunst und schönes Essen in Einklang.

Künstler aus dem Zunftsystem blieben oft anonym.

Wie so oft bietet die Vergangenheit Einblicke, die uns die Gegenwart verstehen und die Zukunft vorhersehen lassen. Manche antiken griechischen Keramiken tragen die Namen des Töpfers und des Malers und zollen ihnen gleichermaßen Anerkennung. So signierten sowohl Euphronios als auch Euxitheos den rotfigurigen Kelchkrater von ca. 515 v. Chr., auf dem der *Tod des Sarpedon* dargestellt wird (Museo Nazionale Archeologico Cerite, Cerveteri). Auf manchen Vasen zeigt die Signatur an, dass Töpfer und Maler identisch waren – keiner dieser Berufe hatte also mehr Prestige als der andere.

Im europäischen Mittelalter wurde die Person, die ein Bild auf eine Holztafel malte, genau wie die Person, die diese herstellte, in einer Zunft ausgebildet und ist daher heute fast ausnahmslos namentlich nicht bekannt. Man unterschied kaum zwischen den Menschen, die wir heute als Künstler oder Kunsthandwerker bezeichnen, da dieselbe Person nicht nur Gemälde und Skulpturen, sondern auch Möbel, Geschirr, Buchumschläge, Waffen, Kleidung und Wandteppiche entwarf – also eigentlich alles.

Während der Renaissance änderte sich das. Da man nun glaubte, künstlerische Inspiration sei göttlichen Ursprungs, galten Künstler für von Gott bevorzugt. Dennoch war der Künstler Hans Holbein der Jüngere nicht nur Porträtist König Heinrichs VIII. von England, sondern entwarf auch Buchumschläge, königliche Siegel, Zeremonialwaffen, Schmuck und Tafelsilber für den König – wie es auch Benvenuto Cellini für Franz I. von Frankreich tat.

Die Diskussion um die Unterscheidung zwischen Künstlern und Kunsthandwerkern sowie zwischen schönen Künsten und Handwerk dauert bis heute an. Wenn hochwertige Einzelstücke von Handwerkern sowohl schön als auch funktional sind und Werke von Künstlern rein ästhetisch sind, sollten wir diesen Objekten dann einen höheren Wert beimessen, weil sie keine Funktion haben? Das würde Warhols Definition eines Künstlers stützen, als »jemand, der Dinge herstellt, die die Menschen nicht haben müssen«.

DIE TECHNISCHE AUSFÜHRUNG ALS KRITERIUM?

Sind sorgfältig und präzise hergestellte Gemälde oder Skulpturen, die ordentlich und exakt gefertigt sind, bessere Kunst als grob gefertigte? Sollten wir also den künstlerischen Wert nur an der Idee bemessen oder auch an der technischen Ausführung dieser Idee?

Die entstehenden Kunstakademien verdrängten die Zünfte.

In Kulturen, die nicht zwischen Künstlern und Kunsthandwerkern unterschieden, wurden die Menschen, die als Maler und Bildhauer arbeiteten, oft durch Familienmitglieder und/oder eine lange Lehrzeit in einer Zunft ausgebildet – wie vermutlich jeder, der ein Handwerk oder Gewerbe beherrschte. So war es zumindest im mittelalterlichen Europa. Ein Schüler musste die gelehrten technischen Fähigkeiten umsetzen; die Entwicklung eines eigenen künstlerischen Stils gehörte nicht zum Lehrplan. Ziel war es, zum Meister zu werden, was am Ende durch die Herstellung eines »Meisterstücks« demonstriert wurde und der Person erlaubte, andere auszubilden. Entsprechend wichtig war es, wie gut jemand ein Werk technisch ausführte und wie gründlich die notwendigen Fähigkeiten angewendet wurden.

Thomas Rowlandson und Augustus Pugin
Exhibition Room, Somerset House, 1808
Aquatinta und Radierung, Blattgröße 24,7 x 29 cm
The Metropolitan Museum of Art, New York

Joshua Reynolds, der erste Präsident der Royal Academy of Art in London, entwarf ähnlich wie Charles Lebrun, der Direktor der Académie Royale de Peinture et de Sculpture in Paris, Theorien und Regeln für die Kunst. Reynolds' 15 *Discourses* bestehen aus starren Regeln, die von seinen Zeitgenossen willkommen geheißen wurden.

Die entstehenden Kunstakademien verdrängten dieses System allmählich. Im italienischen Bologna gründete die Malerfamilie Carracci, mit den Brüdern Annibale und Agostino sowie ihrem Cousin Ludovico, 1582 eine Kunstakademie, und entzog damit den Zünften den Einfluss. Frankreich etablierte 1648 in Paris die Académie Royale de Peinture et de Sculpture (Königliche Akademie für Malerei und Bildhauerei). Charles Lebrun, ab 1663 ihr Direktor, richtete ein strenges Ausbildungssystem in Theorie und Praxis ein. Da er für alle Kunstprojekte von Ludwig XIV. verantwortlich war, kamen mit der Zeit alle Künstler unter die Kontrolle der Académie. Lebrun gab die Regeln vor, legte Standards fest und diktierte Themen und Stil der französischen Kunst, was der Originalität einen empfindlichen Dämpfer versetzte. England schuf mit der Gründung der Royal Academy of Arts 1768 ein ähnliches System (oben).

In der zweiten Hälfte des 19. Jahrhunderts kam es in Frankreich zu einer grundlegenden Änderung. Mit den jährlichen Ausstellungen in Paris, den sogenannten Salons, hatte die Académie bestimmt, welche Werke ausgestellt wurden, und damit sowohl den Geschmack des Publikums als auch den Erfolg einzelner Künstler beeinflusst. 1863 lehnte die Jury des Salons mehr als 4.000 Gemälde ab, was einen solchen Aufschrei der abgelehnten Maler und ihrer Unterstützer hervorrief, dass Kaiser Napoleon III. einen zweiten Salon für die abgelehnten Werke ins Leben rief, den sogenannten Salon des Refusés (Salon der Zurückgewiesenen). Damit begann der Niedergang des akademischen Ansatzes; die Jury verlor ihre übermächtige Kontrolle über die französische Kunst.

Maler und Bildhauer, befreit von der Pflicht, die Jury des Salons zufriedenzustellen, wandten sich von den traditionellen Themen Religion, Mythologie, Historie oder Politik ab und zogen ihre Inspiration aus dem Alltag und der Natur. Neue Malmethoden, die Farbe und optische Studien nutzten, um die Prinzipien des Sehens und des Lichts zu untersuchen, rückten in den Mittelpunkt. Die Haltung zu den technischen Aspekten der Malerei wandelte sich: Die glatten Flächen, die sorgfältige Zeichenkunst und die detaillierte Darstellung, die die Akademie lange bevorzugte, verloren an Bedeutung.

Heute ist die technische Ausführung den Künstlern noch weniger wichtig als früher. Das bedeutet aber auch: Manche modernen Kunstwerke bröckeln oder blättern bereits oder bedürfen aus anderen Gründen der Konservierung und/oder Restaurierung.

Unbekannter Künstler
Ti bei der Nilpferdjagd,
ca. 2500–2400 v. Chr.,
4. Dynastie
Wandrelief aus bemaltem Kalkstein, Höhe ca. 114,3 cm
Grab von Ti, Sakkara, Ägypten

Altägyptische Malereien stellen dar, was der Verstand weiß, und nicht, was das Auge tatsächlich sieht. Jedes Objekt wird von seinem charakteristischsten Standpunkt aus dargestellt, um seine Bedeutung zu zeigen. Alle Fische, Nilpferde und Boote werden entsprechend von der Seite gezeigt.

TRADITION VERSUS INNOVATION

Ist es möglich, Kunst nach Regeln und Theorien zu schaffen, wie Charles Lebrun und Joshua Reynolds glaubten? Heute ist man allgemein der Meinung, dass das Erschaffen von Kunst Fantasie, Intuition, Inspiration, sogar Genie erfordert. Wir bewundern Originalität und das Neue, das wir gern als Fortschritt ansehen. Doch auch wenn Künstler nach Einzigartigkeit streben, bleibt das Studium der »alten Meister« eine anerkannte Komponente der Ausbildung. Es bringt Vorteile, die Vergangenheit zu untersuchen; die Studierenden sind besser gerüstet, etwas Neues zu erzeugen: Aus der Nachahmung erwächst am Ende die Innovation.

In der Vergangenheit gab es Zeiten, in denen man das ganz anders sah. Betrachten Sie etwa die zwei altägyptischen Grabmalereien: *Ti bei der Nilpferdjagd*, ca. 2500–2400 v. Chr. (gegenüber) und *Nebamun jagt im Papyrusdickicht*, ca. 1350 v. Chr. (unten). Auch nach 1.000 Jahren gelten die gleichen Darstellungskonventionen. Beide Künstler zeigen Kopf und Beine von der Seite, Auge und Schultern jedoch von vorn; die relative Größe der Figur deutet auf ihre Stellung in der Gesellschaft hin und nicht auf ihre Position im Raum. Die einzige bedeutsame Ausnahme von dieser altägyptischen

Unbekannter Künstler
Nebamun jagt im Papyrusdickicht, aus der Grabkammer des Nebamun, Theben, Ägypten, ca. 1350 v. Chr., 18. Dynastie
Bemalte Gipswand, 83 x 98 cm
British Museum, London

An den Wänden ägyptischer Gräber vereint sich Naturalismus ganz ungezwungen mit einer gewissen dekorativen Abstraktion. Die hieroglyphischen Texte betonen die flache Bildebene.

Ehrfurcht vor Wiederholung und Tradition, die nicht nur in der Kunst galt, gab es während der 18. Dynastie unter Pharao Amenhotep IV. (auch bekannt als Echnaton, gestorben ca. 1336/1334 v. Chr.) – die von ihm eingeführten Änderungen verschwanden nach seinem Tod zum Großteil wieder.

Im Gegensatz zu den alten Ägyptern, die ihre etablierten Ideale über Jahrtausende kaum änderten, wechselten die antiken Griechen und Römer mehrfach ihre Vorstellungen von ästhetischer Perfektion. Ihre intellektuellen Theorien kombinierten Wissenschaft und Kunst und nutzten mathematische Verhältnisse, um sowohl den menschlichen Körper als auch ihre Bauten ideal zu proportionieren.

Das Interesse an der menschlichen Figur ist in der Geschichte der Kunst ungebrochen.

Der *Speerträger* (*Doryphoros*), die römische Marmorkopie einer Bronzestatue des griechischen Bildhauers Polyklet (ca. 450–440 v. Chr.), zeigt die idealen Proportionen eines Mannes während der klassischen Periode mit einer Höhe von acht Köpfen (Museo Archeologico Nazionale, Neapel). Später, in der hellenistischen Ära, war das Ideal mit einer Höhe von neun Köpfen schlanker, wie der *Apoxyomenos* beweist, die römische Marmorkopie eines Bronzeoriginals des griechischen Bildhauers Lysipp (ca. 330 v. Chr.; Museo Pio Clementino, Vatikanstadt, Rom). Der römische Architekt und Schriftsteller Vitruvius, der im späten 1. Jahrhundert v. Chr. lebte, bestimmte die idealen männlichen Proportionen mithilfe der Mathematik: Die Kopfgröße bei ihm betrug ein Zehntel der Körpergröße. Leonardo da Vinci verewigte Vitruvius' Beschreibung in seiner berühmten Zeichnung *Der Vitruvianische Mensch* (ca. 1490; Gallerie dell'Accademia, Venedig).

Das Interesse an der menschlichen Figur ist in der Geschichte der Kunst ungebrochen. Moderne Abbildungen sind ausgesprochen vielfältig. Ein Extrem sind die unnatürlich schlanken, langen Figuren des Schweizer Bildhauers Alberto Giacometti, wie etwa *Frau von Venedig III* (1956; gegenüber links). Das Werk des kolumbianischen Bildhauers Fernando Botero dagegen ist durch rundliche, aufgebläht wirkende Figuren gekennzeichnet, wie man es an seiner *Stehenden Frau* (1993; gegenüber rechts) sieht. Fast alle anatomischen Typen und Körperformen – ob weiblich oder männlich – wurden zur einen oder anderen Zeit einmal zum Vorbild erklärt. Glücklich die Person, die zur richtigen Zeit geboren wurde, um dem aktuellen Ideal zu entsprechen. Falls das nicht klappt, können wir uns damit trösten,

Gegenüber links:
Alberto Giacometti
Frau von Venedig III, 1956
Bronze,
118,5 x 17,8 x 35,1 cm
Collection Fondation Alberto & Annette Giacometti, Paris

Der Schweizer Giacometti, ein bedeutender Bildhauer des 20. Jahrhunderts, hatte einen einzigartigen Blick auf den menschlichen Körper. Diese Frau ist kaum mehr als ein Schatten, wenn Giacometti einen übertrieben dünnen Körperbau in eine künstlerische Ästhetik verwandelt.

Gegenüber rechts:
Fernando Botero
Stehende Frau, 1993
Bronze,
73 x 30,5 x 26,5 cm
Edition sechs von sechs
Privatsammlung

Der Kolumbianer Botero hatte eine großzügigere Sicht auf die Anatomie der Frau. Seine korpulenten Figuren mit den üppigen Konturen sind quasi eine Weiterentwicklung des Körpertypus, den der flämische Barockmaler des 17. Jahrhunderts Peter Paul Rubens bevorzugte (siehe Seiten 42–43).

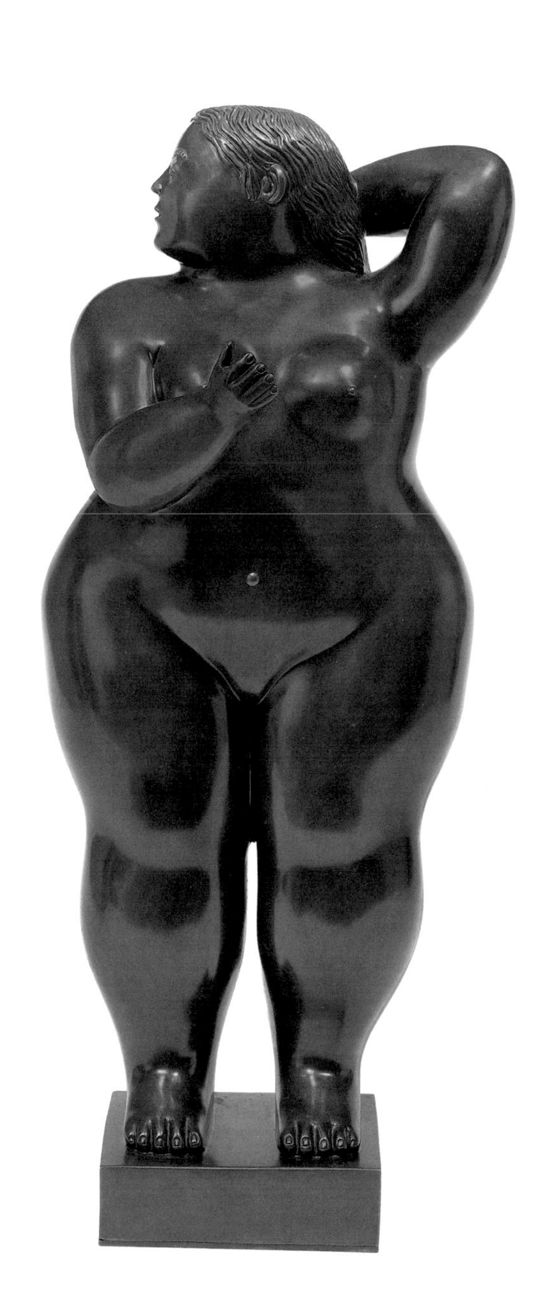

dass wir früher einmal als anatomisch perfekt erachtet und von allen beneidet wurden (oder es künftig sein werden).

SCHÖNHEIT, EMOTION UND BOTSCHAFT IN DER KUNST

Muss ein Kunstwerk schön sein? Attraktiv? Hübsch? Nehmen Sie *Die Schwestern* (1869; unten). Hier malte die französische Impressionistin Berthe Morisot zwei junge, hübsche Damen, die modisch gekleidet, sorgfältig frisiert und entspannt auf ihrem Plüschsofa sitzen. Solch pastellfarbene Nettigkeiten sind typisch für Morisot und den Impressionismus im Allgemeinen. Morisots Malerkollege, der Impressionist Renoir, nur einen Monat jünger als sie, sagte: »Ein Bild sollte eine liebenswürdige Angelegenheit sein, fröhlich und hübsch, ja, hübsch. Es gibt genügend langweilige Dinge in der Welt, ohne dass wir noch mehr davon machen.« Eine ähnliche Empfindung drückte der kanadische Dichter Bliss Carman in *The Making of Personality* (1908) aus: »Sache der Kunst ist es, Fröhlichkeit zu bereiten ... welch eine Schande ist es, die großartige Gabe des Ausdrucks auf abscheuliche und freudlose Themen zu verschwenden.« Der Expressionist Henri Matisse schrieb in seinen *Notes d'un peintre* (Notizen eines Malers; 1908): »Ich träume von einer Kunst des Gleichgewichts, der Reinheit, der Ruhe, ohne beunruhigende und sich aufdrängende Gegenstände, von einer Kunst, die ... ein Beruhigungsmittel ist, eine Erholung für das Gehirn, so etwas wie ein guter Lehnstuhl, in dem man sich von physischen Anstrengungen erholen kann.«

Berthe Morisot
Die Schwestern, 1869
Öl auf Leinwand,
52,1 x 81,3 cm
National Gallery of Art,
Washington, DC

Morisot schuf einladende Landschaften und vor allem Porträts ihrer Familienmitglieder – ihr Lieblingsmotiv war ihr einziges Kind Julie. Indem sie eine Laufbahn als Malerin einschlug, folgte Morisot nicht dem Lebensweg, den ihre wohlhabende Familie von ihr erwartete.

Matthias Grünewald
Isenheimer Altarbild,
1512–16
Öl auf Holz, Mitteltafel,
2,69 x 3,07 m
Unterlinden-Museum,
Colmar

Grünewald, ein deutscher Maler, bemühte sich, beim Betrachter eine starke emotionale Reaktion auszulösen. Selbst die Produzenten heutiger Horrorfilme erschaffen nur selten ein Bild, das so abstoßend ist wie das eines gefolterten, gekreuzigten, fast nackten Mannes.

Das offenkundig groteske und bewusst grauenerregende Bild soll den Betrachter dazu bewegen, mit Christus zu leiden.

Wenn Sie Renoirs Standpunkt zustimmen, wonach ein Kunstwerk »fröhlich und hübsch« sein soll, was halten Sie dann vom *Isenheimer Altarbild* (1512–16; oben) des deutschen Renaissance-Malers Matthias Grünewald? Die Beschreibung dieser entstellten, verkrümmten Figur des gekreuzigten Christus, dessen Fleisch grau-verwest und von Würmern zerfressen scheint, wird kaum die Worte »fröhlich« oder »hübsch« enthalten. Das offenkundig groteske und bewusst grauenerregende Bild soll den Betrachter dazu bewegen, mit Christus zu leiden. Kaum jemand betrachtet das *Isenheimer Altarbild* und bleibt unbewegt, selbst wenn ihm die dargestellte religiöse Geschichte nicht vertraut ist. Macht unsere instinktive Reaktion es mehr zu »Kunst«? Oder weniger?

Soll ein Kunstwerk eine emotionale Reaktion auslösen?

Grünewalds Gemälde wirft eine weitere Frage auf: Soll ein Kunstwerk dem Betrachter eine Emotion vermitteln oder tatsächlich eine

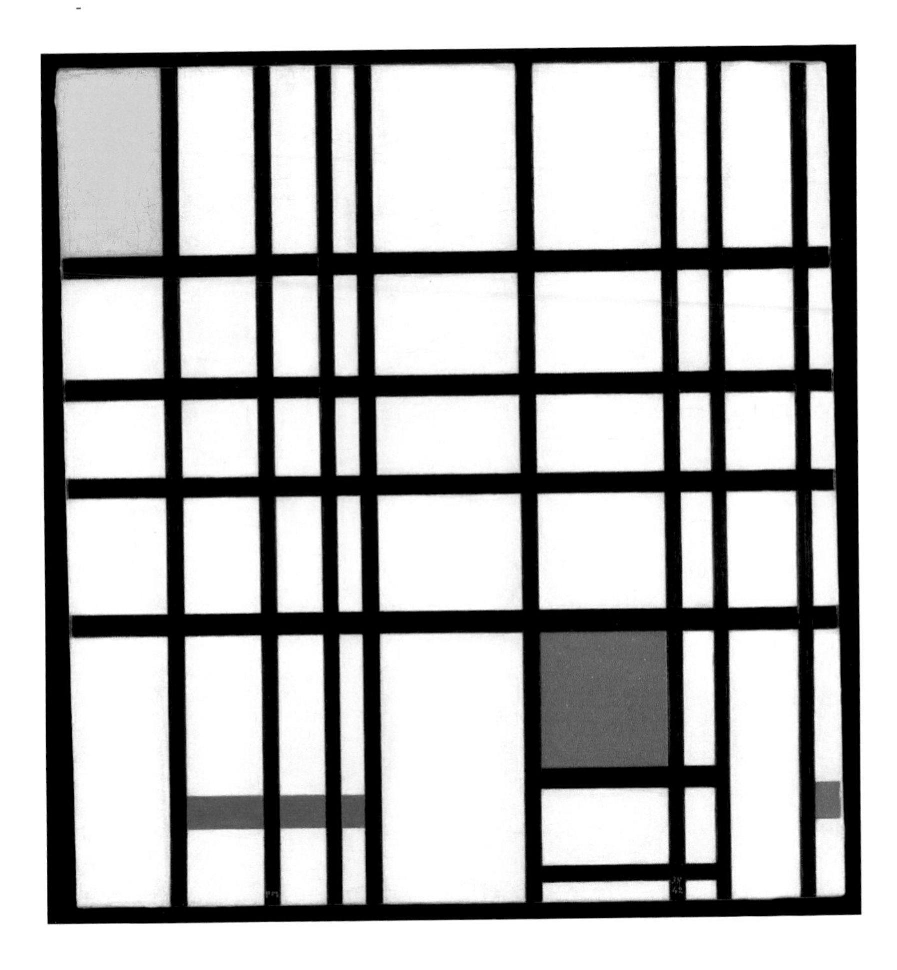

emotionale Reaktion in ihm auslösen? Ist es besser oder erfolgreicher, wenn es das tut? Vergleichen Sie das *Isenheimer Altarbild* mit der *Komposition mit Gelb, Blau und Rot* (1937–42; oben) des niederländischen Malers Piet Mondrian, mit seinem perfekten Gleichgewicht aus Primärfarben, Schwarz, Weiß und geraden Linien. Spüren Sie etwas? In dieser intellektuellen Anordnung, die eher vergeistigt als instinktiv daherkommt, sind nur wenige Emotionen zu finden.

Verbunden mit der Möglichkeit, dass ein Kunstwerk Emotionen transportiert, ist seine Fähigkeit, eine Botschaft zu vermitteln. Ist es wünschenswert, dass ein Kunstwerk dem Betrachter etwas sagt? Muss der Künstler in diesem Fall die ganze Arbeit machen und direkte, unzweideutige visuelle Informationen liefern? Andersherum: Hat der Betrachter mehr von der Erfahrung, wenn er selbst an dem Prozess teilnimmt? Künstler haben absichtlich unfertige Werke

Piet Mondrian
Komposition mit Gelb, Blau und Rot, 1937–42
Öl auf Leinwand,
72,7 x 69,2 cm
Tate Collection,
Großbritannien

Der niederländische Maler Mondrian kam nach und nach von einem figürlichen Malstil zu einem Stil von intellektueller Strenge. Die Natur wurde schließlich zu einem reinen Stil aus sorgfältig angeordneten Grundfarben und rechteckigen Formen vereinfacht.

Auguste Rodin
Der Gedanke, ca. 1895
Marmor, 74,2 x
43,5 x 46,1 cm
Musée d'Orsay, Paris

Die »unvollendete« Skulptur von Camille Claudel des französischen Impressionisten Rodin regt den neugierigen Betrachter an nachzudenken, was der unbehauene Stein enthält – und verbirgt.

produziert, die den Betrachter ermutigen, wenn nicht gar verpflichten, mit dem Künstler zusammenzuarbeiten und das Werk in seinem Geist fertigzustellen. *Der Gedanke* (ca. 1895; vorherige Seite) des französischen Bildhauers Auguste Rodin greift auf diese Idee zurück, indem er das Porträt seiner Mitarbeiterin und Geliebten Camille Claudel nur teilweise aus dem Stein formt und damit andeutet, dass in dem rohen Stein (dem Geist) wunderbare Gedanken zu finden sind.

Die abstrakte Kunst nutzt diese Idee in einem viel größeren Ausmaß. Jeder Mensch sieht etwas anderes in dem rätselhaften Gemälde des armenisch-amerikanischen Künstlers Arshile Gorky, das den gleichermaßen geheimnisvollen Titel *The Liver Is the Cock's Comb* (1944; gegenüber) trägt. Das Kunstwerk regt jeden von uns an, sich seine eigene persönliche Botschaft zu überlegen. Mehr über abstrakte Kunst erfahren Sie auf den Seiten 122–125.

WICHTIGE IDEEN

Zur Definition von »Kunst«:

- Weiterhin schwer fassbar, aber zunehmend inklusiv

Warum wird Kunst erschaffen?

- Einige der vielen Aufgaben von Kunst
- Kunst als Aufzeichnung der Geschichte
- Dokumentarische Beweise

Kunst und Funktionalität:

- Schöne Kunst und Gebrauchskunst
- Rolle von Museen bei der Feststellung, was »Kunst« ist

Technische Ausführung als Kriterium für die Bewertung:

- Zünfte, Akademien und der Salon

Tradition versus Innovation:

- Die menschliche Figur

Schönheit, Emotion und Botschaft in der Kunst:

- »Unvollendete« Kunstwerke als bewusste Entscheidung

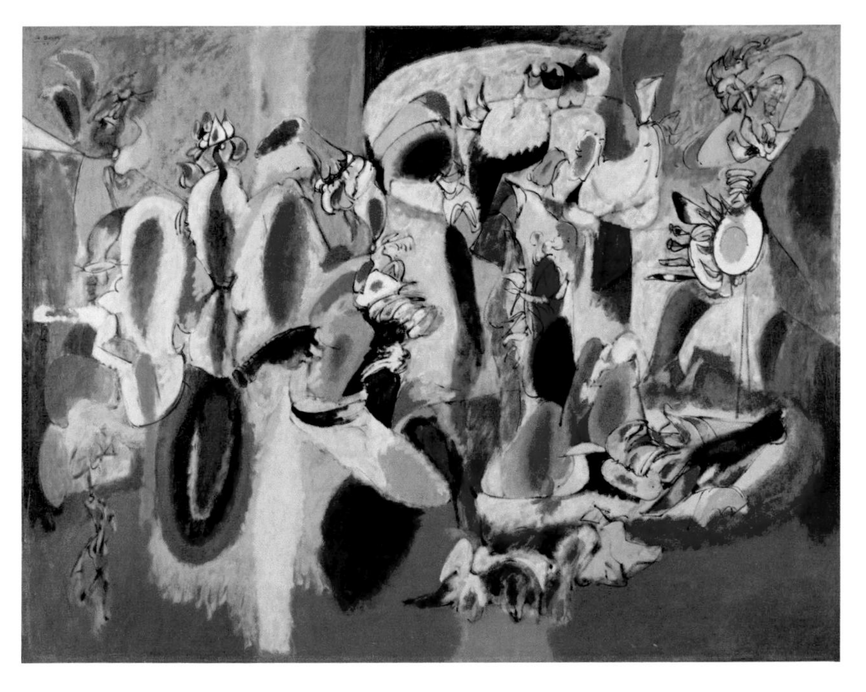

Arshile Gorky
The Liver Is the Cock's Comb, 1944
Öl auf Leinwand,
186 x 250 cm
Albright-Knox Art
Gallery, Buffalo

Der in Armenien geborene Gorky erhielt seine künstlerische Ausbildung in den Vereinigten Staaten und entwickelte einen Stil völliger Abstraktion. Da die Bedeutung nicht festgelegt ist und die Formen nicht durch den Künstler erkennbar dargestellt wurden, bietet ein abstraktes Bild jedem Betrachter ein anderes und ganz eigenes Erleben.

KUNST ERLEBEN, ANALYSIEREN UND WERTSCHÄTZEN

-

Egal welcher Stil, welcher Inhalt oder welches Medium, das Erschaffen von Kunst ist eine visuelle Sprache, die durch Farbe, Linie, Rhythmus, Textur und die Illusion des Raumes spricht.

-

Kay WalkingStick
2020

Die Ideen in diesem Kapitel sollen Ihr Erleben maximieren und Ihnen helfen, Kunst zu analysieren, wertzuschätzen und sogar selbst zu erschaffen. Die Grundelemente der bildenden Kunst sind: Farbe, Linie, Textur, Licht, Raum, Komposition und Emotion. Auch wenn wir uns hier auf Malerei und Bildhauerei konzentrieren, sind doch viele der mit diesen Richtungen verwandten Konzepte auch auf andere Formen darstellender Kunst anwendbar: Ornamentik, Druck, Fotografie, digitale Kunst und sogar Architektur. Künstler müssen keine Regeln hinsichtlich dieser Grundelemente befolgen. Die Kunst profitiert zwar von der Wissenschaft, ist aber selbst keine.

FARBE

Farbpigmente stammen aus natürlichen und künstlichen Quellen. Natürliche Pigmente enthalten chemische Elemente wie Gold, Silber, Zinn und Kohlenstoff, Mineralien wie Metallsalze, farbige Erden wie Ocker, wertvolle Steine wie Ultramarinblau aus Lapislazuli sowie Extrakte aus Pflanzen und Tieren. Künstliche Pigmente entstehen aus der Kombination chemischer Elemente oder der Anwendung von Säuren auf Metall sowie aus der Dekomposition von Salzen und synthetischen Substanzen. Gute Pigmente sollten im Laufe der Zeit weder verblassen noch sich verfärben.

Die Primärfarben aus Farbpigment sind Gelb, Blau und Rot. Aus diesen lassen sich alle Farben bis auf Schwarz und Weiß mischen. Die Sekundärfarben, für die man zwei Primärfarben mischt, sind Grün, Lila und Orange. Komplementärfarben liegen einander auf

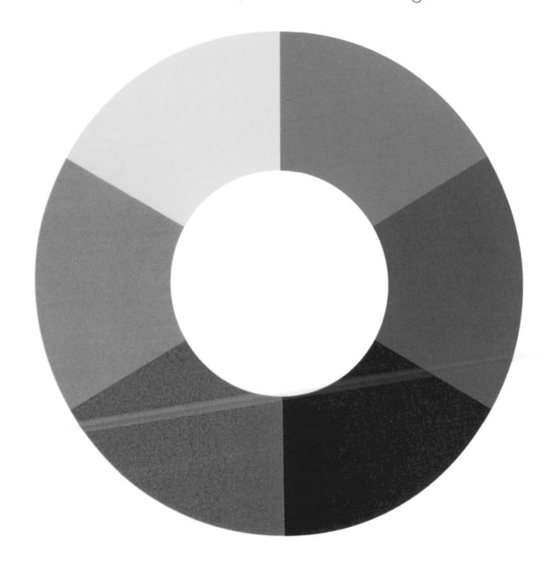

Farbrad
Darstellung der Beziehungen von Farben

Sir Isaac Newton entwickelte das erste Farbrad, als er die Brechung des Lichts durch ein Prisma untersuchte. Ein sich drehendes Farbrad erscheint weiß, da die Farben im Gehirn des Betrachters verschmelzen. Dieses einfache Farbrad verdeutlicht die Beziehung zwischen Primär-, Sekundär- und Komplementärfarben.

Pierre-Auguste Renoir
Ruderer in Chatou, 1879
Öl auf Leinwand,
81,2 x 100,2 cm
National Gallery of Art,
Washington, DC

Der französische Impressionist Renoir nutzte den visuell faszinierenden Effekt, den das Nebeneinander der Komplementärfarben Orange und Blau auslöste. Impressionistische Maler verwendeten leuchtendere, hellere Farben als in früheren Stilen. Dazu gehörte auch das Arbeiten auf weißer Leinwand statt auf dem braunen Malgrund, der lange gebräuchlich war.

dem Farbrad gegenüber (Gegenseite): Gelb und Lila sind komplementär, genau wie Grün und Rot sowie Blau und Orange. Jedes Paar besteht aus einer Primärfarbe und der Sekundärfarbe, die bei der Mischung der beiden anderen Primärfarben entsteht. Sie haben also keine Farbe gemein. Da sie maximalen Kontrast bieten, wirken sie leuchtender und intensiver, wenn man sie nebeneinander setzt.

Dieses visuelle Phänomen nutzten die Impressionisten. In Pierre-Auguste Renoirs *Ruderer in Chatou* (1879; oben) ist das orangefarbene Boot das Komplement zum blauen Wasser und die orangefarbene Jacke der Frau wirkt lebendiger, weil Renoir sie mit einem blauen Rock ergänzte.

Komplementärfarben findet man auch in der Op Art (kurz für Optical Art), wo sie die schwingenden, grellen visuellen Illusionen verstärken. Dieser abstrakte, geometrische Stil exakter Malerei war in den 1960ern immens beliebt. Zu den besten Beispielen zählen die Gemälde des ungarisch-französischen Malers Victor Vasarely (1906–97), der auch als Vater der Op Art gilt. Die faszinierende Wirkung, die durch Komplementärfarben erzielt wird, hilft bei der Erschaffung packender Poster, Verpackungen und Werbedesigns.

Farben können als warm oder kalt und entsprechend als auffallend oder zurückhaltend beschrieben werden.

Farbe besitzt ihre eigene Nomenklatur. Der Farbton bezieht sich auf die eigentliche Farbe, wie Gelb oder Lila. Intensität oder Sättigung bezieht sich darauf, wie lebendig eine Farbe ist – der höchste Grad bezeichnet die reine Farbe. Um die Intensität zu verringern, fügen Sie das Komplement der Farbe hinzu. Wert oder Tonwert bezieht sich darauf, wie hell oder dunkel eine Farbe ist. Um den Wert zu erhöhen, fügen Sie Weiß hinzu – dadurch wird eine Tönung oder eine Pastellfarbe erzeugt; um den Wert zu verringern, fügen Sie Schwarz hinzu, womit Sie eine Schattierung erzeugen. Farben können als warm oder kalt und entsprechend als auffallend oder zurückhaltend beschrieben werden. Warme Farben, wie Rot und Orange, scheinen aus einem Gemälde herauszukommen, während kühle Farben wie Grün und Blau sich zurückzuziehen scheinen.

Farbenblindheit äußert sich meist in der Schwierigkeit, Rot und Grün zu unterscheiden, kann aber auch andere Farben betreffen, die ebenfalls bräunlich-grau wirken. Etwa acht Prozent der Männer haben eine Rot-Grün-Schwäche; bei den Frauen ist ein deutlich geringerer Anteil betroffen. 1798 veröffentlichte der Engländer John Dalton, selbst farbenblind, die erste wissenschaftliche Studie über Farbenblindheit. Heute gibt es Spezialbrillen, deren Gläser spezielle Filter aufweisen und mit denen farbenblinde Menschen zwischen Rot- und Grüntönen unterscheiden können.

Linien lenken den Blick des Betrachters in einem Bild.

LINIEN

Schon die einfachste Linie kann Bedeutung vermitteln, Bewegung oder Stillstand, Aufregung oder Ruhe, Freude oder Traurigkeit andeuten. Linien lenken den Blick des Betrachters in einem Bild. Eine Reihe eng beieinanderliegender Linien kann eine Form bilden und etwa einen Kreis in eine dreidimensionale Kugel verwandeln. Parallele Linien werden als Schraffur, überkreuzende Linien als Kreuzschraffur bezeichnet. Die fließenden Linien des italienischen Renaissance-Malers Sandro Botticelli sind so schön, dass wir ihm die anatomischen Anomalien in seiner *Geburt der Venus* (1485–86; Galleria degli Uffizi, Florenz) verzeihen.

Koba (Wild Horse)
Warten auf Wild, aus Fort Marion, Florida, 1875–78
Bleistift, Tinte und Wasserfarbe auf Papier, 12,7 x 20,3 cm
National Museum of American History, Smithsonian Institution, Washington, DC

Dieses Werk, das ein Krieger der Kiowa auf die Seiten eines Kontobuches malte, erinnert an die auf Tierhäute gemalten Bilder der Ureinwohner Nordamerikas.
Die Männer malten historische Ereignisse, die Frauen abstrakte Designs.

Linien sind besonders effektiv für informative visuelle Geschichten. Bemerkenswert sind hier die Zeichnungen der Prärie-Indianer, die sogenannte Ledger Art, da das Papier dafür aus alten Kontobüchern (Ledger Books) stammte. Ihr Ursprung ist ungewöhnlich: Die US-Regierung hielt Männer verschiedener nordamerikanischer Stämme in Fort Marion, in Saint Augustine, Florida, gefangen. 26 dieser Gefangenen schufen, angeregt von ihren Bewachern, zwischen 1875 und 1878 diese Bilder, in denen sie das Leben ihrer Völker dokumentierten. Die Ledger-Zeichnungen sind sachlich und genau und stellen oft Schlachten zu Pferde dar. Das oben gezeigte Beispiel von Koba (Wild Horse) zeigt Kiowa bei der Jagd. Die Strichellinien verdeutlichen die Schritte der Männer. Die sorgfältig beobachteten Details, festgehalten in ausdrucksstarken Linien und anschließend koloriert, unterstreichen ihren dokumentarischen und künstlerischen Wert.

Poussin organisiert seine fünf Figuren mithilfe impliziter Linien in Form eines Dreiecks.

Implizite Linien können ganz subtil Formen andeuten. Der französische Barock-Maler Nicolas Poussin organisiert in *Die Heilige Familie auf den Stufen* (1648; folgende Seite) seine fünf Figuren mithilfe impliziter Linien in Form eines Dreiecks, einer stabilen geometrischen Form, die von Künstlern häufig als Kompositionshilfe verwendet wird. Die Rechteckform hinter Jesus' Kopf dient dazu, ihn einzurahmen und hervorzuheben.

Anders als Poussin bevorzugte Rubens Farbe statt Linien.

Linie versus Farbe

Wir alle scheinen von Natur aus eine Vorliebe für Linie oder Farbe zu haben und im Zweifel lieber einen Pinsel zum Malen als einen Bleistift zum Zeichnen zu wählen (oder umgekehrt). Poussin, der die Linie der Farbe vorzog, fertigte zuerst eine sorgfältige Zeichnung an, bevor er Farbe auftrug. Er wählte seine Farben ganz bewusst und kleidete die wichtigsten Figuren – Maria und Elisabeth – in die Primärfarben Rot, Blau und Gelb. Um sie herum findet man Sekundärfarben: Joseph trägt Lila, vervollständigt wird der Kreis durch lilafarbene Früchte und grüne Blätter.

Der flämische Barock-Maler Peter Paul Rubens dagegen bevorzugte Farbe statt Linien. *Die Heilige Familie mit der heiligen Elisabeth und dem Johannesknaben* (ca. 1615; gegenüber) zeigt im Prinzip dasselbe Motiv wie bei Poussin, er arbeitete aber direkt mit reichen

Nicolas Poussin
Die Heilige Familie auf den Stufen, 1648
Öl auf Leinwand,
73,3 x 105,8 cm
Cleveland Museum of Art, Cleveland

Der französische Künstler Poussin war zwar im Barock aktiv, bevorzugte jedoch statt dessen Gefühlsbetontheit einen analytischen, intellektuellen Stil, der sich an der Antike orientierte. Er setzte stark auf Linien und eine geometrische Komposition.

Farben. Das gekonnte Nebeneinander aus kontrastierenden Farben verstärkt die typische opulente, sinnliche Qualität der Malereien von Rubens, der es schafft, überzeugende Strukturen aus weichem Fleisch und fließenden Stoffen herzustellen.

Diese beiden unterschiedlichen und gegensätzlichen Ansätze sorgten im 17. Jahrhundert für Konflikte. Die sogenannten Poussinisten, die die Linie bevorzugten, behaupteten, sie sei überlegen, weil sie sich an den gebildeten Geist richte. Die Rubenisten dagegen, die Farbe favorisierten, hielten diese für überlegen, weil sie naturgetreuer sei und allen gefiele. Dieser scheinbar kleine Konflikt hatte weitreichende Auswirkungen. Wenn die Linie den Verstand erfreute, die Farbe dagegen das Auge, bestand dann der Zweck der Malerei darin, unseren Intellekt weiterzubilden und zu stärken oder visuelle Freuden zu bereiten? Diese Probleme warfen grundsätzliche Fragen über den Nutzen der Kunst auf – und das Publikum, für das die Kunst gedacht war.

Peter Paul Rubens
Die Heilige Familie mit der heiligen Elisabeth und dem Johannesknaben, ca. 1615
Öl auf Holztafel,
114,5 x 91,5 cm
Art Institute of Chicago, Chicago

Rubens war einer der erfolgreichsten Künstler der Ära des flämischen Barock – sowohl künstlerisch als auch finanziell. Die Fleischigkeit seiner typisch fülligen Figuren passt zu den reichen Farben und fließenden Pinselstrichen.

TEXTUR

Beim Beschreiben eines Kunstwerks ist mit Textur nicht gemeint, wie es sich *tatsächlich* anfühlt, wenn Sie es berühren würden (was Sie nicht sollten, auch wenn es verlockend ist), sondern wie es sich anzufühlen *scheint* – die implizite Textur. Manche Künstler achten besonders auf die strukturellen Illusionen, wie der spanische Barock-Maler Diego Velázquez. Sein Gemälde *Die Alte beim Eierbraten* (1618; unten) zeigt, wie überzeugend er verschiedene Substanzen darstellen konnte: die polierten Metall- und Terrakottagefäße, die Flüssigkeit, in der die Eier braten, die Glasflasche und die Melone, die der Junge trägt, der aufgehängte Bastkorb, dicke und dünne Stoffe und die Haut des Jungen im Vergleich zu der der alten Frau.

Seurat eliminierte mit seiner innovativen Malmethode die Möglichkeit, Illusionen von Textur zu schaffen.

Diego Velázquez
Die Alte beim Eierbraten, 1618
Öl auf Leinwand, 100,8 x 119,5 cm
Scottish National Gallery, Edinburgh

Velázquez war zu Beginn seiner Laufbahn einer der ersten spanischen Maler, die solche Genreszenen schufen. Die verschiedenen Texturen sind mit solcher Genauigkeit abgebildet, dass sie fühlbar erscheinen. Später wurde Velázquez ein beliebter Maler am spanischen Hof.

Georges Seurat
Ein Sonntagnachmittag auf der Insel La Grande Jatte – 1884, 1884–86
Öl auf Leinwand,
207,5 x 308,1 cm
Art Institute of Chicago, Chicago

Der französische Post-Impressionist Seurat verband wissenschaftliche Erkenntnisse mit dem Farbverständnis in seinen Gemälden. In seiner als Pointillismus bezeichneten Technik vermischen sich die zahllosen Punkte aus reiner Farbe im Auge des Betrachters. Seurats Fokus liegt nicht auf der Textur, sondern auf dem Sehen und der Farbtheorie.

Andere Maler hatten kein Interesse daran, zwischen Texturen zu unterscheiden. Das soll kein Werturteil sein, da der Einsatz von Textur genau wie der Einsatz der anderen Werkzeuge eines Künstlers optional ist. In seinem Gemälde *Ein Sonntagnachmittag auf der Insel La Grande Jatte – 1884* (1884–86; oben) eliminierte der französische Post-Impressionist Georges Seurat mit seiner innovativen Malmethode die Möglichkeit, Illusionen von Textur zu schaffen. Da jeder Farbton in seine Teilfarben zerlegt wird, nennt man dies Divisionismus. Bekannter ist der Begriff Pointillismus – schließlich werden die Farben als Punkte aufgebracht. Nimmt man einen Teil des Bildes aus dem Kontext, dann verrät nur die Farbe, ob Haut, Stoff, Wiese, Blätter, Wasser oder Himmel dargestellt wird.

Die Simulation der Textur einer Substanz durch eine andere in einer antiken griechischen Skulptur ist eine Form der visuellen Täuschung.

Doch auch Bildhauer können die Textur betonen. Betrachten Sie einmal die Simulation von Fleisch, weich und warm, die der altgriechische Bildhauer Praxiteles Mitte des 4. Jahrhunderts v. Chr. für seine *Aphrodite von Knidos* (nächste Seite) aus hartem, kaltem Marmor formte. Die Simulation der Textur einer Substanz durch eine

Nach Praxiteles
Aphrodite von Knidos,
2. Jahrhundert
Römische Kopie eines
griechischen Originals
von Praxiteles,
von Mitte 4. Jahrhundert
v. Chr.
Marmor, Höhe 204 cm
Vatikanische Museen,
Vatikanstadt, Rom

Praxiteles war einer der berühmtesten Bildhauer der griechischen Antike. Das Original dieser Statue war der erste lebensgroße weibliche Akt eines griechischen Bildhauers. Die Illusion einer lebenden Person aus Stein zu erschaffen, erfordert ganz besondere Kunstfertigkeit.

andere in dieser Skulptur ist eine Form der visuellen Täuschung – und ein beeindruckendes Zeugnis für das Können des Bildhauers.

Textur kann aber auch die Fähigkeit bestimmter Materialien hervorheben, Empfindungen zu vermitteln. Nehmen Sie *Der Vogel im Raum* (unten) des rumänischen Bildhauers Constantin Brâncuși. Brâncuși schuf mehrere Versionen davon aus Marmor, doch andere, wie das hier abgebildete, 1928 gegossene Werk, bestehen aus glatter, polierter Bronze und vermitteln ganz besonders effektiv den Eindruck eines aufsteigenden Vogels.

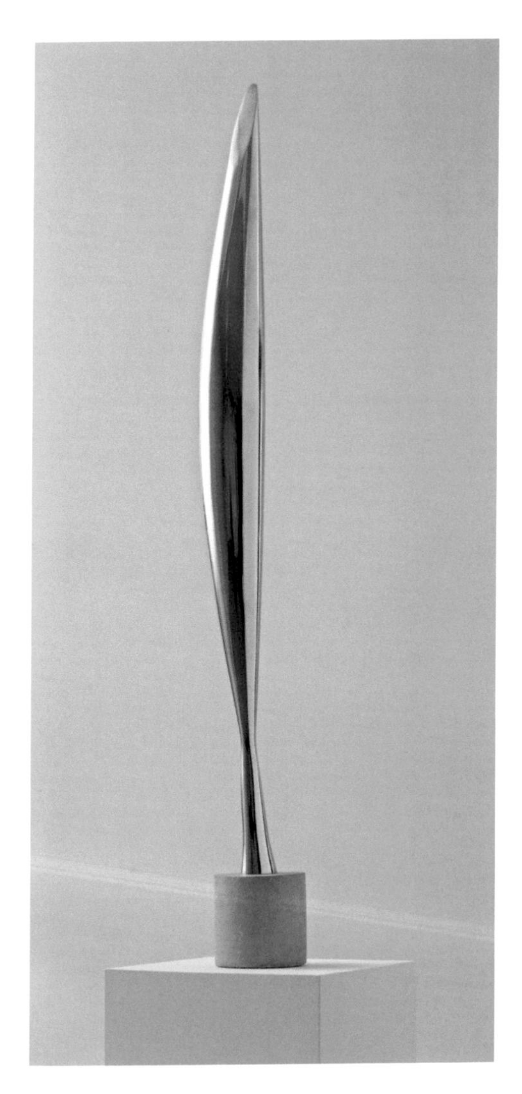

Constantin Brâncuși
Der Vogel im Raum,
gegossen 1928
Bronze,
137,2 x 21,6 x 16,5 cm
Museum of Modern Art,
New York

Brâncuși verfolgte eine abstrakte Herangehensweise an die Bildhauerei: Er strebte danach, das Wesen eines Motivs darzustellen statt seiner exakten Form. Entsprechend deutet er mit dieser glatten und glänzenden schlanken Form das Auffliegen des Vogels an und nicht den Vogel selbst.

Aus der Werkstatt von Rembrandt
Kreuzabnahme, 1650–52
Öl auf Leinwand,
142 x 110,9 cm
National Gallery of Art,
Washington, DC

Rembrandt verstand es meisterhaft, die Aufmerksamkeit des Betrachters mithilfe von Licht zu lenken – eine Fertigkeit, die er an seine Schüler weitergab. Licht verleiht der Komposition Gleichgewicht, weist auf die wichtigsten Figuren hin und erzeugt emotionales Drama.

LICHT

Licht dient, unterschiedlich eingesetzt, verschiedenen Zwecken in Malerei, Bildhauerei und anderen bildenden Künsten. Die niederländischen Barock-Künstler legten in ihren Gemälden besonderen Wert auf Lichteffekte. In *Kreuzabnahme* (1650–52; gegenüber), das heute als Werk aus Rembrandts Werkstatt gilt, ist die von dem Mann auf der Leiter gehaltene Fackel in der Mitte des Bildes die Lichtquelle. Das Licht zieht die Aufmerksamkeit des Betrachters auf die wichtigsten Personen – wie auf einer Bühne steht Christus im Rampenlicht. Seine Mutter Maria steht an zweiter Stelle, sodass klar ist, welche Geschichte hier erzählt wird.

Die französischen Impressionisten analysierten Licht durch die innovative Methode der gebrochenen Farbe, bei der jeder Farbton in seine Bestandteile zerlegt wird. Wenn ein Bereich also grünes Gras zeigen soll, werden Gelb und Blau eingesetzt, die sich aus der Ferne betrachtet mischen und die Leuchtkraft der Farben erhöhen. Claude Monet, der von Licht fasziniert war, nutzte gebrochene Farben, um die flüchtigen Effekte in seinen vielen Bildern der Kathedrale von Rouen einzufangen, vertreten hier durch *Kathedrale von Rouen: Das Portal (Sonnenlicht)*. Obwohl die gotische Kathedrale eigentlich aus grauem

Claude Monet
Kathedrale von Rouen: Das Portal (Sonnenlicht), 1894
Öl auf Leinwand, 99,7 x 65,7 cm
Metropolitan Museum of Art, New York

Ganz im Sinne der französischen Impressionisten studierte Monet die Lichtverhältnisse. Er entschied sich für die mittelalterliche Kathedrale von Rouen, weil er von seinem Zimmer auf der anderen Seite des Platzes aus das sich ändernde Licht beobachten und festhalten konnte. Er wählte das Motiv nicht aus religiösen Gründen (Monet war Agostiker), sondern weil es, wie er sagte, ihm die Möglichkeit bot, den Raum zwischen seinen Augen und der Fassade zu malen.

Stein besteht, nutzte Monet in seiner Analyse des Lichts keine graue Farbe. 1892 und 1893 malte er vor Ort mehr als 30 Bilder der Fassade, die er 1894 in seinem Atelier vollendete. Er arbeitete gleichzeitig an mehreren Leinwänden, indem er entsprechend der Lichtverhältnisse zu unterschiedlichen Tageszeiten zwischen ihnen wechselte.

Der innovative amerikanische Künstler Dan Flavin nutzt das Licht ganz anders in seiner Lichtskulptur *untitled (in honor of Harold Joachim) 3* (1977; unten). Flavin verwendete einen Großteil seiner Karriere darauf, die ästhetischen Möglichkeiten von Licht zu entdecken – nicht des natürlichen Lichts, das Monet so faszinierte, sondern des künstlichen Lichts! Flavin, der zu den Begründern des Minimalismus gehörte und einfache Formen bevorzugte, nutzte Leuchtstoffröhren, die er zu Kompositionen aus Formen und strahlenden Farben anordnete. Kritiker haben infrage gestellt, ob Konstruktionen aus Leuchtstoffröhren (die gefährliche Quecksilberdämpfe enthalten) als Kunst gelten dürfen.

Dan Flavin
untitled (in honor of Harold Joachim) 3, 1977
Neonleuchten und Metallhalterungen,
243,8 x 243,8 x 25,4 cm
The Dan Flavin Art Institute / Dia Bridgehampton, New York

Flavin verwendete ganz normale Neonleuchten. Normalerweise wird Licht verwendet, um ein Kunstwerk zu beleuchten, hier jedoch dient es selbst als künstlerisches Medium.

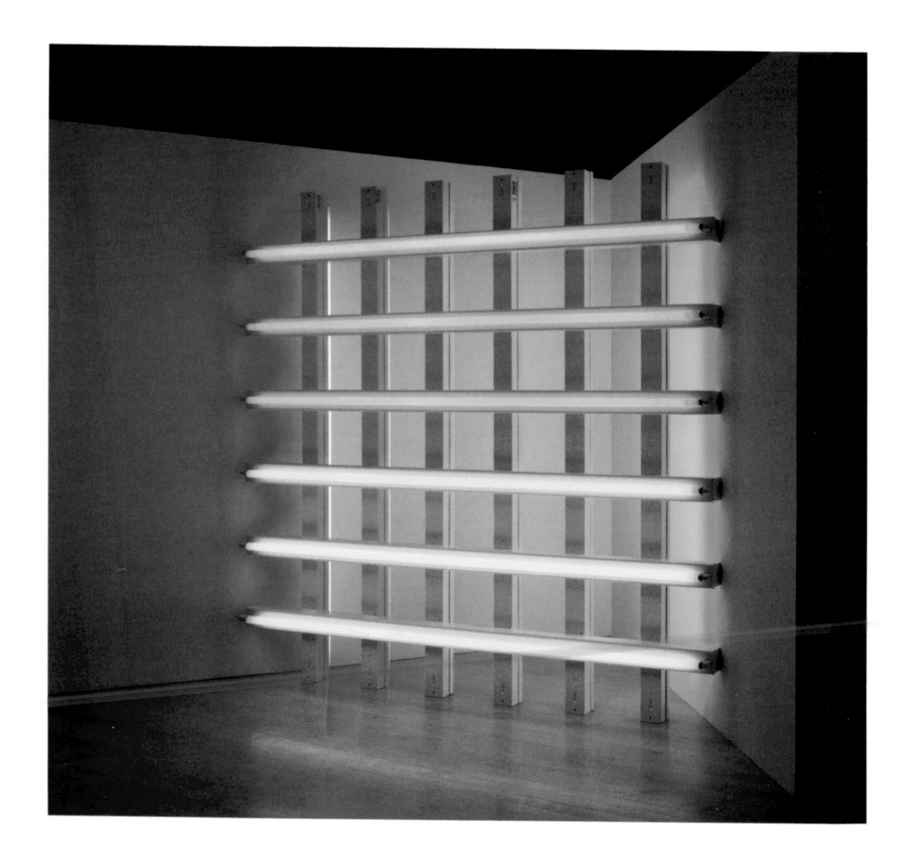

Raffael
Die Schule von Athen,
1509–11
Fresko, 5 x 7,70 m
Stanza della Segnatura,
Apostolischer Palast,
Vatikanstadt, Rom

Raffael, einer der größten Maler der italienischen Hochrenaissance, arbeitete häufig im Vatikan. Seine Gemälde werden für ihren scheinbar mühelosen Charme und ihre perfekten Kompositionen gepriesen. Durch die Kombination verschiedener Methoden, darunter der Linearperspektive, scheint Raffael die Bildebene aufzulösen und die Illusion eines gewaltigen Bildraums zu erschaffen.

RAUM

Künstler nutzen verschiedene Methoden, um auf zweidimensionalen Flächen die Illusion von drei Dimensionen zu schaffen. Wenn man sie konsistent und gemeinsam einsetzt, ist es möglich, dem Auge des Betrachters vorzugaukeln, dass die gemalte Szene in einem Raum hinter der Bildebene – der Oberfläche, auf der sich das Bild befindet – existiert. Der Bilderrahmen wird zu einem Fenster, durch das wir schauen, oder zu einem Torbogen, durch den wir die Welt des Künstlers betreten können.

Raffaels *Schule von Athen* (1509–11; oben), ein großes Fresko, nutzt viele der Methoden, die dem Künstler zur Verfügung stehen. Der vielleicht einfachste Indikator für einen Ort im Raum ist die Überschneidung, die anzeigt, dass ein Objekt vor oder hinter einem anderen liegt. Relative Größe nutzt die Tatsache, dass größere Objekte näher wirken als kleinere. Objekte, die in einer Komposition niedriger positioniert sind, scheinen dichter am Betrachter zu sein als höher positionierte. Spitzlichter und Schatten lassen ein Objekt dreidimensional erscheinen, indem sie Veränderungen an den Oberflächen andeuten. Das Verkürzen einer Figur oder eines Objekts zeigt, dass es nicht parallel zur Bildebene steht, sondern in einem schrägen Winkel in die Tiefe verläuft.

Maler nutzen oft Linear- und Luftperspektive, um ein Gefühl von Tiefe zu erzeugen. Die Linearperspektive ist besonders effektiv für überzeugende Illusionen von dreidimensionalen Innenräumen

Thomas Cole
View from Mount Holyoke, Northampton, Massachusetts, after a Thunderstorm – The Oxbow, 1836
Öl auf Leinwand, 130,8 x 193 cm
Metropolitan Museum of Art, New York

Cole, Gründer der Hudson River School, konzentrierte sich auf bewegende Ansichten der Landschaft des Hudson Valley im Staat New York. Während Raffael die Linearperspektive einsetzte, nutzte Cole die Luftperspektive, um seiner Landschaft Tiefe zu verleihen.

und Außenansichten von Gebäuden. Diagonale Linien scheinen in den Raum zurückzuweichen, wenn man sie auf einen oder mehrere »Fluchtpunkte« auf der Horizontlinie zulaufen lässt. Das Gefühl von Tiefe in der baulichen Anordnung von Raffaels *Schule von Athen* ist das Ergebnis einer Zentralperspektive mit einem Fluchtpunkt.

-

Die Luftperspektive nutzt das Prinzip der hervortretenden und zurückweichenden Farben.

-

Die Luftperspektive erreicht einen Tiefeneindruck, indem mithilfe von Farbe die optische Tatsache kopiert wird, dass die Atmosphäre unsere Wahrnehmung von entfernten Objekten verändert – sie wirken weniger deutlich und ihre Farben weniger intensiv. Die Luftperspektive nutzt das Prinzip der hervortretenden und zurückweichenden Farben (siehe S. 40). Landschaftsmaler machten davon Gebrauch, darunter die Maler der amerikanischen Hudson River School, wie man an Thomas Coles *View from Mount Holyoke, Northampton, Massachusetts, after a Thunderstorm – The Oxbow* (1836; oben) sieht.

Bildhauer nutzen den Raum auf andere Weise. Der Vergleich zweier Versionen desselben Motivs, beide von italienischen Bildhauern aus Marmor gefertigt, verdeutlicht dies. Michelangelo, der in der Hochrenaissance wirkte, zeigt seinen *David* (unten links), entstanden 1501–04, nachdenklich. Das Gewicht ist auf ein Bein verlagert, er schaut in der antiken *Kontraposto*-Haltung auf seinen Feind. Michelangelos *David* bewegt sich nicht – seine Stärke ist verborgen.

Der Raum zwischen den zwei Gegnern ist voller Anspannung.

Im Gegensatz dazu dreht sich der überaus lebhafte *David* (unten rechts) des Barock-Bildhauers Gianlorenzo Bernini, entstanden 1623–24, also mehr als ein Jahrhundert später, dramatisch im Raum, bevor er den Stein schleudert. Um das Bild von Berninis *David* zu vervollständigen, denkt sich der Betrachter implizit den Goliath hinzu, wodurch der Raum zwischen den zwei Gegnern voller Anspannung ist. Die Illusion ist so komplett, dass Besucher der Galerie es vermeiden, sich in die gedachte Schusslinie zu stellen!

Unten links:
Michelangelo
David, 1501–04
Marmor, Höhe 5,17 m
Galleria dell'Accademia, Florenz

Bei Michelangelo ist der Schäferjunge David statisch und sieht dem Kampf mit Goliath voller Ruhe entgegen.

Unten rechts:
Gianlorenzo Bernini
David, 1623–24
Marmor, Höhe 1,70 m
Galleria Borghese, Rom

Bernini studierte Michelangelos Werk in Rom, entwickelte aber einen dynamischeren Stil.

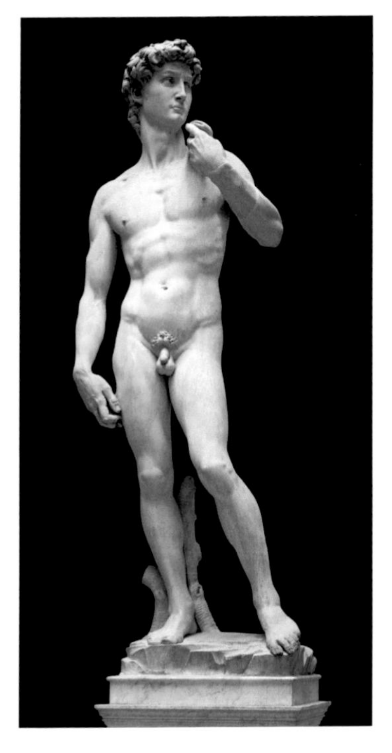

KOMPOSITION

Bei einem Kunstwerk erzeugt die Anordnung der visuellen Elemente die Komposition. Eine erfolgreiche Komposition zeichnet sich durch die Prinzipien Gleichgewicht, Proportion und Einheit aus.

Gleichgewicht

Die menschliche Natur sucht das Gleichgewicht – damit fühlen wir uns behaglich. Die einfachste Form von Gleichgewicht ist die Symmetrie. Wird eine Komposition durch eine Linie in zwei identische Spiegelbilder zerlegt, weist sie eine perfekte bilaterale Symmetrie auf, wie z. B. Flavins Lichtskulptur (S. 50). Sind die zwei Seiten dagegen ähnlich, aber nicht identisch, ist es eine leichte bilaterale Symmetrie, wie in Raffaels *Schule von Athen* (S. 51). Bei zwei völlig verschiedenen Seiten einer Komposition handelt es sich um Asymmetrie. Die *Kreuzabnahme* aus Rembrandts Werkstatt (S. 48) ist asymmetrisch, trotzdem wirkt die Komposition wegen der genialen Verteilung der hellen und dunklen Bereiche ausgewogen.

Die Mitte einer Komposition strahlt eine gewisse Kraft aus.

Damit in einer Komposition Gleichgewicht herrscht, kann ein Künstler eine visuelle Kraft (ein visuelles Gewicht) einsetzen. Manche Aspekte eines Kunstwerks wecken eher und länger unsere Aufmerksamkeit als andere – sie sind auffälliger. Im Allgemeinen wirken Formen, die größer, leuchtender gefärbt und deutlicher texturiert sind sowie Bewegung andeuten, visuell kraftvoller als kleine, matt gefärbte, undeutlich texturierte und statische Formen. Auch die Mitte einer Komposition strahlt eine gewisse Kraft aus und zieht unseren Blick an – wir sind es gewohnt, das »Zentrum der Aufmerksamkeit« im physischen Zentrum einer Komposition zu finden. Wenn der Künstler es uns nicht bietet, dann ergänzen wir es implizit selbst. Der italienische Künstler Giotto nutzte dieses visuelle Phänomen geschickt in seinem Fresko *Jesu Einzug in Jerusalem* (ca. 1305; gegenüber): Der nächste Schritt des Esels bringt Jesus direkt in die Mitte des Bildes und impliziert damit eine Bewegung.

Proportionen

Dies bezieht sich auf die relative Größe der Komponenten in einer Komposition. Die Idee, dass bestimmte mathematisch abgeleitete Proportionen visuell befriedigender sind als andere, stammt schon aus der Antike. Die alten Griechen erfanden den Goldenen Schnitt.

Giotto
Jesu Einzug in Jerusalem, ca. 1305
Fresko, 200 x 185 cm
Arenakapelle, Padua

Der italienische Maler Giotto, eine wichtige Figur in der Geschichte der westlichen Malerei, brach mit dem früheren mittelalterlichen flachen, zweidimensionalen Stil und führte raumgreifendere Figuren sowie menschliche Emotionen ein. In *Jesu Einzug in Jerusalem* verschieben wir Jesus visuell in die Mitte der Komposition, weil wir instinktiv das Gefühl haben, dass er dorthin gehört.

Salvador Dalí
Das Abendmahl, 1955
Öl auf Leinwand,
166,7 x 267 cm
National Gallery of Art,
Washington, DC

Salvador Dalí schuf eine exzentrische surrealistische Persönlichkeit, die im Einklang mit seinem Malstil stand. Für die Festlegung der Maße dieser Leinwand und des am Himmel schwebenden Dodekaeders – das eine Referenz auf die zwölf Apostel darstellt – griff er auf den Goldenen Schnitt zurück.

Ausdrücken lässt er sich als: (a+b)/a = a/b, oder das kleinere von zwei Maßen verhält sich zum größeren wie das größere Maß zum Ganzen. Bei einer Berechnung ergibt sich das exakte Verhältnis als 1,61803398875:1. Damit kann man z. B. die Maße für ein angenehm proportioniertes Rechteck bestimmen. Der spanische Surrealist Salvador Dalí verwendete den Goldenen Schnitt für sein Gemälde *Das Abendmahl* (oben) von 1955.

Künstler sind schon lange von den idealen Proportionen des menschlichen Körpers fasziniert. Die Griechen und Römer der

Antike ermittelten mithilfe der Mathematik die gewünschten Maße (siehe S. 28). Diese Idee zog sich durch die Geschichte der Kunst: Das Ideal der italienischen Hochrenaissance in Michelangelos *David* (1501–04; S. 53 links) geht auf das klassische Ideal zurück.

Einheit

Eine Komposition erscheint als Einheit, wenn alle Teile verbunden und zusammenhängend wirken. Die Wiederholung von ähnlichen Formen, Pinselstrichen, Texturen, Farben oder anderen Elementen kann die Einheit eines Kunstwerks bewirken. So hält z. B. Seurats pointillistische Maltechnik in *Ein Sonntagnachmittag auf der Insel La Grande Jatte – 1884* (S. 45) die Komposition durch die konsistente Form und Größe der Pinselstriche zusammen. Monets dicke Pinselstriche gebrochener Farbe bei der *Kathedrale von Rouen* (S. 49) ergibt eine grobe Oberfläche, die alle Teile des Gemäldes eint.

Das vereinigende Element in Picassos *Die Tragödie* (1903; gegenüber) ist das Blau – auch im Sand und der Haut der Menschen. Treibt man allerdings die Nutzung ähnlicher Elemente in einem Kunstwerk zu weit, führt dies zu Monotonie. Es ist daher ratsam, sowohl auf Einheit als auch auf Vielfalt zu setzen, indem man Elemente verwendet, die ähnlich, aber nicht identisch sind.

Pablo Picasso
Die Tragödie, 1903
Öl auf Holz,
105,3 x 69 cm
National Gallery of Art,
Washington, DC

Picasso wird oft als der größte Künstler des 20. Jahrhunderts betrachtet. Im Laufe seiner langen Karriere bediente er sich vieler Stile, darunter seiner frühen Blauen Periode, die durch dieses Gemälde repräsentiert wird. Im Anschluss folgten seine Rosa Periode, verschiedene innovative Formen des Kubismus, seine Klassische Periode ... und mehr. (Siehe S. 154–159)

-

***Die Tragödie* ist ein extremes Beispiel für den Einsatz der Farbe Blau, um Emotionen hervorzurufen.**

-

EMOTIONEN

Mit den Elementen der Kunst lassen sich machtvolle Emotionen vermitteln – positive, negative und alles dazwischen. Auch wenn nicht klar ist, welcher Art die Tragödie ist, drücken die dominante Farbe Blau, die schroffen schwarzen Linien, die gebeugte Haltung der Figuren und ihre gesenkten Blicke in Pablo Picassos *Tragödie* eine tiefe Traurigkeit aus. Die Verbindung zwischen körperlicher Lage oder Richtung und Emotion wird deutlich, wenn jemand »sich niedergeschlagen« fühlt oder wir ihm sagen »Kopf hoch, das wird schon«. Emotionale Assoziationen, die über Farben vermittelt werden, sind ebenfalls in unserer Sprache verankert: Wir sehen etwas »rosarot« oder »schwarz« und wissen, was das bedeutet.

-

Farben können eine Bedeutung vermitteln.

-

Die Tragödie ist ein extremes Beispiel für den Einsatz von Blau zum Ausdrücken einer Emotion. Farben tragen eine Bedeutung. Wir sagen z. B., dass jemand »rot« sieht oder »grün hinter den Ohren ist«. Die psychologischen Auswirkungen von Wandfarben für verschiedene Arten von Räumen sind bekannt: Die beruhigenden Farben von Wartezimmern in Krankenhäusern wird man kaum in einem Nachtclub finden.

1903
Picasso

STIL IN DER KUNST

Der Stil eines Kunstwerks ergibt sich aus der Verwendung der visuellen Elemente. Es ist der persönliche Stil des Künstlers, der Auguste Rodins *Kuss* (unten) von ca. 1882 so sehr von Constantin Brâncuşis Version des gleichen Motivs (gegenüber unten) von 1916 unterscheidet. Die beiden Skulpturen, entstanden unter zeitlich, räumlich und kulturell ähnlichen Bedingungen, zeigen, wie sich der persönliche Stils des jeweiligen Künstlers auswirkt.

»Stil« bezeichnet nicht nur die persönliche Herangehensweise eines Künstlers, sondern auch Perioden in der Kunstgeschichte. Dies sind vereinfacht gesagt die wichtigsten Epochen der Kunst Westeuropas: Vorgeschichte, griechische und römische Antike, frühes Mittelalter, Romanik, Gotik, Früh- und Hochrenaissance, Manierismus, Barock, Rokoko, Klassizismus, Romantik, Realismus, Impressionismus und Post-Impressionismus, Fauvismus, Kubismus, Futurismus, Dadaismus, Surrealismus, Minimalismus, Postmodernismus und die zahllosen »ismen« der letzten Jahre.

Auguste Rodin
Der Kuss, ca. 1882
Marmor,
181,5 x 112,5 x 117 cm
Musée Rodin, Paris

Rodin begehrte gegen die bildhauerischen Normen seiner Zeit auf und sagte nach einer Reise nach Italien: »Michelangelo hat mich von der akademischen Bildhauerei befreit.« Rodin nutzte den menschlichen Körper, dargestellt in außerordentlich naturalistischem Stil, als Mittel, um ohne Worte Gefühle zu transportieren.

Man unterschied Kunststile früher auch nach ihrer geografischen Lage – italienische Renaissance, französischer Impressionismus usw. Das ist kaum noch sinnvoll. Die zunehmende Globalisierung und die Leichtigkeit, mit der Ideen sich international verbreiten, sorgen dafür, dass sich Kunstrichtungen kaum noch mit bestimmten Ländern verknüpfen lassen.

Stattdessen ist inzwischen immer häufiger zu beobachten, dass mehrere Stile gleichzeitig an Popularität gewinnen und nicht mehr ein einziger Stil dominiert. Die Palette reicht aktuell vom fotografischen Hyperrealismus bis zur völligen Abstraktion. Das eine Extrem sind Werke, die das Auge des Betrachters geschickt täuschen und uns überzeugen, dass wir etwas sehen, was gar nicht da ist. Solche Arbeiten sind naturalistisch und so sorgfältig ausgeführt, dass sie ganz echt wirken. Andere Werke sind stilisiert, die Unvollkommenheiten der Natur überdeckt oder vielleicht aus ästhetischen Gründen modifiziert. Entfernen wir uns noch weiter von der beobachtbaren Realität: Wenn ein Kunstwerk kein erkenn- oder identifi-

Constantin Brâncuși
Der Kuss, 1916
Kalkstein,
58,4 x 33,7 x 25,4 cm
Philadelphia Museum of Art, Philadelphia

Im Gegensatz zu Rodin schuf Brâncuși seine Skulptur, als der Kubismus in Mode war. Sein vereinfachtes Paar ist alles andere als natürlich, formt im wahrsten Sinne einen Kubus und hat praktisch nur Augen füreinander.

zierbares Motiv enthält, ist es der abstrakten Kunst zuzurechnen. Ob nun als geistige Vereinfachung von Primärfarben und geometrischen Formen oder aller Farben und Linien – abstrakte Kunst hat keine Verbindung zur sichtbaren Welt.

WORAUF ES BEIM ANALYSIEREN VON KUNST ANKOMMT

Worauf sollten Sie achten, wenn Sie ein Kunstwerk analysieren? Es gibt einen Unterschied zwischen einfacher Beschreibung und durchdachter Analyse. Die Farben in Picassos *Tragödie* (S. 59) als verschiedene Blautöne zu beschreiben, ist akkurat, aber oberflächlich. Informativer ist es, bei der Analyse zu bemerken, dass die vielen kühlen Blautöne das Gefühl der Traurigkeit verstärken, das dieses Gemälde durchdringt. Ein Blick in Picassos Leben platziert es in die Blaue Periode des Künstlers, 1901–04, als seine Bilder fast monochromatisch blau waren und oft traurige, arme Menschen zeigten. Der autobiografische Aspekt: Picasso war zu der Zeit verarmt und sein Freund Carles Casagemas hatte sich im Februar 1901 das Leben genommen.

Sie können den Genuss eines Kunstwerks noch stärken, indem Sie etwas über den Schöpfer dieses Werks in Erfahrung bringen. Versuchen Sie bei einem unbekannten Künstler, etwas über die Kultur zu verstehen, die das Kunstwerk repräsentiert. Ist es typisch für den Künstler und/oder die Ära? Betrachten Sie das abgebildete Motiv und seine Bedeutung (siehe S. 98–129). Was sagt Ihnen der Stil des Künstlers? Wie haben die verwendeten Materialien und Techniken das Ergebnis beeinflusst?

Besonders erhellend kann es sein, wenn ein Motiv von zwei Künstlern zu unterschiedlichen Zeiten und Orten gemalt wurde.

Bestimmte Eigenschaften eines Kunstwerks werden offensichtlicher, wenn man es zu einem anderen Werk in Beziehung setzt. Wenn Sie einen frühen mit einem späten Rembrandt vergleichen, erhalten Sie einen Einblick in den Verlauf seines Lebens und seiner Karriere. Besonders erhellend kann es sein, wenn ein Motiv von zwei Künstlern zu unterschiedlichen Zeiten und Orten gemalt wurde: Ein Vergleich von Tizians *Venus und Adonis* aus den 1550ern mit Rubens' Version aus der Mitte der 1630er (beide im Metropolitan Museum of Art, New York) verrät uns etwas über die Renaissance in Venedig bzw. den Barock in Flandern.

Camille Claudel
La Valse (Der Walzer),
1889–1905
Glasiertes Steinzeug,
41,5 x 37 x 20,5 cm
Musée Camille Claudel,
Nogent-sur-Seine

Claudel war zunächst Schülerin des viel älteren Rodin, wurde dann aber seine Geliebte und war ihm ebenbürtig in ihrem Können als Bildhauerin. Sie ist bekannt für die offen zur Schau gestellte Sinnlichkeit ihrer Figuren. Tragischerweise wurde sie nach dem Tod ihres Vaters und Beschützers auf Veranlassung ihrer Familie für die letzten 30 Jahre ihres Lebens in eine psychiatrische Anstalt eingewiesen.

Wenn wir Werke vergleichen, die von einem Künstler und seinem Schüler geschaffen wurden, erfahren wir etwas über ihr Können und die Beziehung zwischen ihnen. Der junge Leonardo da Vinci ging bei Andrea del Verrocchio in die Lehre und malte Teile von Verrocchios *Taufe Christi* (ca. 1470–75; Galleria degli Uffizi, Florenz). Giorgio Vasari berichtete im 16. Jahrhundert in den *Lebensbeschreibungen der Künstler*, dass dies die besten Teile des Bildes seien und Verrocchio in seinem Ärger »nie wieder Farbe anrührte«. Die Beziehung zwischen dem französischen impressionistischen Bildhauer Auguste Rodin und seiner Schülerin Camille Claudel ging ganz anders aus: Sie wurde sein Modell, seine Mitarbeiterin und Geliebte. Ihr Stil war fast nicht zu unterscheiden – sie entdeckte zu ihrem Verdruss gar, dass Rodin ihre Arbeiten mit seinem Namen signiert hatte.

Beachten Sie die Beschränkungen des Mediums, in dem der Künstler gearbeitet hat.

Wie lässt sich die Qualität eines Kunstwerks abschätzen? Das Können des Künstlers sollte zumindest ausreichen, um die gewünschten Ideen visuell zu vermitteln. Soll die Einschätzung darüber hinaus fair sein, müssen die Grenzen, denen der Künstler vielleicht begegnete, und das, was entsprechend möglich war, berücksichtigt werden. Beachten Sie die Beschränkungen des Mediums, in dem der Künstler gearbeitet hat: Ei-Tempera, das einzige Mittel für die Tafelmalerei im Mittelalter, trocknet schnell und bildet eine einheitlich matte Oberfläche, sodass sich kaum die Illusion von Textur erzeugen lässt. Ölfarbe dagegen, in der Renaissance weiterentwickelt, trocknet langsam, ist unterschiedlich viskos und erlaubt es dem Maler, jeden visuellen Effekt zu erzeugen, dessen er fähig ist. Wenn man andererseits einen Mosaikkünstler für den mangelnden Naturalismus in seinem Werk kritisiert, betrifft dies eigentlich eine Eigenschaft des Mediums und nicht das Können des Künstlers (siehe nächstes Kapitel).

Bis zu einem gewissen Maß haben alle kreativen Errungenschaften mit der Vergangenheit zu tun.

Was macht »große« Kunst aus? Auf diese wichtige Frage gibt es kaum eine einzige, weithin akzeptierte Antwort. Warum faszinieren uns einige Stile, wie der klassisch griechische, und einige Künstler, wie Rembrandt, dauerhaft, andere dagegen nicht? Das gilt auch für andere Gebiete wie Musik und Literatur. Sie könnten sich fragen, ob ein Werk intelligent und frisch ist. Kreativ und innovativ? Vielleicht sogar wirklich neu und einzigartig? Heute sehen die meisten Menschen diese Eigenschaften positiv. Oder ist es gar nicht originär? Nur eine Wiederholung der Ideen früherer Künstler? Bis zu einem gewissen Maß haben alle kreativen Errungenschaften mit der Vergangenheit zu tun. Die Welt, in der wir leben, und die Vergangenheit, die diese Welt geformt hat, beeinflussen selbst jene Künstler, die sich als »Autodidakten« oder »naiv« bezeichnen.

Sie müssen nicht unbedingt alle Kunstwerke mögen, die Sie sehen, sollten aber in ihrer Bewertung aufgeschlossen sein. Schauen Sie in Museen, Galerien und anderen Orten, die Kunst ausstellen, auch Werke aus fremden, vielleicht zeitlich oder örtlich entfernten

Kulturen an und nehmen Sie neue Ideen auf. Legen Sie die fast unvermeidlichen vorgefertigten Meinungen und Vorurteile ab. Bemühen Sie sich, jedem Werk die seiner Ästhetik und seinem Zweck angemessene Beachtung zu schenken. Denken Sie daran, dass die Definition von »Kunst« in nichtwestlichen Kulturen die Vorstellung dessen verkomplizieren kann, was »gute Kunst« ausmacht. Manche Menschen messen Objekten der sogenannten »primitiven Kunst« oder »Volkskunst« einen geringeren Status zu als den schönen Künsten. Dabei ist dies eine moderne westliche Haltung, die den Kulturen, auf die wir sie anwenden, unbekannt ist.

WICHTIGE ELEMENTE

Farbe:

- Primär-, Sekundär-, Komplementärfarben
- Farbton, Intensität/Sättigung, Tonwert, Tönung/Pastell, Schattierung
- Farbenblindheit

Linien:

- Schraffur, Kreuzschraffur
- Implizite Linien und Formen
- Diskussion Linie versus Farbe

Textur:

- Implizierte statt tatsächliche

Licht:

- Gebrochene Farbe
- Künstliches Licht

Raum:

- Überschneidung, relative Größe, Modellierung, Verkürzung
- Linearperspektive, Luftperspektive
- *Kontraposto*

Komposition:

- Gleichgewicht
- Proportion
- Einheit
- Visuelle Kraft

Emotionen:

- Rolle der physischen Position
- Einsatz von Farbe

Stil in der Kunst:

- Persönlicher Stil
- Stile in der Geschichte der Kunst von Hyperrealismus bis Abstraktion

MATERIALIEN UND TECHNIKEN

-

Wer mit seinen Händen arbeitet, ist ein Arbeiter;
Wer mit seinen Händen und seinem Geist arbeitet,
ist ein Kunsthandwerker;
Wer mit seinen Händen, seinem Geist und seinem
Herzen arbeitet, ist ein Künstler.

-

Boys' Club Federation, New York City
1923

Unbekannter Künstler
Porträt einer jungen Frau von einer Fayum-Mumie, römisch-ägyptisch, 90–120 n. Chr.
Enkaustik und Blattgold auf Lindenholz, 38,1 x 18,4 cm
Metropolitan Museum of Art, New York

Bei der Enkaustik wird Wachs als Bindemittel verwendet. Enkaustik-Mumienporträts wurden in ganz Ägypten gefertigt, doch die am besten erhaltenen Exemplare sind die faszinierend lebensecht wirkenden Bilder aus dem Fayum-Becken. Enkaustik wird auch heute noch praktiziert.

Wenn Sie wissen, wie Künstler Gemälde, Skulpturen und andere Werke herstellen, werden Sie viel mehr Vergnügen an ihnen finden. Welche Ressourcen, Werkzeuge und Methoden hatte und hat ein Künstler? Was kann ein geschickter Künstler in einem Medium erreichen und was nicht? Wie beeinflusst das Medium das Ergebnis?

MALEREI UND VERWANDTE MEDIEN

Alle Typen von Farbe bestehen aus Pigmenten in Form gemahlener Partikel farbigen Materials und eines Bindemittels, das die Pigmente zusammenhält und sie auf einem Untergrund haften lässt.

Enkaustik

Für die Enkaustik, eine der ältesten Maltechniken, wird das Pigment mit heißem Wachs (traditionell Bienenwachs) als Bindemittel gemischt. Das Wachs ist je nach Temperatur flüssig oder pastös. Mit dieser Farbe malt der Künstler dann auf einer Holztafel, wie bei den Mumienporträts aus dem Fayum-Becken in Ägypten (gegenüber), den ältesten noch vorhandenen Enkaustik-Gemälden.

Die Vorzüge der Enkaustik liegen in ihrer Beständigkeit und der Permanenz der Farben. Poliert man die Oberflächen, nehmen sie einen weichen Glanz an. Nachteilig ist die Notwendigkeit, das Wachs beim Arbeiten warmzuhalten, wofür eine relativ aufwendige Ausrüstung nötig ist. Werden Enkaustik-Gemälde größerer Hitze ausgesetzt (mehr als 90° C), dann schmelzen sie.

Heute gibt es elektrische Paletten, Maleisen und Heißluftgeräte, und Künstler können kleine Blöcke aus farbigem, gereinigtem Bienenwachs, gemischt mit Kunstharz oder synthetischem Wachs, in den unterschiedlichsten Farben kaufen. Der Zusatz von Kunstharz und anderen Stoffen, die die Elastizität erhöhen, erlaubt es, auf flexiblen Oberflächen, wie Papier und Leinwand, zu malen.

Fresko

Große Gemälde auf Wänden und Decken werden üblicherweise als Fresko ausgeführt. Die zwei Grundtypen sind *buon fresco* (auch: *fresco buono*), gemalt auf feuchten Putz, und *fresco secco*, gemalt auf trockenen Putz. Die Namen sind italienisch und bedeuten: *fresco*: »frisch«, *buon*: »gut« und *secco*: »trocken«. Die Fresko-Technik, die bereits im alten Rom hoch entwickelt war, wie man an den ausgegrabenen Häusern von Herculaneum und Pompeji sehen kann, die durch den Ausbruch des Vesuv im Jahre 79 konserviert wurden, hatte ihre Blütezeit während der italienischen Renaissance.

Michelangelo
Die Erschaffung Adams,
Detail der Decke, ca. 1512
Fresko,
2,80 x 5,70 m
Sixtinische Kapelle,
Vatikanstadt, Rom

Ein berühmtes Beispiel ist die von Michelangelo bemalte Decke der Sixtinischen Kapelle im Vatikan (1508–12; oben und S. 102–103).

Für ein Fresko wird die Oberfläche mit mehreren Schichten Gipsputz geglättet, wobei man mit grobem Putz beginnt und immer feineres Material aufträgt. Die *Giornàta*, italienisch: Tagwerk, wird mit einer sehr feinen, dünnen Gipsschicht bedeckt, der *Intonaco*. Der Künstler malt mit fein gemahlenem, in Wasser angerührtem Pigment auf den feuchten Putz. Wichtig ist, schneller zu malen, als der Putz trocknet. Beim Trocknen werden die Pigmente absorbiert und in die Calciumkarbonat-Kristalle des Gipsputzes eingebettet. Da sich die Farbe beim Trocknen mit dem Putz verbindet, ist *buon fresco* außerordentlich beständig.

Ein Künstler kann ein *buon fresco* mithilfe der *fresco secco*-Technik nachbearbeiten und Details mit Ei-Tempera ausführen. Keines von beiden haftet jedoch gut, da sie nur eine oberflächliche Schicht bilden. Nicht alle Pigmente eignen sich für *buon fresco*: Aufgrund der Alkalität des Putzes sind fast alle Farben pflanzlichen Ursprungs chemisch

Beim *buon fresco* wird Farbe, die nur aus Pigmenten und Wasser besteht, auf eine Oberfläche aus frischem Putz aufgetragen. Da das Pigment den Putz beim Trocknen durchdringt, ist ein echtes Fresko sehr beständig. Michelangelo lag beim Arbeiten an der Decke der Sixtinischen Kapelle auf dem Rücken, hoch über dem Boden auf einem Gerüst, wobei ihm die Farbe ins Gesicht tropfte.

inkompatibel. Da die Farben beim Trocknen aufhellen, muss man sie dunkler auftragen als gewünscht und es ist schwierig, an aufeinanderfolgenden Tagen farbgenau zu arbeiten.

Beim *fresco secco* wird ein trockener Kalkputz am Abend vor dem Bemalen und am Tag des Malens gründlich mit Kalkwasser getränkt. Während die Wand feucht ist, malt der Künstler mit einer Mischung aus gemahlenem Pigment, Wasser und Kalkwasser oder mit gemahlenem Pigment und einem Bindemittel wie Kasein, einem Pulver, das aus getrocknetem Quark gewonnen wird. Oder man malt mit Tempera (nicht zu verwechseln mit Ei-Tempera) auf den getrockneten Putz, einer Mischung aus Erdfarben und einem Bindemittel pflanzlichen oder tierischen Ursprungs. Ein ausgezeichnetes Beispiel für *fresco secco* ist das Gewölbe des Mittelschiffs der Kirche von Saint-Savin-sur-Gartempe in Frankreich, das Ende des 11. bis Anfang des 12. Jahrhunderts mit Szenen aus dem Alten Testament bemalt wurde.

Mosaik

Beim Mosaik nutzt man wie beim *buon fresco* feuchten Putz. Statt darauf zu malen, presst der Künstler kleine Mosaiksteine aus farbigem Material, die sogenannten Tesserae (vom griechischen Wort für »vier« wegen der vier sichtbaren Ecken), in den Putz. Im letzten Schritt werden die Zwischenräume mit Mörtel verfugt.

Die Technik war im alten Rom schon ausgereift und wurde oft eingesetzt. Römische Mosaikkünstler nutzten Marmor und andere Steinarten und beschränkten sich auf die natürlich vorhandenen Farben. Im 4. Jahrhundert begann man dann, mit farbigem Glas und goldenen Teilen zu arbeiten, was die Farbvielfalt und die möglichen Effekte deutlich steigerte. Die Mosaiken des byzantinischen Kaisers Justinian und der Kaiserin Theodora (ca. 547; oben) in der Kirche San Vitale in Ravenna glänzen mit Glas-Tesserae. Die Künstler variierten die Größe der Teile: Sie nutzten kleinere Mosaiksteine für die Gesichter und größere für den Hintergrund. Theodoras Krone und Halskette enthalten runde Perlmuttscheiben.

Die Tesserae können aber auch aus farbiger Paste gefertigt werden, indem man Pigment mit Zement und gemahlenem Glas mischt, wie in der Palastkapelle von Palermo. Statt Würfel aus reinem Gold zu verwenden, wurde Blattgold auf einen Glaswürfel aufgebracht oder zwischen zwei durchsichtige Glasstücke gelegt. Sogenanntes Musivgold aus Zinndisulfid, ein preiswertes, goldglänzendes

Unbekannter Künstler
Kaiserin Theodora mit ihrem Gefolge, ca. 547
Mosaik, 2,64 x 3,66 m
Kirche San Vitale, Ravenna

Frühe Mosaike bestanden aus Stein, während spätere Mosaike vor farbigem Glas und Gold glänzten und blinkten, vor allem wenn man sie bei Kerzenlicht betrachtete. Unter Theodoras Ehemann, Kaiser Justinian (dargestellt in einem weiteren Mosaik in San Vitale), erlebte die Byzantinische Kunst eine Blütezeit.

Pigment, diente schon im 13. Jahrhundert als wirksamer Ersatz für Blattgold und Goldpulver.

Der Künstler kann gleichförmige Flächen bewusst mit Glas und Gold in schimmernde, kristallene Bilder verwandeln.

Ein Mosaik an großen Flächen wie Decken, Wänden und Fußböden ist beständig und kann sowohl innen als auch außen eingesetzt werden. Der Künstler kann die dekorative Qualität des Mediums unterstreichen, indem er Gold und Glas verarbeitet, um gleichförmige Flächen in schimmernde, prächtige, kristallene Bilder zu verwandeln. Da die Mosaiksteine jedoch gut erkennbar sind (ausgenommen beim seltenen Mikromosaik), besteht kaum die Möglichkeit, wirklich naturgetreue Bilder zu erschaffen.

Buchmalerei

Das Wort Manuskript kommt von den lateinischen Wörtern *manus* (»Hand«) und *scribere* (»schreiben«). Sind die Bilder in den Manuskripten nicht nur farbig, sondern sogar vergoldet, spricht man von Illuminationen. Eine Seite eines Manuskripts wird als Folio bezeichnet; die Vorderseite heißt *recto*, kurz *r*, und die Rückseite *verso*, kurz *v*. Das *Book of Kells* etwa aus dem Jahre 800, eines der berühmtesten illustrierten Manuskripte, enthält die *Symbole der vier Evangelisten* (folgende Seite): Matthäus (der Mann), Markus (der Löwe), Lukas (der Stier) und Johannes (der Adler).

Für Manuskript-Folios wurde meist Tierhaut verwendet: Pergament oder Vellum. Das Wort Pergament leitet sich von der griechischen Stadt Pergamon in der westlichen Türkei ab. Der römische Naturforscher Plinius der Ältere (gest. 79) schrieb, dass König Eumenes II. von Pergamon (197–158 v. Chr.) Pergament erfand, als Ägypten den Export von Papyrus verbot. Vellum lässt sich auf französisch *veau* (»Kalb«) zurückführen. Es wird aus Kälberhaut gefertigt; die allerfeinste Qualität liefert die Haut eines totgeborenen Kalbes. Es können aber auch die Häute anderer Tiere verwendet werden.

War die Arbeit des Schreibers abgeschlossen, begann der Illustrator, mithilfe verschiedener Bindemittel die Farben aufzubringen. Ein übliches Bindemittel im Mittelalter war mit Wasser verrührtes Eiklar, eine als »übelriechend« beschriebene Mischung. Gummi arabicum, ein wasserlöslicher Baumsaft, bildet in Wasser ein dünnes Gelee. Durch Auskochen von Pergament und Haut gewonnener

Unbekannter Künstler
Symbole der vier Evangelisten, Folio 27v im *Book of Kells*, Evangeliar, Text in Latein, hergestellt in Britannien oder Irland, ca. 800
Vellum, beschnitten: 33 x 25,5 cm
Trinity College Library, Dublin

Manuskripte (von Hand gefertigte Bücher, vor allem aus der Zeit vor Erfindung des Buchdrucks) haben Folios (Seiten) aus Pergament oder Vellum (Tierhaut). Das *Book of Kells* – ein lateinisches Evangeliar, benannt nach der Abtei Kells, wo es lange aufbewahrt wurde – gehört zu den schönsten illustrierten Manuskripten, die im frühen Mittelalter entstanden sind.

tierischer Leim eignete sich besonders für Blautöne. Eigelb in einem der Bindemittel ergab glänzende und strahlende Farben. Bläschen im Eiklar verhinderte man durch das Hinzufügen von – tatsächlich – Ohrenschmalz. Hatte der Illustrator die Formen gezeichnet, ging er mit schwarzer Tinte über das Bild.

Ei-Tempera

Ei-Tempera verwendet eine Emulsion aus Eigelb und Wasser als Bindemittel. Ihren Höhepunkt erreichte diese Technik im späten Mittelalter, wie Duccios Predella-Tafel *Christi Geburt* (1308–11; gegenüber) von seiner *Maestà* (S. 21) beweist. Der Künstler arbeitete auf einer älteren Holztafel, die mit einer Schicht Leim, gefolgt von mehreren Schichten Gesso versiegelt war, sodass sich eine glatte Oberfläche bildete. Das Blattgold im Hintergrund und die Heiligenscheine, die man aus mittelalterlichen Gemälden kennt, wurden vor dem eigentlichen Malen aufgebracht. Es war üblich, die Haut wichtiger Figuren mit Grün zu unterlegen, weil man glaubte, dass dies den rötlichen Hautton verstärkte. Leider führte die Abnutzung der oberen Farbschicht nun zu einer grünlichen Blässe.

Ein Nachteil von Ei-Tempera ist, dass es extrem schnell trocknet.

Zu den Vorteilen von Ei-Tempera gehört, dass es scharfe Bilder und leuchtende Farben (das Gelb des Eigelbs verschwindet) ergibt, die sich über die Jahrhunderte kaum ändern. Das Medium ist sehr beständig, was der ausgezeichnete Zustand vieler mittelalterlicher Gemälde zeigt. Obwohl der Künstler Ei-Tempera mit Wasser verdünnen kann und es in feuchtem Zustand wasserlöslich ist, ist die Farbe nach dem Trocknen unlöslich.

Ein Nachteil von Ei-Tempera ist, dass es extrem schnell trocknet, sodass es schwierig ist, Farben zu mischen. Außerdem können nur kleine Pinselstriche verwendet werden. Es lässt sich kaum die Illusion einer Textur erreichen, da die Oberfläche gleichförmig matt trocknet. Glänzende Flächen wie bei der Ölmalerei sind nicht möglich. Zudem enthält das Weiße des Eis Schwefel, der bestimmte Pigmente nachdunkeln lässt, weshalb sie ungeeignet für Ei-Tempera sind. Der Farbumfang ist also begrenzt. Da Ei-Tempera eine gewisse Transparenz aufweist, ist es schwierig, Fehler zu korrigieren. Und da es nicht flexibel ist, kann der Künstler es nur auf einer festen Oberfläche anwenden und nicht auf Leinwand.

Duccio di Buoninsegna
Christi Geburt mit den Propheten Jesaja und Ezechiel, 1308–11
Ei-Tempera und Gold auf Pappelholz, inkl. Originalrahmen
48 x 86,8 x 7,9 cm
National Gallery of Art, Washington, DC

Ei-Tempera, das bevorzugte Medium für die Tafelmalerei des Mittelalters in Westeuropa, nutzt Eigelb als Bindemittel. Die schnell trocknende und matte Oberfläche begrenzt zwar die möglichen Effekte, das Bild ist aber sehr beständig. Große Gemälde bestehen aus mehreren verbundenen Tafeln. Altarbilder besaßen oft kleinere Predella-Tafeln wie diese, die einst zu Duccios *Maestà* (S. 21) gehörte.

Ölfarbe

Ei-Tempera wurde nach und nach durch Ölfarbe ersetzt – in einer Übergangsphase zunächst mittels einer gemischten Technik. Ihren Anfang nahm sie in Flandern, als Melchior Broederlam seine Tempera-Gemälde mit Öl lasierte, wie *Mariä Verkündigung und Heimsuchung* (1394–99; Musée des Beaux-Arts, Dijon). Eine Ölschicht, die auf eine Schicht aus Ei-Tempera folgt, nutzt die Vorteile beider Medien. Das schnell trocknende Ei-Tempera eignet sich gut als Untermalung, weil der Künstler fast sofort in Öl weiterarbeiten kann. Da das eine Medium wasserbasiert, das andere aber ölbasiert ist, zerfließen die Schichten nicht ineinander.

Da Öl langsam trocknet, lassen sich Farben gut mischen und feine Abstufungen sowie strukturelle Illusionen erreichen.

Am gebräuchlichsten ist Leinöl, das durch Auspressen der Samen des Gemeinen Lein (Gattung *linum*) gewonnen wird. Da Öl langsam trocknet, lassen sich Farben gut mischen und feine Abstufungen sowie strukturelle Illusionen erreichen, die mit Ei-Tempera nicht möglich sind. Der Künstler kann die Arbeit jederzeit unterbrechen und unbefriedigende Teile übermalen – was bei anderen Medien wie *buon fresco* nicht unbedingt funktioniert.

Anders als wasserbasierte Medien, die beim Trocknen heller werden, ändern sich Ölfarben nicht, sodass der Künstler bereits beim Malen das Zusammenspiel der Farben erkennen kann. Und da es keine chemischen Unverträglichkeiten gibt, ist die Farbpalette der Ölfarben größer als die von Fresken oder Ei-Tempera. Ölfarben sind gesättigt, reich, dicht und intensiv mit einem natürlichen Glanz. Der Maler kann die Viskosität variieren – von dünner, transparenter Lasur aus wenig Pigment und viel Öl, wie in Rembrandts Nachtwache (1642; S. 140–41), bis zu einem dicken Impasto aus viel Pigment und wenig Öl, wie in Vincent van Goghs Sternennacht (1889; S. 146). Ein Gemälde kann aber auch beide Möglichkeiten und alle Zwischenstufen ausschöpfen wie Der Raub der Europa (1562; gegenüber), gemalt vom venezianischen Künstler Tizian.

Da Ölfarbe flexibel ist, muss der Künstler sich nicht auf eine feste Holztafel beschränken, sondern kann auf Leinwand malen. Leinwand, die das erste Mal Anfang des 16. Jahrhunderts in Italien benutzt wurde, ist ein fester Stoff aus den Fasern des Gemeinen Lein. Das Präparieren einer Leinwand ist weniger teuer und zeitaufwendig als das Vorbereiten einer Holztafel. Ab Ende des 18. Jahr-

Tizian
Der Raub der Europa, 1562
Öl auf Leinwand,
178 x 205 cm
Isabella Stewart Gardner
Museum, Boston

Ölfarbe nutzt Pflanzenöl als Bindemittel und kann bis zur gewünschten Konsistenz angerührt werden. Diese Vielseitigkeit erlaubt es dem Maler, eine Vielzahl von Effekten zu erzielen. Tizian, der zu den ersten Künstlern in Italien gehörte, die mit Öl auf Leinwand malten, begründete im 16. Jahrhundert die venezianische Malschule, die Farbe stärker schätzte als Linien.

hunderts konnte man Ölfarben in Metalltiegeln, im 19. Jahrhundert dann auch in Tuben kaufen. Zu dieser Zeit kamen auch chemisch hergestellte Pigmente auf, die eine Vielzahl neuer Farben mit sich brachten.

Ölfarbe hat allerdings Probleme, die oft erst nach vielen Jahren offenbar werden. Öl neigt dazu, dunkel und gelb zu werden. Auch die Transparenz kann zunehmen, sodass Überarbeitungen einer Komposition sichtbar werden können – etwa wenn eine Figur plötzlich mehr Gliedmaßen oder sogar Köpfe zu haben scheint! Die braune Untermalung (die bis Ende des 19. Jahrhundert üblich war) kann stärker hervortreten als gewünscht und das ganze Bild abdunkeln. Darüber hinaus war es üblich, ein fertiges Ölbild mit einer Schicht Firnis zu schützen, die ebenfalls im Laufe der Zeit dunkel und gelblich wurde. Im Allgemeinen ist Öl nicht so beständig wie Ei-Tempera. Und für ungeduldige Künstler oder ungeduldige Auftraggeber mit einer engen Deadline ist der langwierige Trocknungsprozess von Öl definitiv ein Nachteil.

Helen Frankenthaler
Grey Fireworks, 1982
Acryl auf Leinwand,
182,9 x 301 cm
Privatsammlung

Synthetische Farben lassen sich leicht verarbeiten, weil sie in feuchtem Zustand wasserlöslich sind und durch den Zusatz verschiedener Substanzen ein breites Spektrum an Effekten erlauben. Frankenthaler, eine Vertreterin des Abstrakten Expressionismus, entwickelte mit ihrer »Soak Stain«-Technik eine neue Methode der Malerei, bei der direkt auf der unbehandelten Leinwand gearbeitet wird.

Synthetische Farbe

Die Dispersion von Pigment in einer Acrylpolymer-Emulsion ergibt Acrylfarbe. Nach ihrer Einführung als Industrie- und Hausfarben entdeckten Mitte des 20. Jahrhunderts auch Künstler diese Farben. Aufgrund ihrer Flexibilität kann man auf einer Leinwand arbeiten, die mit einer Polymer-Grundierung präpariert wurde. Synthetische Farben sind robust, beständig und vergilben nicht. Sie widerstehen klimatischen Änderungen, Licht und Hitze besser als Öl oder Ei-Tempera. Synthetische Farben können in vielen Schichten aufgetragen werden. Acrylfarbe trocknet schnell, doch mit einem Verzögerer lässt sich die Verarbeitungszeit verlängern. Modellierpaste hilft beim Erzeugen von Texturen. Helen Frankenthalers Bild *Grey Fireworks* (1982; oben) demonstriert die Vielseitigkeit von Acrylfarbe und einige der möglichen Effekte.

Synthetischen Farben fehlt allerdings die ölige Fülle von Ölfarbe, und bestimmte alkaliempfindliche Pigmente sind inkompatibel mit Acrylen. Nach dem Trocknen ist Acrylfarbe wasserunlöslich und kann nur mit einem starken Lösungsmittel entfernt werden. Sie eignet sich nicht für eine öl-präparierte Leinwand oder als Untermalung für Ölfarben, da sie ihre Elastizität länger behält als Ölfarben und dies deren Haftung behindert. Nicht alle Acrylfarben-Marken lassen sich gut mit anderen mischen.

Wasserfarbe und Gouache

Wasserfarbe und Gouache bestehen aus Pigmenten, gemischt mit Wasser, einem Bindemittel wie Gummi arabicum und Zutaten wie

Glyzerin und/oder Honig zum Verbessern von Konsistenz und Farbe sowie Konservierungsmitteln. Während Wasserfarbe durchscheinend ist, ist Gouache aufgrund der größeren Partikel und des höheren Anteils an Pigmenten dicker und besser deckend. Wasserfarben und Gouache können kombiniert werden, wie *Mending the Nets* (1882; unten) des amerikanischen Künstlers Winslow Homer zeigt.

Heute gibt es Wasser- und Gouache-Farben in Tuben und kleinen Farbtabletten. Da sie sich gut transportieren lassen und schnell trocknen, werden sie gern für die Freiluftmalerei genutzt. Sie eignen sich aber auch für Studien und Skizzen. Allerdings wirken die Farben feucht anders als trocken, sodass die finale Wirkung beim Malen schwer einzuschätzen ist.

Winslow Homer
Mending the Nets, 1882
Wasserfarbe und Gouache über Grafit auf Papier, 69,5 x 48,9 cm
National Gallery of Art, Washington, DC

Wasserfarben, die schnell trocknen und gut transportiert werden können, eignen sich ideal für Skizzen. Da allerdings jeder Pinselstrich sichtbar ist und Fehler nicht übermalt werden können, bieten sie auch die größte Herausforderung unter den Malmedien. Der amerikanische Künstler Winslow Homer verwendete Wasserfarben und Gouache, um das Leben in seiner Umgebung zu dokumentieren.

Drucke

Drucke sind Kunstwerke, die in mehreren Kopien auf Papier hergestellt werden. Die Editionen sind limitiert und die Drucke nummeriert. So bedeutet z. B. 3/24 in der unteren linken Ecke eines Druckes, dass dies der dritte Druck von insgesamt 24 ist.

Relieftechniken

Für ein Relief schneidet der Grafiker den Entwurf mit einem Meißel oder Messer in einen Holzklotz und entfernt die Bereiche, die nicht gedruckt werden sollen. Die Tinte wird mit einer Rolle auf die erhabenen Bereiche aufgebracht und dann auf ein Blatt Papier übertragen, indem man es mit einem löffelartigen Werkzeug andrückt. Auch ohne Druckerpresse sind mehrere Drucke möglich. Beispielhaft sind die Holzschnitte von Katsushika Hokusai (ca. 1831–32; unten). Eine Kolorierung erfolgt entweder von Hand oder wie bei Hokusai durch zusätzliche Holzplatten. Für einen Holzschnitt wird der Block *mit* der Faser des Baumes geschnitten, während der Block für einen Holzstich *quer* zur Faser geschnitten wird, sodass der Meißel in alle Richtungen auf den gleichen Widerstand trifft.

Tiefdrucktechniken

Im Gegensatz zum Reliefdruck, bei dem die Oberfläche druckt, wird beim Tiefdruck die Tinte gedruckt, die die Einkerbungen unter der

Katsushika Hokusai
Der Inume-Pass in der Provinz Kai (Kōshū Inume tōge), aus der Serie *36 Ansichten des Berges Fuji (Fugaku sanjūrokkei)*, ca. 1831–32
Farbholzschnitt,
25,1 x 37,8 cm
Metropolitan Museum of Art, New York

Der japanische Künstler Katsushika Hokusai schuf *Ukiyo-e* (»Bilder der fließenden Welt«) – farbige Holzschnitte mit Landschaften. Seine Faszination mit dem Berg Fuji stand im Einklang mit seinen buddhistischen Überzeugungen und der Verbindung zwischen diesem Berg und der Unsterblichkeit.

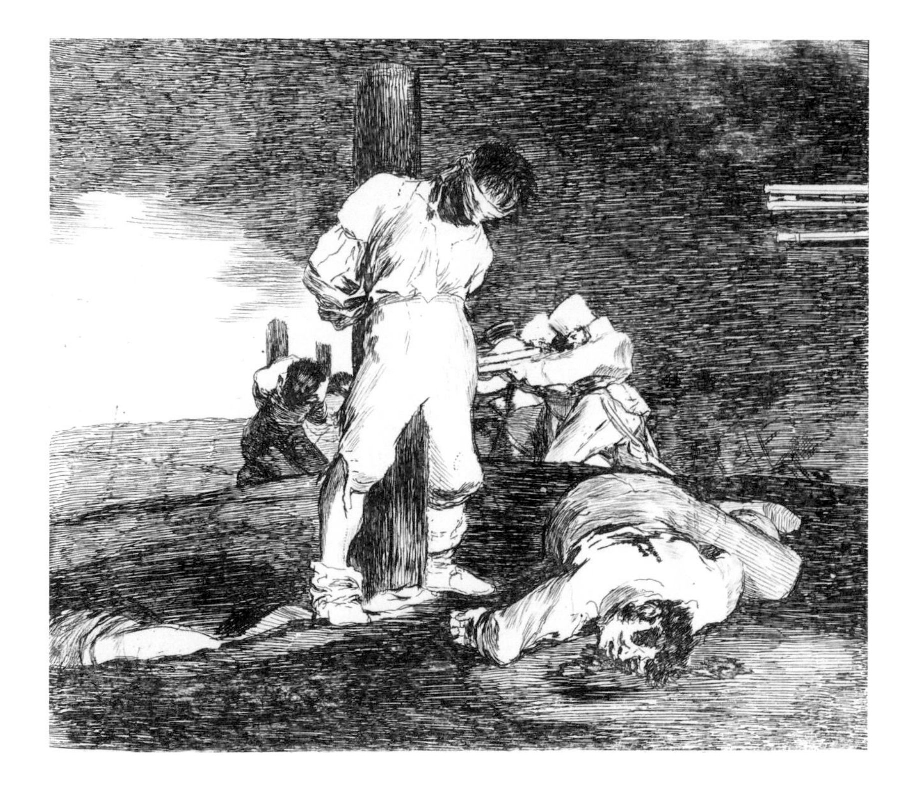

Francisco Goya
Und es gibt kein Entrinnen, aus der Serie *Schrecken des Krieges*, 1810
Radierung,
Tafel 14 x 16,7 cm
Metropolitan Museum of Art, New York

Der spanische klassizistische Künstler Goya wurde, obwohl nach einer nicht diagnostizierten Krankheit ertaubt, zum Hofmaler der Familie Karls IV.
Die Radierungen *Schrecken des Krieges* wurden allerdings wegen ihrer aufrührerischen Antikriegshaltung erst 1863 veröffentlicht, 35 Jahre nach Goyas Tod.

Oberfläche einer Metallplatte füllt. Es gibt mehrere Methoden, die Einschnitte herzustellen. Für einen Stich schneidet der Grafiker mit einem Meißel oder Stichel Rillen in die Metallplatte. Bei einer Radierung kratzt er mit einem spitzen Werkzeug über die Platte, ohne Metall zu entfernen, drückt aber fest genug, sodass ein Grat auf beiden Seiten des Striches entsteht. Eine Ätzradierung erfordert weniger Kraftaufwand: Der Grafiker bedeckt die Platte mit einer wachsartigen, säurebeständigen Schicht und kratzt dann mit einem spitzen Werkzeug Linien hinein. Ein Säurebad ätzt die Linien in die Platte. Weitere Techniken sind Aquatinta und Mezzotinto, mit denen auch Grautöne erzielt werden können. Der spanische Künstler Francisco Goya kombinierte verschiedene Tiefdrucktechniken in *Und es gibt kein Entrinnen* (1810; oben).

Ungeachtet der Technik zum Erzeugen der Vertiefungen ist der Druckprozess beim Tiefdruck immer gleich: Der Grafiker reinigt und erwärmt die Platte, tupft dann Tinte auf die Oberfläche, die er in die Vertiefungen drückt, und wischt anschließend die Fläche sauber, sodass nur in den eingeritzten Linien Tinte verbleibt. Die Platte wird dann auf die Druckpresse gelegt und mit einem angefeuchteten

Divan Japonais
75 rue des Martyrs
Ed Fournier
directeur
HLautrec

Henri de Toulouse-Lautrec
Divan Japonais (Der japanische Diwan),
1892–93
Lithografie in vier Farben, gedruckt auf Velinpapier,
80,8 x 60,8 cm
Metropolitan Museum of Art, New York

Der Post-Impressionist Toulouse-Lautrec war ein Abkömmling des französischen Adels, doch aufgrund seiner Kleinwüchsigkeit entfernte er sich von diesem Lebensstil. Seine lithografischen Plakate führen uns stattdessen in das Pariser Nachtleben des ausgehenden 19. Jahrhunderts.

Blatt Papier sowie einem Druckfilz bedeckt. Die Platte wird in beide Richtungen durch die Presse bewegt. Dabei drückt sich das weiche Papier in die Vertiefungen und nimmt die Farbe auf.

Lithografie

Drucker nutzen ganz verschiedene Materialien. Beim Holzschnitt (Relief) entsteht das zu druckende Bild im Holz, bei Radierung, Stich und Ätzradierung (Tiefdruck) im Metall, bei der Lithografie dagegen auf Stein. Beim Reliefdruck druckt die Oberfläche und beim Tiefdruck drucken die Vertiefungen unter der Oberfläche. Bei einer Lithografie wird nicht das Niveau der Oberfläche verändert, sondern mithilfe einer Säure eine chemische Veränderung auf der Oberfläche eines Kalksteinblocks vorgenommen. Der deutsche Schauspieler Alois Senefelder erfand die Lithografie 1796 auf der Basis der einfachen Tatsache, dass Öl und Wasser sich nicht mischen. Der Begriff leitet sich von den griechischen Wörtern für »Stein« (*lithos*) und »schreiben« oder »zeichnen« (*graphein*) ab.

Für eine Lithografie zeichnet man das Bild mit einer fettigen Substanz wie einer Wachskreide auf einen glatten Kalkstein. Das Bild wird mit einer Mischung aus milder Säure und Gummi arabicum behandelt, die eine chemische Veränderung in den Bereichen bewirkt, die nicht durch das Fett geschützt sind. Der Lithograf nimmt den Stein aus dem Säurebad, hält ihn aber weiterhin feucht. Ölbasierte Farbe, die auf den Stein gerollt wird, haftet nur auf den fettigen Stellen. Der Stein wird auf die Druckpresse gelegt, mit Papier bedeckt und durch die Presse bewegt. Für einen mehrfarbigen Druck braucht man mehrere Steine oder ein Stein wird zwischen den Farben abgeschliffen und neu gezeichnet.

Das Können des französischen Post-Impressionisten Henri de Toulouse-Lautrec als Lithograf zeigt sich in *Divan Japonais* (1892–93; gegenüber). In jüngerer Zeit haben Lithografen Metall- und sogar Plastikplatten statt Stein benutzt. Die Offset-Lithografie ist ein kommerzieller Prozess (siehe S. 105); das Bild wird vor dem endgültigen Blatt auf ein Zwischenmedium gedruckt, sodass die Qualität der Originalplatte erhalten bleibt.

Siebdruck

Obwohl die Serigrafie schon seit der Song-Dynastie (960–1279) in China bekannt ist, tauchte der Begriff erst in den 1930ern auf, um Siebdruck für Kunstgrafiken vom gewerblichen Siebdruck zu unterscheiden. Er leitet sich vom lateinischen *sericum* für »Seide« und dem griechischen *graphein* für »schreiben« oder »zeichnen« ab.

Andy Warhol
Campbell's Soup I: Chicken Noodle, 1968
Siebdruck auf Papier,
88,9 x 58,7 cm
Andy Warhol Museum,
Pittsburgh

Andy Warhol, der führende amerikanische Künstler der Pop Art, begann seine Karriere als Illustrator. Er arbeitete mit einer Vielzahl von Medien, doch am bekanntesten ist er wohl für seine Siebdrucke. Mit dieser kommerziellen Drucktechnik schuf er Bilder von Alltagswaren (siehe S. 161).

Ein feines Seidengewebe wird über einen Holzrahmen gespannt und fungiert quais als Sieb. Mit einer Schablone aus Papier, Plastik oder einem anderen dünnen Material werden die Bereiche blockiert, die nicht gedruckt werden sollen. Der Drucker legt ein Blatt Papier unter das Sieb. Nachdem er am oberen Rand des Siebs dickflüssige Farbe aufgebracht hat, zieht er diese mit einem Rakel gleichmäßig über das Sieb und drückt sie damit durch das Seidengewebe auf das Papier.

Die Technik ergibt gleichmäßige Farbflächen. Heute werden meist synthetische Gewebe und Metallrahmen verwendet. Der amerikanische Pop-Art-Künstler Andy Warhol nutzte den Siebdruck, etwa für *Campbell's Soup I: Chicken Noodle* (oben) von 1968.

DEKORATIVE KUNST

Dekorative Kunst bezieht sich auf Objekte, die sowohl einen ästhetischen als auch einen praktischen Wert besitzen, also etwa Emaillen, Buntglas, Tapisserien, Keramik, Schmuck und Möbel.

Emaille

Emaille ist Pulver oder Paste aus farbigem Glas, die auf Metall aufgebracht und bei hoher Temperatur gebrannt wird, sodass das Material schmilzt und eine deckende Schicht bildet. Das Ergebnis ist eine leuchtend farbige Oberfläche, die glänzend poliert werden kann. Die Ägypter nutzten Emailleverzierungen bereits im 2. Jahrtausend v. Chr. Die Technik erreichte einen Höhepunkt im Mittelalter mit den beiden Haupttypen Cloisonné und Champlevé.

Der Begriff Cloisonné leitet sich von *cloison* ab, französisch für »Zelle«, und bezieht sich auf die kleinen, abgegrenzten Flächen, die durch Verlöten dünner Goldstreifen auf einer goldenen Platte entstehen und die Farben trennen. Die Technik entstand vermutlich in Byzanz. Ein bedeutendes Beispiel ist das große *Haho-Triptychon* mit

Nikolaus von Verdun
Noah und die Arche,
Tafel vom Altar aus dem Stift Klosterneuburg (*Verduner Altar*), signiert und datiert 1181
Champlevé-Emaille auf vergoldetem Kupfer,
20,3 x 16,5 cm
Stift Klosterneuburg, nahe Wien

Emaille wird oft mit Gold kombiniert, um juwelenartige Schmuckgegenstände herzustellen. Für viele Kunsthistoriker ist Nikolaus von Verdun der beste Emaille-Künstler des ausgehenden 12. Jahrhunderts. Er signierte seine Werke, was ungewöhnlich für diese Zeit war.

ursprünglich 115 Cloisonné-Platten, die zwischen dem 8. und dem 12. Jahrhundert in Georgien und Konstantinopel hergestellt wurden (Georgisches Kunstmuseum, Tiflis). Später gewann die Technik in China an Popularität, obwohl dort statt Gold Kupfer oder Bronze verwendet wurde.

Die Champlevé-Technik, französisch: »erhöhter Grund« oder »erhöhtes Feld«, lässt sich bis in das alte Rom zurückverfolgen und wurde besonders für christliche Objekte wie Reliquiare und Altarbilder eingesetzt. Anders als Cloisonné ist Champlevé eine westeuropäische Spezialität. Es nutzt eine dickere, vergoldete Kupfer- oder Bronzeplatte. Der Künstler schneidet oder schleift mit einem Stichel Vertiefungen für die Emaillemasse. Ein schönes Beispiel ist das Altarbild des maasländischen Künstlers Nikolaus von Verdun im Stift Klosterneuburg von 1181 (vorherige Seite).

Sogenannte *Bleiruten* halten die kleinen Glasstücke zusammen.

Unbekannter Künstler
Die Kindheit Jesu,
Detail des unteren Fensterteils, Westfassade, ca. 1150
Kathedrale von Chartres

Buntglasfenster lassen im Innenraum Muster aus farbigem Licht erscheinen, die über die Oberflächen tanzen und sich mit der Bewegung der Sonne und der Wolken ändern. Die Fenster in der Kathedrale von Chartres bedecken eine Fläche von etwa 2.600 Quadratmetern und wurden vermutlich von wenigstens zwei verschiedenen Werkstätten gefertigt.

Buntglas

Diese Kunstform erreichte ihren Höhepunkt bei der Gestaltung mittelalterlicher Kirchenfenster. Ein frühes Rezept für Glas verlangt nach zwei Teilen Buchenholzasche (Pottasche, ein Alkali) und einem Teil Flusssand (Quarzsand). Beim Erhitzen lässt das Alkali den Quarzsand zu einem grünlichen Glas verschmelzen. Wird die Masse länger gekocht, verfärbt sie sich gelblich oder rötlich; das Zusetzen von Metalloxidpulver liefert eine ganze Palette an Farben. Sogenannte *Bleiruten*, schmale Stege aus weichem Blei, halten die kleinen Glasstücke zusammen (gegenüber).

Die einzelnen Glasstücke können ganz unterschiedlich behandelt werden. Grisaille, von französisch »grau«, dient zum Malen feiner Details wie Gesichtszüge, Finger und Falten. Silber, sogenanntes *jaune d'argent* oder »Gelb aus Silber«, erzeugt lebhafte gelbe Glanzpunkte und kann auch über andere Farben gesetzt werden – etwa über Blau, um Grün zu erzeugen. Ein Mineral aus Eisenoxiden namens *Rötel* erzeugt Rot. Bestimmte Farben, besonders Rottöne, so dunkel, dass sie nahezu blickdicht sind, wurden für Überfangglas verwendet. Dies ist eine sehr dünne Schicht aus farbigem Glas, das mit Klarglas verschmolzen wird, indem man das Klarglas in die farbige Glasmasse taucht. Beim *Sgraffito* werden transparente Linien in die farbige Schicht des Überfangglases gekratzt.

Im 16. und besonders im 17. Jahrhundert stellten Künstler Emaille aus gemahlenem Glas und farbigen Metalloxiden her, um damit auf

Glas zu malen. Das Ergebnis war eine grundlegende Konzeptänderung – Schmuckfenster bestanden nun aus größeren, hellen Glasstücken, die bunt bemalt wurden.

FOTOGRAFIE

Das Wort Fotografie leitet sich vom Griechischen her und bedeutet so viel wie »Zeichnen mit Licht«. Analogfotografie hält Bilder auf lichtempfindlichen Fotoplatten oder flexiblem Zelluloid-Film fest. Unabhängig voneinander entwickelten der französische Erfinder Nicéphore Niépce, der mit dem Künstler Louis Daguerre zusammenarbeitete, und der englische Erfinder William Fox Talbot in den 1830ern diese Technik. Ab 1885 gab es Film in Rollenform. Die üblicherweise mit 24 oder 36 Bildern hergestellten Rollen mussten nach dem Belichten chemisch in einer Dunkelkammer behandelt werden, um das Bild auf dem Film hervorzubringen, das dann als Negativ zum Ausdrucken oder als »Positiv« zum Projizieren dient.

Bei der 1975 vom amerikanischen Elektroingenieur Steven Sasson erfundenen Digitalfotografie werden Bilder mithilfe eines fotoelektrischen Sensors aufgenommen und auf einem winzigen Speicherchip abgelegt. Dann ist es möglich, sie auf einem Computer mit einer Software wie Photoshop zu bearbeiten, direkt auf einem Digitaldrucker auszugeben, zu projizieren, zu übertragen oder elektronisch zu archivieren.

Ein Digitalfotograf ist nicht auf die Bilder beschränkt, die er zu einem bestimmten Zeitpunkt aufgenommen hat, da der Speicherchip Tausende von Bildern speichern kann. Ein weiterer Vorteil ist, dass das Bild sofort begutachtet werden kann und nicht erst wie Analogfilm entwickelt werden muss. Die amerikanische Fotografin Cindy Sherman, berühmt für ihre Selbstporträts in verschiedenen Rollen (gegenüber), betonte, wie wichtig das ist: »Früher hätte ich z. B. zwei Filme aufgenommen und mich dann abgeschminkt, umgezogen, den Film ins Labor gebracht und dann einige Stunden gewartet, während er entwickelt wurde.« Zur Digitalfotografie merkte sie hingegen an: »Ich kann loslegen, auch wenn ich noch keine richtige Idee habe, vor der Kamera herumspielen, ein paar Bilder machen und sie mir auf dem Computer anschauen …«

Cindy Sherman
Untitled #475, 2008
Chromogener Farbabzug,
219,4 x 181,6 cm

Die Fotografie, eine relativ aktuelle Technik, ist nach und nach in den künstlerischen Status aufgestiegen. Nachdem die Amerikanerin Sherman einen ersten Fotografiekurs am College nicht bestanden hatte, wiederholte sie ihn mit viel besseren Ergebnissen. Sie ist Empfängerin einer MacArthur Fellowship, einer Auszeichnung, die oft als Genie-Preis bezeichnet wird.

COLLAGE

Der Begriff Collage stammt von *coller*, französisch für »kleben«. Für eine Collage werden unterschiedliche Materialien wie Zeitung, Fotos, Stoff sowie andere Objekte, wie Etiketten und Spielkarten,

auf einer flachen Oberfläche zusammengesetzt. Ein Beispiel ist Pablo Picassos *Stillleben mit Rohrstuhl*, entstanden 1912 aus Ölfarbe, Öltuch und Seil, auf eine Leinwand geklebt (Musée Picasso, Paris).

Unbekannter Künstler
Dharmapala auf einem Löwen, Tibet, ca. 16. Jahrhundert
Stein mit Spuren von Goldfarbe, eingelegt mit Türkis,
21,6 x 14,6 x 5,7 cm
Metropolitan Museum of Art, New York

Für Skulpturen werden viele unterschiedliche Steinarten verwendet, die nach Farbe, Körnung und Härte oder Weichheit der Textur ausgewählt werden. Dieser sorgfältig behauene *Dharmapala* repräsentiert einen der zornigen Götter, die das buddhistische Gesetz (*Dharma*) und die Buddhisten schützen.

BILDHAUEREI

Seit vorgeschichtlichen Zeiten haben Künstler mithilfe subtraktiver (Schnitzen) und additiver (Modellieren oder Zusammensetzen) Methoden dreidimensionale Skulpturen hergestellt. Bei der ersten Methode kommen feste Materialien wie Stein, Holz und Elfenbein zum Einsatz, die feste Maße haben, in denen sich der Bildhauer bewegen muss. Die zweite Methode nutzt Substanzen wie Wachs, Mörtel, Terrakotta und Plastillin, die keine festen Formen oder Maße haben und frei gestaltet werden können.

Stein

Guter Stein ist konsistent strukturiert und ohne Löcher oder Einschlüsse im Inneren. Bei Marmor, Kalkstein und Sandstein handelt es sich um Calciumcarbonat, entsprechend sind sie chemisch und geologisch eng miteinander verwandt. Sie unterscheiden sich aber in ihrer Kristallstruktur und damit in Aussehen und Verwendung. Marmor ist hart mit einer glatten Struktur, die es dem Bildhauer erlaubt, ihn glänzend zu polieren. Normalerweise fast weiß, gibt es Marmor aber auch in vielen anderen Farben. Kalkstein ist weicher und oft cremefarben, kann aber auch mehrfarbig sein. Polierter Kalkstein hat nicht den Glanz von Marmor, sondern eine eher matte Oberfläche. Sandstein ist körnig und beständig, wodurch er sich gut für Skulpturen im Freien eignet. Im Gegensatz dazu hat Alabaster, also weißer oder leicht getönter Gips (Calciumsulfat), eine zarte Textur, die ihn für feine Schnitzereien empfiehlt, allerdings nur für den Innenbereich.

Zur Zierde sind Farben und Intarsien möglich, wie die tibetische Darstellung des *Dharmapala auf einem Löwen* (gegenüber) zeigt.

Holz

Holzarten unterscheiden sich in Textur, Farbe und Faserung – eine feinere Faser erlaubt feinere Details. Holz ist anfällig für Verziehen, Rissbildung, Verwitterung und Insektenfraß. Dennoch beweisen altägyptische Skulpturen aus jahrtausendealten Gräbern, dass es unter günstigen Bedingungen äußerst beständig ist. Das Behauen von Stein verlangt zwar größere körperliche Kraft als das Schnitzen von Holz, jedoch erfordert dieses größeres Geschick, da sich die Faser je nach Richtung des Meißels anders verhält. Der Bildhauer

Unbekannter Künstler
Minjemtimi, Ahnenfigur des Sawos-Volkes, Papua-Neuguinea, 19. Jahrhundert oder früher
Holz, Farbe und Fasern, 182,9 x 32,4 x 25,1 cm
Metropolitan Museum of Art, New York

Wie beim Stein gibt es viele unterschiedliche Arten von Holz mit verschiedenen Farben, Maserungen und Texturen, die das Ergebnis des Bildhauers beeinflussen. Die Clans des Volkes der Sawos von Papua-Neuguinea fühlen sich bestimmten Ahnen zugehörig; diese lebensgroße Statue erinnert an einen Vorfahren namens Minjemtimi.

Unbekannter Künstler
Sitzender Ganesha,
Orissa, Indien,
14.–15. Jahrhundert
Elfenbein, Höhe 18,4 cm
Metropolitan Museum
of Art, New York

Nur der Elefantenstoßzahn besteht aus echtem Elfenbein. Der Hindu-Gott Ganesha, der Zerstörer von Hindernissen, ist als rundliches Kind mit einem Elefantenkopf dargestellt. Die Legende berichtet, dass dies an einem unglücklichen Unfall liegt, bei dem er von Vishnu geköpft wurde, der daraufhin Ganeshas ursprünglichen Kopf durch den eines Elefanten ersetzte.

kann sich die Arbeit erleichtern, wenn er mit der Faser schnitzt, wie die Ahnenfigur aus Papua New Guinea (gegenüber) zeigt.

Elfenbein

Elfenbein, die Stoßzähne von Elefanten, war lange ein begehrtes Material für Skulpturen. Es handelt sich um Zahnbein, ein faseriges, kalkhaltiges Material. Zwischen dem zentralen Nervenkanal mit der Pulpa, die zu weich, und dem Zahnzement, der zu hart ist, sind weniger als 60 Prozent des Zahns für filigrane Arbeiten, wie den indischen *Sitzenden Ganesha* (oben), geeignet. Elfenbein fühlt sich glatt an, hat einen natürlichen Glanz und kann wegen seines Kollagen poliert werden. Da es jedoch Feuchtigkeit, Salze und andere Substanzen aus der Umgebung aufnimmt, ist es nicht sehr beständig. Es kann nachdunkeln, gelblich oder bräunlich und fleckig werden. Wird es zu trocken, kann es sich auch verziehen und reißen.

Alternative Materialien sind Knochen von Pferden und Kühen. Sie lassen sich polieren, sind jedoch aufgrund der porösen Struktur brüchiger. Walknochen, Stoßzähne vom Narwal und Geweihe sind ebenfalls zum Schnitzen geeignet.

Vera Manzi-Schacht
Remembrance, 2014
Terrakotta,
48,3 x 45,7 x 38,1 cm
Sammlung von D'Achille-Rosone, Little Silver, New Jersey

Die weichen, von Hand in einem additiven Medium wie Terrakotta modellierten Formen, in denen man die Fingerabdrücke der Künstlerin zu sehen meint, sind ganz anders als subtraktive Steinskulpturen, die mit Hammer und Meißel gehauen werden. Die amerikanische Bildhauerin Manzi-Schacht ist Kunstprofessorin am New Yorker Institute of Technology.

Gips und Terrakotta

Bildhauer arbeiten oft mit Gips und Terrakotta, die beim Bearbeiten weich sind, nach dem Trocknen an der Luft jedoch hart werden; im Gegensatz dazu härtet Plastillin, eine ölbasierte Knetmasse, nicht aus. Skulpturen, die aus diesen weichen Materialien modelliert werden, benötigen möglicherweise im Inneren ein Gerüst als Stütze.

Zu den ungewöhnlicheren Skulpturen, die aus Gips gefertigt sind, gehören sicher die nicht essbaren Speisen des Pop-Art-Künstlers Claes Oldenburg, wie seine *Two Cheeseburgers with Everything (Dual Hamburgers)* aus gipsgetränktem Sackleinen und Farbe (1962; Museum of Modern Art, New York).

Terrakotta (ital.: »gekochte Erde«), mit einem rötlich-braunen Ton, wird schon lange für Skulpturen verwendet, wie die im chinesischen Xi'an ausgegrabenen Terrakotta-Krieger, erschaffen 210–209 v. Chr., beweisen. Nach dem Modellieren und vollständigen Trocknen wird das Stück in einem Brennofen bei einer Temperatur gebrannt, die ausreicht, um den Trocknungs- und Härtungsprozess vollständig abzuschließen. Dabei wird der Ton chemisch so verändert, dass er dauerhaft fest wird. Terrakotta wird auch heute noch als künstlerisches Medium eingesetzt. Die amerikanische Bildhauerin Vera Manzi-Schacht nutzt ihn für eindringliche Bilder von großer Empfindsamkeit, wie *Remembrance* (2014; gegenüber), die mit Gedichten von Rainer Maria Rilke (1875–1926) verziert sind.

Flüssiges Metall, das in die Form gegossen wird, ersetzt das Wachs.

Metallguss

Das Wachsausschmelzverfahren, manchmal auch Verfahren mit verlorener Form oder französisch: *cire perdue* (verlorenes Wachs) genannt, dient zum Gießen hohler Objekte. Der Bildhauer modelliert einen hitzebeständigen Kern in der Form der Skulptur und ummantelt diesen mit einer Wachsschicht, die so dick ist wie die gewünschten Metallwände. Auf der Wachsoberfläche wird ein *Angusssystem* aus Wachsstäben befestigt. Damit die Teile an ihrer

Unbekannter Künstler
Kopf eines Oba (Königs), Edo-Völker, Hof von Benin, Nigeria, 16. Jahrhundert
Messingguss, 23,5 x 21,9 x 22,9 cm
Metropolitan Museum of Art, New York

Das Wachsausschmelzverfahren zum Gießen von Metallskulpturen ermöglicht es, detaillierte, einzigartige Kunstwerke zu erschaffen. Die Edo-Völker von Nigeria entwickelten bereits im 13. Jahrhundert eine ausgefeilte Metallgusstradition.

vorgesehenen relativen Position bleiben, setzt der Künstler gleichmäßig verteilte Metallstifte durch das Wachs in den Kern. Die Stifte reichen bis in die Formschale aus Ton und Sand oder Steinpulver, die die Gussform bilden. Beim Erhitzen schmelzen Wachsschicht und -stäbe – das Wachs ist »verloren«, wenn es aus dem System herausläuft. Flüssiges Metall, das in die Form gegossen wird, ersetzt das Wachs. Nach dem Abkühlen entfernt der Bildhauer die Form, den Kern und die Metallstifte und stellt die feinen Details von Hand fertig, wie bei dem aus dem 16. Jahrhundert stammenden *Kopf eines Oba* aus Nigeria (vorherige Seite). Jeder Guss mit diesem Verfahren erzeugt ein Unikat; der Bildhauer muss die Formschale zerstören, um sie zu entfernen (verlorene Form). Eine Dauerform dagegen wird aus mehreren Teilen konstruiert, die man zerstörungsfrei entfernen und entsprechend wiederverwenden kann, um exakt die gleiche Form erneut zu gießen.

Calders sorgfältig ausbalancierte Mobiles bewegen sich mit der kleinsten Brise und ändern damit ihr Aussehen.

Alexander Calder
Untitled, ca. 1938
Metallfolie, Holz, Aluminium, Bindfaden und Farbe
122 x 207 x 207 cm
Privatsammlung
Dauerleihgabe in der Tate, Großbritannien

Der aus einer Bildhauerfamilie stammende Amerikaner Calder schuf in vielerlei Medien alles Mögliche – von Gemälden bis zu Schmuck und Skulpturen. Er erfand eine neue Art von Skulptur, bei der Bewegung ein Element der Komposition ist.

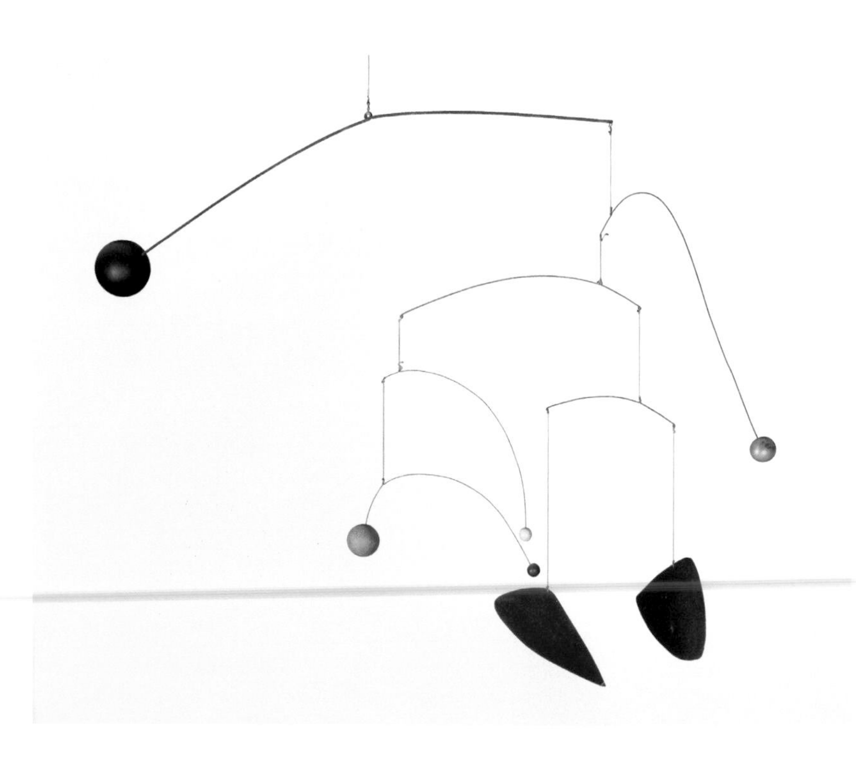

Konstruktionen und Assemblagen

Neben dem Schnitzen und Modellieren kann ein Künstler eine Skulptur auch durch Zusammensetzen herstellen – ich nenne dies »Kunst durch Amalgamierung«. Die in der Ukraine geborene amerikanische Bildhauerin Louise Nevelson baute große, mauerartige Konstruktionen aus beliebigen Holzteilen, die sie in Kisten aus demselben Material organisierte, die sie wiederum aufeinanderstapelte und in einer einheitlichen Farbe, meist Schwarz, bemalte. Ein typisches Beispiel dafür ist die *Sky Cathedral* von 1958, 3,40 m hoch (Museum of Modern Art, New York).

Der Amerikaner Alexander Calder erfand eine neue Art von Skulptur, bestehend aus einzelnen Formen, die mit Drähten verbunden sind. Das Ganze steht nicht auf dem Boden, sondern hängt an der Decke. Calders *Untitled* (ca. 1938; gegenüber) ist ein frühes Beispiel für eine kinetische Skulptur, bei der Bewegung eine wichtige Rolle spielt. Calders sorgfältig ausbalancierte Mobiles bewegen sich mit der kleinsten Brise und ändern damit ihr Aussehen; nach und nach enthüllt ein Mobile seine zahllosen Kompositionen.

WICHTIGE MEDIEN

Malerei und verwandte Medien:

- Enkaustik, Fresko, Mosaik, Manuskriptillustration, Ei-Tempera, Mischtechnik, Ölfarbe, synthetische Farbe (Acryl), Wasserfarbe und Gouache

Drucke:

- Relief, Tiefdruck, Lithografie und Siebdruck

Dekorative Kunst:

- Emaille (Cloisonné, Champlevé) und Buntglas

Fotografie:

- Analog und digital

Bildhauerei:

- Subtraktive (Stein, Holz und Elfenbein), additive (Wachs, Gips, Terrakotta und Plastillin), Metallguss (verlorene Form), Konstruktionen und Assemblagen und kinetische Skulpturen

ABER WAS BEDEUTET DAS?

-

Ich verstehe sie einfach nicht. Sie sind keine Literatur. Sie sind lediglich malerische Ausgestaltungen von Bildern, die mich verfolgen ... Die Theorien, die ich mir ausdenken könnte, um mich selbst zu erklären, und die, die andere mit meinem Werk in Verbindung bringen, sind Unsinn ...

-

Marc Chagall
Vor 1946

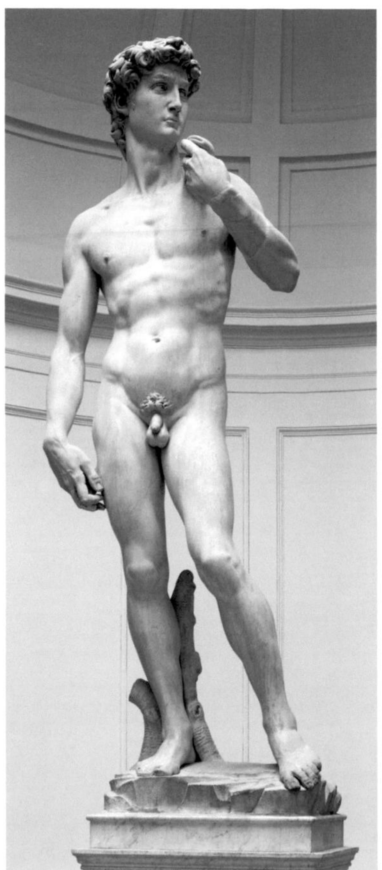

Der russisch-französische Maler Marc Chagall bestand darauf, dass Theorien, die seine symbolisch anmutenden Bilder erklären sollten, »Unsinn« seien. Eigentlich könnten wir uns also davon befreit fühlen, alles in einem Kunstwerk erklären zu müssen. Dennoch wollen wir aus reiner Neugier verstehen, was der Künstler zu vermitteln versucht.

MOTIVE

Die Kategorisierung eines Kunstwerks nach seinem Motiv kann ein erster Schritt sein, um seine Bedeutung zu verstehen. Kein Klassifizierungssystem kann jedoch absolut präzise sein, denn je nach Inhalt oder Thema kann ein Werk in mehrere sich überschneidende Kategorien passen. Vereinfacht gesagt, sind die Kategorien, die Kunsthistoriker als hilfreich empfunden haben, der Mensch, Porträt,

Gegenüber links:
Nach Praxiteles
Aphrodite von Knidos,
2. Jahrhundert n. Chr.
Römische Kopie des
griechischen Originals
von Praxiteles,
Mitte des 4. Jahrhunderts
v. Chr. (siehe S. 46)

Gegenüber rechts:
Michelangelo
David, 1501–04
(siehe S. 53)

Mythologie, Religion, Geschichte, Politik, Genreszenen, Landschaft, Stillleben und abstrakte Kunst.

-

Künstler haben viele verschiedene Körpertypen geschaffen, wobei die naturgetreue Darstellung stark variiert.

-

Unter allen von Künstlern dargestellten Themen erscheint die menschliche Figur am häufigsten. In einigen Fällen erfordert die Erzählung, wie zum Beispiel die Geschichte von Adam und Eva, die Darstellung des nackten männlichen und weiblichen Körpers. Aber auch andere Akte sind so zahlreich, dass man sich fragen könnte, warum sich Künstler so oft auf den menschlichen Körper konzentrieren? Ist es die angeborene Schönheit der menschlichen Form? Sicher, wie in Praxiteles *Aphrodite von Knidos* (gegenüber links) und Michelangelos *David* (gegenüber rechts). Doch die Künstler interessieren sich nicht nur für den schönen jungen Körper: Die Anatomie des muskulösen David steht im Gegensatz zu der des ägyptischen *Sitzenden Schreibers* (S. 16), einer akkuraten Darstellung der eher älteren Anatomie. Der idealisierte Naturalismus der *Aphrodite von Knidos* unterscheidet sich deutlich von Giacomettis expressiv abstrahierter *Frau von Venedig III* (S. 29 links). Obwohl die Natur eine breite Palette von Körpertypen hervorgebracht hat, haben Künstler eine Vielzahl weiterer Typen geschaffen, wobei die naturgetreue Darstellung stark variiert.

-

Verschiedene berühmte Künstler haben mehrere Selbstporträts geschaffen, die wie visuelle Tagebücher die Schwankungen in ihrem Leben festhalten.

-

Die Porträtmalerei erlangte in gewissen Kulturen besondere Bedeutung. Porträts reichen von präzisen Aufzeichnungen jedes Fältchens im Gesicht, jedes Details (wie bei altrömischen Steinporträts, die auf Totenmasken aus Wachs basieren) bis hin zu neueren abstrakten Porträts, in denen der Dargestellte kaum noch als Mensch zu erkennen ist. Porträts aus dem römischen Ägypten, wie *Junge Frau* (S. 68), ermöglichten es, dass ihr *ka* und *ba* (grob übersetzt als Lebenskraft und Seele) ihre Mumie erkennt. Rembrandt (S. 143) und Frida Kahlo (S. 151–153) gehören zu berühmten Künstlern, die mehrere Selbstporträts schufen, die wie visuelle Tagebücher die Schwankun-

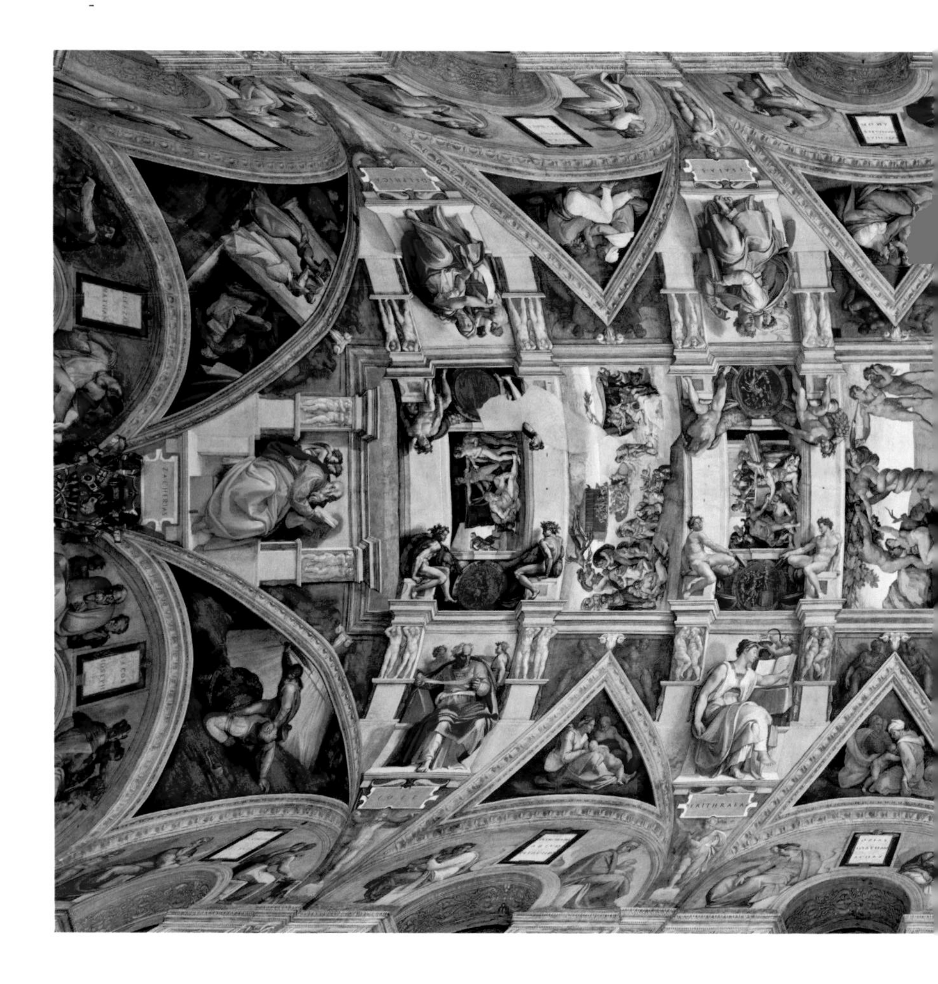

gen in ihrem Leben festhalten. Das wohl berühmteste Gemälde der Welt ist ein Porträt – die *Mona Lisa* (S. 137) von Leonardo da Vinci.

Themen aus der Mythologie, vor allem die der griechischen und römischen Gottheiten, sind bei Künstlern seit Langem beliebt. Während einige mythologische Erzählungen erschrecken, bezaubern andere. Beispiele für erstere sind zahlreich: monströse Kreaturen wie der dreiköpfige Hund Cerberus oder der grimmige Minotaurus, halb Mensch und halb Stier. Ansprechender sind vielleicht die Liebesgeschichten wie *Amor und Psyche* oder *Pygmalion und Galatea*, gemalt von Jean-Léon Gérôme (S. 120).

Die Religion ist der Antrieb für viele Kunstwerke, die visuelle Schönheit nutzen, um die Spiritualität zu steigern, und mit ihrer Bildersprache die Botschaft unterstützen. Die Gotteshäuser verschiedener Religionen werden mit Wandmalereien, Skulpturen, Glasma-

Michelangelo
Decke der Sixtinischen Kapelle, 1508–12
Fresko, 40,54 x 14,02 m
Vatikanstadt, Rom

Michelangelo malte die Decke der Sixtinischen Kapelle auf dem Höhepunkt der italienischen Hochrenaissance für Papst Julius II. Doch tat er dies nur widerwillig, denn er behauptete, Malerei sei etwas für Frauen und Bildhauerei etwas für Männer, wie er mit seinem einige Jahre zuvor geschaffenen David (S. 100 rechts) demonstrierte.

lereien, dekorativer Kunst und kostbaren Materialien geschmückt. So malte Michelangelo neun Szenen der Schöpfungsgeschichte an die tonnengewölbte Decke der Sixtinischen Kapelle (1508–12; oben) im Vatikan. Papst Julius II. gab dieses gewaltige Projekt in Auftrag, um die Lehren der römisch-katholischen Kirche zu vermitteln. *Die Erschaffung Adams* ist die berühmteste Szene (S. 70–71).

Historiengemälde halten Ereignisse fest, die sich zu Lebzeiten des Künstlers abgespielt haben können, aber nicht müssen. Jacques-Louis David stellte den *Tod des Sokrates* (S. 118) dar, der sich im Jahr 399 v. Chr. ereignete, sowie den *Tod des Marat*, seines Freundes, im Jahr 1793 (S. 119). Der Realismus in Historiengemälden soll Betrachter davon überzeugen, dass das Ereignis tatsächlich stattgefunden hat, und ähnelt dabei der Fotografie. Historiengemälde haben oft politische Ziele.

-

Kunst und Politik sind miteinander verflochten, spätestens seit der Zeit König Narmers von Ägypten (ca. 3100 v. Chr.).

-

Tatsächlich diente die Kunst schon lange dazu, politische Ziele voranzutreiben. Francisco Goya schuf kraftvolle Anti-Kriegs-Gemälde und -Grafiken, darunter *Und es gibt kein Entrinnen* (S. 81) aus der Serie *Schrecken des Krieges*, in der weder die Spanier noch die Franzosen heldenhaft erscheinen und Goya den Krieg verurteilt. Goyas spanischer Landsmann Pablo Picasso malte während des Spanischen Bürgerkriegs aus Protest *Guernica* (S. 158–159), kurz nachdem deutsche Bomber diese Stadt angegriffen hatten. Kunst und Politik sind spätestens seit der Zeit König Narmers miteinander verflochten, dem ersten König der ersten ägyptischen Dynastie, dessen Errungenschaften auf der Narmer-Platte festgehalten sind, ca. 3100 v. Chr. (Ägyptisches Museum, Kairo) – bis hin zu Shepard Faireys Hope-Wahlplakaten (2008; nebenstehend) zur Unterstützung von Barack Obama.

Shepard Fairey
Obama Hope, 2008
Offset-Lithografie,
61 x 91,4 cm
Obey Giant Art,
Los Angeles

Das kraftvolle Bild des Straßenkünstlers und Aktivisten Fairey mit seiner unmissverständlichen und willkommenen Botschaft der Hoffnung trug dazu bei, dass Barack Obama der erste afroamerikanische Präsident der USA wurde.

-

Motive aus dem Alltagsleben, die vorher nicht als darstellungswürdig betrachtet wurden, rückten schrittweise in den Blick der Öffentlichkeit.

-

Genreszenen aus dem gewöhnlichen Alltagsleben tauchten in Kalenderzyklen auf, wie z. B. im Stundenbuch *Les Très Riches Heures* der Brüder von Limburg aus dem frühen 15. Jahrhundert, das für Johann von Berry angefertigt wurde. Obwohl Darstellungen des bäuerlichen Lebens und sogar bürgerlicher Aktivitäten ungewöhnlich waren, finden sie sich in niederländischen Gemälden des 16. und 17. Jahrhunderts wie denen von Pieter Bruegel dem Älteren (Seite 11) und Johann Vermeer (z. B. *Das Konzert*, gestohlen aus dem Isabella Stewart Gardner Museum, Boston). Ende des 19. Jahrhunderts dominierten Genresujets die Gemälde des französischen Impressionismus; Pierre-Auguste Renoirs *Ruderer bei Chatou* (S. 39) zeigt Mitglieder der Bourgeoisie beim Bootfahren, einem beliebten Zeitvertreib. Motive aus dem Alltagsleben, die vorher nicht als darstellungswürdig betrachtet wurden, rückten schrittweise in den Blick der Öffentlchkeit.

Ebenso wurden Landschaften, lange lediglich als Hintergrund in der westlichen Kunst verwendet, zunehmend auch als selbstständige Motive beachtet. *View from Mount Holyoke, Northampton, Massachusetts, after a Thunderstorm – The Oxbow* (S. 52), 1836 gemalt von

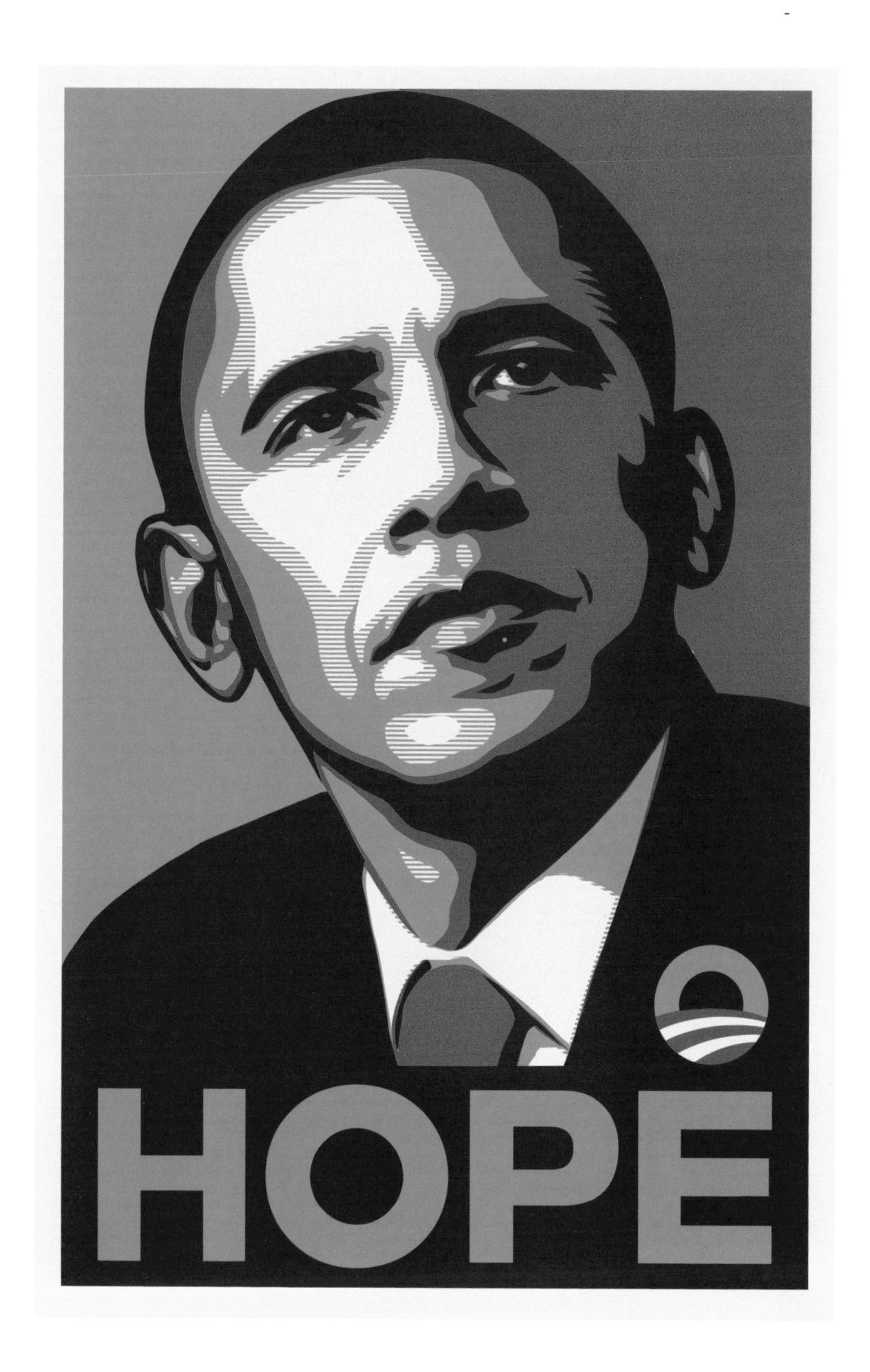
HOPE

Guo Xi
Vorfrühling, 1072
Hängende Rolle, Tusche und helle Farbe auf Seide, 158,3 x 108,1 cm
Nationales Palastmuseum, Taipeh

In der chinesischen Malerei, so der Hofkünstler Guo Xi aus dem 11. Jahrhundert, kann die Landschaft aus mehr als einem Blickwinkel betrachtet werden. Seine Gemälde zeigen verschiedene malerische Bäume – alt und knorrig im Kontrast zu jung und hochgewachsen – sowie Wasserläufe, Klippen und Felsen, Teile davon hinter Wolken angedeutet.

dem Amerikaner Thomas Cole, Gründer der Hudson River School für Landschaftsmalerei, deutet auf diese veränderte Einstellung hin. Im Gegensatz dazu blickt die Landschaftsmalerei in China auf eine lange Geschichte zurück und wurde gegenüber anderen Sujets sogar bevorzugt. Guo Xis berühmtestes Werk, *Vorfrühling* (gegenüber) von 1072 zeugt von einer langen künstlerischen Tradition.

Während westliche Landschaftsbilder in der Regel ein Querformat haben, bevorzugen asiatische Landschaftsbilder eher ein vertikales, wie bei dieser hängenden Schriftrolle aus Seide. Das westliche Konzept des Bildraums ist eher ein kontinuierlicher Schwung vom Vordergrund über den Mittelgrund bis zum fernen Hintergrund, während der asiatische Bildraum die Augen des Betrachters die Bildebene hinaufführt, wobei die Verbindungen zwischen den Landschaftsabschnitten oft durch Nebel verdeckt werden. Guo Xi schrieb in seiner Abhandlung *Berge und Wasser*: »Die Wolken und Dämpfe der realen Landschaften sind in den vier Jahreszeiten nicht gleich. Im Frühling sind sie leicht und diffus, im Sommer reich und dicht, im Herbst verstreut und dünn, im Winter dunkel und einsam.«

Der französische Begriff für Stillleben ist *nature morte*, wörtlich heißt das »tote Natur«.

Stillleben, ästhetisch arrangierte Kompositionen aus natürlichen (z. B. Blumen, Früchte, Lebensmittel) und künstlichen Gegenständen (z. B. Flaschen, Schalen, Teller), sind seit der Antike bei Künstlern beliebt. Der französische Begriff für Stillleben ist *nature morte*, wörtlich heißt das »tote Natur«, obwohl nicht alles, was in einem Stillleben dargestellt wird, einmal lebendig war. Das *Stillleben* von Rachel Ruysch (S. 117) enthält eine beeindruckende Vielfalt an gut erkennbaren Blumen. Da für Stilllebenbilder keine lebenden Modelle benötigt werden, können Künstler sie nutzen, um neue Ideen zu entwickeln und ihre Fähigkeiten zu verfeinern. Der französische Post-Impressionist Paul Cézanne malte viele Stillleben, aber er arbeitete so langsam (bis zu 20 Minuten zwischen den Pinselstrichen), dass die Blumen fast verwelkten und die Früchte faulten, bevor er fertig war.

Abstrakte Kunst hingegen zeigt keine erkennbaren Motive. Zum Beispiel sind Hilma af Klints *Gruppe IV, Die zehn Größten, Nr. 3, Jugend* (S. 123) und Kasimir Malewitschs Bild mit dem deskriptiven Titel *Weiß auf Weiß* (S. 125) gänzlich nicht-gegenständlich. Um die »lästige« Frage der Bedeutung abstrakter Kunst geht es weiter hinten in diesem Kapitel (siehe S. 122–125).

Dieric Bouts der Ältere
Das letzte Abendmahl,
mittlere Tafel des
Abendmahlsaltar,
1464–68
Öl auf Tafel,
180 x 150 cm
Sint-Pieterskerk, Leuven

Die antiken römischen Wandmaler benutzten die annähernde Linearperspektive, aber sie setzte sich im Mittelalter nicht durch. Bouts war einer der frühesten niederländischen Maler der Renaissance, der sich die Ein-Punkt-Linearperspektive zunutze machte, obwohl diese weder wissenschaftlich noch konsistent. Er stieg zum Stadtmaler von Louvain (heute Leuven in Belgien) auf. Die wissenschaftliche Linearperspektive wurde in der Renaissance hoch entwickelt.

NARRATIVE KONVENTIONEN

Narrative Konventionen – Mittel, die von Künstlern eingesetzt werden, um Bedeutung visuell zu vermitteln – sind im Wesentlichen eine Form der nonverbalen Kommunikation. Solche Mittel sind besonders nützlich für ein analphabetisches Publikum. Wenn sie konsequent und in Kombination eingesetzt werden, können auch äußerst subtile und anspruchsvolle Ideen visuell zum Ausdruck gebracht werden. Zu diesen Mitteln gehören Linearperspektive, relative Größe, fortlaufende Erzählung, Körpersprache und Ikonografie.

Die Linearperspektive kann verwendet werden, um die Botschaft eines Gemäldes zu verdeutlichen – oder zu verwirren. Im *Letzten Abendmahl* benutzt der frühe niederländische Maler Dieric Bouts d. Ä. (1464–68; oben) die zentralisierte Ein-Punkt-Linearperspektive, um das Renaissance-Ziel der Bedeutungsklarheit zu erreichen. Die großen orthogonalen Vertiefungslinien der Balkendecke und des Kachelbodens ziehen sich zu einem Fluchtpunkt hinter dem Kopf Jesu zurück und führen so den Blick des Betrachters direkt zu ihm. So verdeutlicht die lineare Perspektive gleichzeitig den ideellen Gehalt des Bildes und schafft einen kubischen Raum.

Jacopo Tintoretto
Letztes Abendmahl,
1592–94
Öl auf Leinwand,
3,65 x 5,68 m
Basilica San Giorgio Maggiore, Venedig

Die Gemälde des italienischen Manieristen Tintoretto zeichnen sich durch schwungvolle perspektivische Linien aus, die auf starken Diagonalen in die Tiefe führen. Obwohl es sich um eine gewöhnliche Taverne handelt, verleihen die übernatürlichen Elemente des Lampenrauchs, der sich zu Engeln formt, und des glühenden Heiligenscheins Jesu dieser Szene zusätzliche Dramatik. Tintoretto erhielt den Spitznamen Il Furioso (Der Wütende), weil er mit Geschwindigkeit und Leidenschaft malte.

Die Bedeutung der Position des Fluchtpunktes wird offensichtlich, wenn man Bouts Gemälde mit dem des venezianischen Malers Tintoretto vergleicht, der dasselbe Thema mehr als ein Jahrhundert später während der manieristischen Ära schuf, in der die Künstler Botschaften absichtlich verschleierten. In seiner Version des *Letzten Abendmahls* (1592–94; oben) platzierte Tintoretto den Fluchtpunkt weit außerhalb des Gemäldes und lenkte so den Blick des Betrachters von Jesus weg, was es schwierig machte, ihn in dem unübersichtlichen Raum zu finden – wären da nicht seine zentrale Position und sein heller Heiligenschein.

Künstler können die physische Größe nutzen, um den Rang einer Person in der Gesellschaft darzustellen.

Die relative Größe kann auf die Bedeutung einer Person im Vergleich zu einer anderen verweisen. So zeigt die physische Größe nicht die Position einer Figur innerhalb des Bildraumes, sondern in der sozialen Hierarchie. Im Gemälde *Jagd im Papyrusdickicht* aus der altägyptischen Grabkapelle des Nebamun (S. 27) zeigt allein die Größe Nebamuns Herrschaft über die anderen an. Da die Figur zwischen seinen Beinen sein Schienbein ergreift, kann ihre geringe Größe nicht bedeuten, dass sie im Hintergrund steht. Dieses einfache, leicht verständliche Mittel, um die Wichtigkeit einer Figur

anzuzeigen, kommt in der christlichen Kunst des Mittelalters häufig vor. So ist in der *Mission der Apostel* (S. 113) Jesus im Vergleich zu seinen Anhängern riesig. In dieser Hierarchie der Größe sind Figuren von Göttinnen und Göttern größer als einfache Sterbliche, und religiöse Figuren sind größer als Königinnen und Könige, die wiederum Mitglieder niedrigerer Klassen überragen können.

Die fortlaufende Erzählung ist ein effektives Mittel, um eine Geschichte zu erzählen, die mehrere separate Ereignisse umfasst. Der Betrachter weiß, dass diese Ereignisse nacheinander stattgefunden haben, doch der Künstler stellt sie gleichzeitig dar, anstatt sie in lauter Einzelbildern zu erzählen. Die alten Römer setzten die kontinuierliche Erzählung geschickt auf der Trajanssäule (107–113 n. Chr.; oben) ein, um die Geschichte von Kaiser Trajans militärischer Eroberung Dakiens zu erzählen. Trajan ersetzte einen bedeutenden Teil der dakischen Bevölkerung durch pensionierte römische Legionäre und schuf so Rumänien. Steinreliefbänder, die 155 Szenen darstellen, ziehen sich spiralförmig die Säule hinauf und dokumentieren die Ereignisse chronologisch und sehr detailliert.

Apollodorus von Damaskus (?)
Detail der Trajanssäule, 107–113 n. Chr.
Carrara-Marmor, Höhe ca. 30 m, inkl. Fuß 35 m,
Trajansforum, Rom

Auf die Gedenksäule Trajans folgte die Säule des Mark Aurel in Rom, die in ähnlicher Weise mit einem spiralförmigen Band aus einer Reihe von aufeinanderfolgenden, in Relief gemeißelten Szenen einen militärischen Sieg dokumentiert.

Viele Jahre später nutzten romanische Künstler ebenfalls die fortlaufende Erzählung, um die verschiedenen Ereignisse eines anderen historisch bedeutenden militärischen Sieges zu dokumentieren – allerdings auf eine ganz andere Art und Weise. Der sogenannte Wandteppich von Bayeux (eigentlich eine Stickerei auf Leinen) zeigt 70 Szenen der Invasion Englands im Jahr 1066 durch Wilhelm den Eroberer. Körpersprache, die Kommunikation durch körperliche Gesten und Körperhaltungen anstelle von Worten, kann eine Geschichte wirkungsvoll erzählen. Zu den einfachsten Beispielen gehören *Adam und Eva, die von Gott getadelt werden* (um 1015; unten), eine der Szenen aus der Schöpfungsgeschichte, die als Relief auf den Bronzetüren dargestellt sind, die Bischof Bernward im frühen 11. Jahrhundert in Auftrag gab und die sich heute im Mariendom in Hildesheim befinden.

Gott beugt sich vor und zeigt mit anklagendem Finger auf Adam und Eva, die unterwürfig vor ihm kauern. Adam, der die verbotene Frucht vom Baum der Erkenntnis gegessen hat und sich seiner Nacktheit bewusst ist, bedeckt sich mit einer Hand und zeigt mit der anderen auf Eva, um ihr die Schuld zuzuschieben. Eva wiederum bedeckt sich mit einer Hand und weist mit der anderen auf die Schlange, die sie in Versuchung geführt hat. So wird die Geschichte mithilfe nonverbaler Kommunikation erzählt. Weder Adam noch Eva übernehmen die Verantwortung für ihr Handeln, was darauf hinweist, dass dieser Aspekt der menschlichen Natur eine lange Geschichte hat.

Unbekannter Künstler
Die Vertreibung aus dem Paradies, eine von 16 Tafeln der Bernwardtür, ca. 1015
Bronzerelief,
ca. 58,3 x 109,3 cm,
Dom zu Hildesheim

Da zu dieser Zeit nur ein kleiner Teil der Bevölkerung des Lesens und Schreibens mächtig war, war eine klare erzählerische Darstellung für das Geschichtenerzählen unerlässlich.
Dieses Relief zeigt, dass ein Bild eine Botschaft effektiver und einprägsamer vermitteln kann als eine schriftliche Beschreibung.

IKONOGRAFIE – DIE SPRACHE DER SYMBOLE

Gerade die religiöse Kunst nutzt häufig Symbole. Das Bild eines Fisches (oben) diente frühen Christen als geheimes Symbol in der Hoffnung, so einer Verfolgung zu entgehen. Das altgriechische Wort für »Fisch«, *Ichthys* (oder *Ichthus*), ist ein Akrostichon für Jesus Christus, Gottes Sohn, Erlöser. Ein vereinfachtes Bild eines Fisches markierte diskret christliche Gebäude und Gläubige und machte sie nur für diejenigen erkennbar, die seine Bedeutung kannten.

Die Ikonografie ermöglicht es den Künstlern, vielschichtige Botschaften zu übermitteln. In der romanischen Kirche Sainte-Marie-Madeleine in Vézelay ist in das Tympanon der Eingangshalle eine Darstellung der *Mission der Apostel* (1120–32; gegenüber) gehauen, die die Lehren Jesu zu allen Jahreszeiten und in der ganzen Welt verbreiten sollen. Doch wie kann selbst der geschickteste Bildhauer diese Idee ohne Worte vermitteln? Die Strahlen, die sich von den Fingerspitzen Jesu bis zum Kopf jedes Apostels erstrecken, deuten darauf hin, dass seine Ideen in ihre Köpfe gelangen, um sie zu verbreiten. Die Tierkreiszeichen am Rand machen deutlich, dass sich ihre Mission

Unbekannter Künstler
Ichthys, christliches Fisch-Symbol, frühe christl. Bestattungsstele vom Vatikanischen Friedhof, Rom, frühes 3. Jahrhundert n. Chr., Marmor, 30,5 x 33,2 x 6,7 cm
Museo Nazionale Romano, Terme di Diocleziano, Rom

Die Ikonografie verwendet Dinge wie Gegenstände, Formen, Farben, Zahlen, Tiere und Pflanzen, um Ideen darzustellen. Obwohl das Edikt von Mailand im Jahr 313 n. Chr. die Christenverfolgung im Römischen Reich beendete, bleibt der Fisch bis heute ein Symbol des Christentums.

über das ganze Jahr erstreckt. Die Apostel müssen der ganzen Welt predigen, sogar den imaginären Wesen, die auf der inneren Archivolte und dem Türsturz dargestellt sind, wie den hundeköpfigen Menschen, die sich anbellen, und den Panotti, deren Ohren so groß sind, dass sie als Decke dienen, wenn dem Besitzer kalt ist, oder auch als Flügel, um wegzufliegen, wenn er sich erschreckt.

Narrative Konventionen ermöglichen es, äußerst subtile und anspruchsvolle Ideen zu vermitteln.

Die Bedeutung bestimmter Symbole ist allgemein bekannt oder lässt sich leicht aus dem Kontext ableiten. Zum Beispiel ist der Apfel ein gängiges Symbol des Bösen in der christlichen Kunst. Denn zum einen hat Gott Adam und Eva verboten, diese Frucht im Garten Eden zu essen, und zum anderen bedeutet malum im Lateinischen, der Sprache der christlichen Kirche, sowohl »böse« als auch »Apfel«. Reste der frühen Ikonografie sind bis heute erhalten geblieben. Zum Beispiel ist der Hund seit der Antike ein Symbol für Treue – im Lateinischen bedeutet *fidus* oder *fides* »treu«, daher Fido, »der beste Freund des Mannes (und der Frau)«. Auch die Redewendung »fleißig wie eine Biene« geht auf die Antike zurück. Eine Person kann als »schüchtern wie ein Veilchen« beschrieben werden, ein mittelalterliches Symbol für Bescheidenheit.

Unbekannter Künstler
Mission der Apostel,
Tympanon, 1120–1132
Sandsteinrelief,
Breite: 9,25 m
Sainte-Marie-Madeleine,
Vézelay

In diesem komplexen französisch-romanischen Tympanon werden mehrere erzählerische Mittel, wie die Verwendung ikonografischer Symbole und die relative Größe der Figuren, kombiniert. Das Ergebnis ist ein didaktisches Bild, das die Gläubigen belehrt und gleichzeitig die Kirche dekorativ verschönert.

WIDERSPRÜCHLICHE BEDEUTUNGEN

Die Bedeutung die einer Person, einem Tier, einem Gegenstand, einer Farbe oder einer Zahl beigemessen wird, ist oft nicht einheitlich und, was die Sache noch komplizierter macht, die Bedeutungen können sich sogar widersprechen. Entscheidend für das Entschlüsseln der Ikonografie ist der spezifische Kontext, in dem ein Symbol erscheint.

In den verschiedenen Kulturen kann ein Tier, insbesondere ein imaginäres, mit sehr unterschiedlichen Bedeutungen konnotiert sein. In westlichen Kulturen sind Drachen bösartige Kreaturen, die mit der Schlange in Verbindung gebracht werden, die Adam und Eva verführte. Als Symbole des Bösen sind Drachen mit ihrem feurigen

Unbekannter Künstler
Drachenrobe, 18. Jahrhundert, Qing-Dynastie, China
Seide, 139,7 x 170,2 cm
Metropolitan Museum of Art, New York

Ein Symbol kann je nach Kontext, in dem es auftaucht, unterschiedliche Bedeutungen haben. Obwohl der Drache in westlichen Kulturen den Teufel und das Böse repräsentiert, ist der Drache in asiatischen Kulturen ein gutes Geschöpf, das positive Eigenschaften wie Weisheit, Stärke und Glück symbolisiert. Der Kaiser von China wird durch den Drachen repräsentiert.

Atem zerstörerische Wesen und versuchen, schöne Jungfrauen zu verschlingen. So muss der heilige Georg die Prinzessin Cleodolinda vor einem Drachen retten. Doch in Asien gilt der Drache seit Jahrtausenden als gutes Geschöpf und ist das Symbol des chinesischen Kaisers.

Die Anzahl der Klauen eines Drachen ist ein Statussymbol; je mehr Klauen, desto höher der Status, wobei fünf die maximale Anzahl sind.

Der Drache ist ein wohlwollendes Tier, das Glück bringt und der mythische Vorfahre des chinesischen Volkes ist. Mehrere Drachen, typischerweise lang und gelenkig, schmücken das nebenstehende Festgewand aus dem 18. Jahrhundert. Die Anzahl der Klauen eines Drachen ist ein Statussymbol; je mehr Klauen, desto höher der Status, wobei fünf die maximale Anzahl von Klauen pro Pfote ist und den Sohn des Himmels oder den Kaiser kennzeichnet. Die fünfklauigen Drachen auf dieser Robe zeigen, dass sie von einem Mitglied der kaiserlichen Familie getragen wurde. Drachen mit niedrigerem Status können vier oder drei Klauen pro Pfote haben.

Selbst innerhalb einer einzigen Kultur können Symbole mehrere und widersprüchliche Bedeutungen haben. Der Löwe, das in der westeuropäischen mittelalterlichen Kunst am häufigsten dargestellte Tier, kann ein Symbol für Jesus sein. So erklärt das mittelalterliche Bestiarium (Book of Beasts), eine Art Erbauungsbuch mit allegorischen Tierdichtungen, das besonders im Frankreich und England des 12. Jahrhunderts beliebt war, dass Löwen tot geboren, aber drei Tage später von ihrem Vater wiederbelebt werden, so wie Gott Christus drei Tage nach seinem Tod wieder zum Leben erweckt hat. Da die Menschen des Mittelalters glaubten, dass Löwen mit offenen Augen schliefen, dienten Bilder von Löwen als Wächter an Eingängen und Gräbern. In der Heraldik stehen Löwen für militärische Stärke und Mut. In jedem dieser Beispiele ist der Löwe ein positives Symbol.

Der Löwe erscheint aber auch in der Bibel immer wieder als Sinnbild des Bösen. In Psalm 7,2 heißt es: »damit niemand wie ein Löwe mein Leben zerreißt, mich packt und keiner ist da, der rettet«, und in Psalm 22,22: »Rette mich vor dem Rachen des Löwen und vor den Hörnern der Büffel!« Die Geschichte von Daniel, der von Gott vor den Löwen verschont wurde (Daniel 6,22), wurde in der mittelalterlichen Kunst dargestellt, zum Beispiel auf einem Kapitell aus dem 12./13. Jahrhundert aus dem Kloster von Saint-Guilhem-le-Désert, Frankreich (The Cloisters, New York). So hat dieselbe Kultur in derselben Zeit diesem Tier widersprüchliche ikonografische Konnotationen zugeschrieben.

Hieronymus Bosch
Garten der Lüste, Detail der rechten Tafel,
1490–1500
Öl auf Eiche,
Gesamtmaße des Triptychons
2,06 x 3,85 m
Museo Nacional del Prado, Madrid

Bosch kritisierte geschickt eine kirchliche Praxis, als er ein Schwein in Nonnenkleidung darstellte, das einen Sterbenden dazu zwang, sein Vermögen der Kirche zu überschreiben. Tiere spielen auch heute noch solche Rollen, so verwendet z. B. der anonyme britische Straßenkünstler Banksy (S. 17) oft Bilder von Ratten.

SUBTILE SYMBOLIK

Ikonografie kann subtil in der Darstellung sein und dennoch eine tiefgreifende Bedeutung haben, wobei Symbole verwendet werden, um eine Botschaft zu verschlüsseln. In dem Triptychon des niederländischen Renaissance-Malers Hieronymus Bosch, bekannt als *Garten der Lüste* (1490–1500), lässt ein Großteil der komplexen Symbolik Raum für Diskussionen. Die Bedeutung des Schweins, das einen Mann umarmt (oben), in der unteren rechten Ecke der rechten Tafel ist jedoch eindeutig. Ein Schwein, gekleidet wie eine römisch-katholischen Nonne, umarmt einen sterbenden Mann – angedeutet durch seine Nacktheit. Sie taucht den Federkiel in das Tintenfass, das ihr von einer monströsen Kreatur angeboten wird. Bosch verweist hier auf die erzwungenen Testamente (über den linken Oberschenkel des Mannes drapiert), die der Kirche zugutekommen. Die Ersetzung eines Menschen durch ein Schwein tarnt Boschs Kritik an dieser kirchlichen Praxis und macht sie sowohl humorvoll als auch einprägsamer, während er persönliche Konsequenzen vermeiden kann.

Eine andere Art von Symbolismus erscheint in floralen Stillleben, in denen sich hinter der Schönheit der Oberfläche eine unheilvolle moralisierende Botschaft verbirgt. Ein *Vanitas*-Gemälde wie auch ein *Memento-mori*-Gemälde erinnert die Menschen daran, dass der Tod unvermeidlich ist. Einige der Symbole, wie z. B. ein Totenkopf, sind offensichtlich. Aber andere Symbole für die Kürze des Lebens sind weniger direkt, wie z. B. eine schwach brennende Kerze oder eine Sanduhr, die abläuft.

Rachel Ruysch
Stillleben mit Rosen, Tulpen, einer Sonnenblume und anderen Blumen in einer Glasvase mit Biene, Schmetterling und anderen Insekten auf Marmortisch,
1710
Öl auf Leinwand,
88,9 x 71,1 cm
Privatsammlung

Ruysch gehörte zu einer Reihe von Blumenmalern, die im 18. Jahrhundert in Holland arbeiteten, aber sie wurde international bekannt für ihre akribischen, symbolträchtigen Stillleben. Überreste der Blumensymbolik des 17. und 18. Jahrhunderts sind bis heute erhalten geblieben. So werden Rosen weithin als Symbol für Liebe und Romantik verstanden, während Chrysanthemen mit Beerdigungen und Tod assoziiert werden.

Noch subtiler sind Darstellungen von einst schönen Blumen und üppigen Früchten, die verwelken, verrotten oder von Insekten gefressen werden – Verweise auf unseren unausweichlichen Verfall. Besonders beliebt waren *Memento-mori*-Blumenstillleben in den Niederlanden des 17. und 18. Jahrhunderts, wie etwa jene der niederländischen Barockmalerin Rachel Ruysch (1710; unten), die eine beeindruckende Vielfalt von Blumen und Insekten zeigen. Die kurzlebige Schönheit der Blumen impliziert die Vergänglichkeit irdischer Genüsse und damit ihre Unbedeutsamkeit. *Vanitas*- und *Memento-mori*-Bilder erinnern den Betrachter daran, seine Missetaten und Sünden zu bereuen und ein besseres Leben zu führen, solange er noch kann.

Jacques-Louis David
Tod des Sokrates, 1787
Öl auf Leinwand,
129,5 x 196,2 cm
Metropolitan Museum
of Art, New York

David und andere neoklassische Künstler suchten in der Antike nach Geschichten, die ethische Konzepte vermitteln. Sein *Tod des Sokrates* verherrlicht den griechischen Philosophen, der für seine Prinzipien stirbt, und sein Gemälde der antiken römischen Geschichte *Der Schwur der Horatier* (1784; Louvre, Paris) plädiert dafür, das Land über die Familie zu stellen.

MANCHE GESCHICHTEN MUSS MAN KENNEN

In bestimmten Kunstwerken kann die Absicht des Künstlers einem Betrachter nicht klar werden, wenn er mit der dargestellten Geschichte nicht vertraut ist. Dies gilt insbesondere dann, wenn die Darstellung eines tatsächlichen historischen Ereignisses eine moralisierende Botschaft vermittelt. Eine Reaktion auf die Vergnügungen des Rokoko zeigt sich in den neoklassischen Gemälden, die in der zweiten Hälfte des 18. und der ersten Hälfte des 19. Jahrhunderts geschaffen wurden und sich nun mit moralischer Strenge befassen.

Ethische Fragen liegen dem *Tod des Sokrates* (1787; oben) des französischen Neoklassizisten Jacques-Louis David zugrunde. Vor die Wahl gestellt, seinen Überzeugungen abzuschwören oder durch Gift zu sterben, entschied sich der antike griechische Philosoph für Letzteres und beging 399 v. Chr. im Gefängnis durch das Trinken von Schierling Selbstmord. Sokrates zeigt nach oben, ein Hinweis auf die Unsterblichkeit der Seele. Am Fußende des Bettes sitzt sein Schüler Platon, der zwar nicht anwesend war, aber die Geschichte in seinem *Phaidos* erzählt.

David dokumentierte auch Ereignisse wie den *Tod des Marat* (gegenüber), gemalt 1793, dem Jahr der Ermordung seines Freundes Jean-Paul Marat. Charlotte Corday erstach Marat, einen Führer der Französischen Revolution, in seinem Bad; er hält ihren Brief noch immer in der Hand. Corday stand auf der Seite der gemäßigten Girondins, die von dem radikalen Jakobiner Marat verdrängt wurden. Corday starb später für den Mord an Marat durch die Guillotine.

Jacques-Louis David
Tod des Marat, 1793
Öl auf Leinwand,
165 x 128 cm
Königliches
Kunstmuseum, Brüssel

David stellte seine künstlerischen Fähigkeiten in den Dienst seiner politischen Ansichten, seine Bilder dienten sowohl als Moralgeschichte als auch als Dokumentation. Verstrickt in die Politik seiner Zeit, gehörte David zu den Anführern der Französischen Revolution. Als Jakobiner wurde er wegen seiner politischen Aktivitäten ins Gefängnis geworfen. Er sollte später Napoleons Maler werden.

Die Namen Marat und Corday sind zwar beide in dem Gemälde enthalten, aber ein Betrachter, der die Umstände kennt, kann das Gemälde auf einer tieferen Ebene schätzen.

Die Werke, bei denen der Betrachter Vorkenntnisse über das dargestellte Thema benötigt, sind sehr unterschiedlich. Warum küsst zum Beispiel ein Mann eine Statue auf dem Gemälde *Pygmalion und Galatea* (um 1890; oben) des französischen Künstlers Jean-Léon Gérôme? Diese Geschichte aus der griechischen Antike, die der römische Dich-

Jean-Léon Gérôme
Pygmalion und Galatea, ca. 1890
Öl auf Leinwand, 88,9 x 68,6 cm
Metropolitan Museum of Art, New York

Die Geschichte von Pygmalion und Galatea, die der französische Künstler Gérôme dargestellt hat, ist eine von vielen antiken Mythen, die visuell umgesetzt wurden. Besonders beliebt sind die Arbeiten des Herakles, das Urteil des Paris sowie Apollo und Daphne.

ter Ovid in seinen *Metamorphosen* aufgezeichnet hat, erzählt von dem Bildhauer Pygmalion, der eine Figur einer schönen Frau schafft. Er ist so begeistert von dieser idealen Frau, dass er Aphrodite, die Göttin der Liebe, um eine solche Frau bittet. Als er nach Hause zurückkehrt und die Statue küsst, erwacht sie zum Leben und erwidert seine Zuneigung.

In einem anderen Beispiel, das weder einen historischen noch mythologischen, sondern einen literarischen Bezug hat, illustrierte der spanische Künstler Pablo Picasso die Geschichte von *Don Quijote von La Mancha* (unten), dem Roman des spanischen Autors Miguel de Cervantes aus dem 17. Jahrhundert. Der Gentleman Don Quijote, inspiriert von zahlreichen Rittergeschichten, ist mit seinem Kumpel Sancho Panza, die Lanze in der Hand, auf der Suche nach Abenteuern. Gemäß Cervantes' Beschreibung stellte Picasso Don Quijote als groß und schlank (auf seinem entsprechend dünnen Pferd) dar,

Pablo Picasso
Don Quijote und Sancho Panza, 1955
Tuschezeichnung auf Papier, Maße unbekannt, Standort des Originals unbekannt

Mit einer einfachen Tuschezeichnung, ohne die Hilfe von Farbe, vermittelt der spanische Künstler Picasso ein Gefühl für die Charaktere, ihre Beziehung und die Geschichte von Don Quijote von La Mancha. Auf Picasso wird im folgenden Kapitel noch eingegangen.

während Sancho Panza klein und rund ist (auf seinem entsprechend bauchigen Esel). Im Hintergrund hat Picasso die Windmühlen eingefügt, auf die Don Quijote zusteuert, weil er sie für Riesen hält.

Hilma af Klint
Group IV, Die zehn Größten, Nr. 3, Jugend, 1907
Tempera auf Papier, auf Leinwand montiert, 3,21 x 2,4 m
The Hilma af Klint Foundation, Stockholm. Moderna Museet, Stockholm

Af Klints Gemälde übertragen die spirituellen Botschaften, die sie erhielt, in eine visuelle Sprache und nutzen die Abstraktion, um die unsichtbare geistige Welt sichtbar zu machen. Af Klint bevorzugt präzise geometrische Formen, einige ähneln Diagrammen, mit Spiralen, die wiederkehren und die Kompositionen vereinen.

ABSTRAKTE KUNST

Weil sie nicht-figurativ und nicht-gegenständlich ist, ohne ein erkennbares Motiv, betrachten manche die abstrakte Kunst als eine reinere Kunstform als die gegenständliche Kunst. Aber wenn es kein erkennbares Subjekt gibt, gibt es dann eine Bedeutung? Und wenn es eine Bedeutung gibt, wer liefert sie – der Künstler oder der Betrachter? Abstrakte Kunst fördert eine aktivere Rolle des Betrachters als gegenständliche Kunst – tatsächlich arbeiten Künstler und Betrachter zusammen. Die Rolle des Betrachters bei der Interpretation nicht-gegenständlicher Kunst ist eine persönliche und intellektuelle, denn ohne eindeutige Hinweise des Künstlers wird das Verständnis des Kunstwerks bei jedem Einzelnen unterschiedlich ausfallen. Der Betrachter muss sich anstrengen, um zu einer Interpretation zu gelangen, und kann daher mehr davon haben, wenn er sich an dem Prozess beteiligt, als wenn er ein passiver, unhinterfragter Beobachter ist. Abstrakte Kunst appelliert an unsere Emotionen, Erinnerungen und Erfahrungen – was für den einen tief bewegend ist, kann für den anderen bedeutungslos sein.

Was halten Sie von Kunstwerken mit der Bezeichnung »Ohne Titel«? Oder solchen, die nichts weiter als eine Nummer oder eine Farbliste zur Kennzeichnung haben? Sollte der Künstler dem Betrachter zumindest einen Hinweis darauf geben, welche Absichten er bei der Schaffung dieses Kunstwerks hatte?

Af Klint war die erste Malerin echter abstrakter Kunst.

Der russische Maler Wassili Kandinsky galt aufgrund seiner Gemälde aus den Jahren 1910–11 als Begründer der abstrakten Kunst. Als früheste völlig abstrakte Werke werden jedoch heute die der schwedischen Mystikerin Hilma af Klint angesehen. Obwohl sie Porträts und Landschaften in einem naturalistischen und stark gegenständlichen Stil schuf, malte sie zu gleicher Zeit (mindestens schon 1906) in einem völlig abstrakten Stil, ohne dass dies der Öffentlichkeit bekannt war. Andere Künstler, in deren Werk frühe abstrakte Bilder zu finden sind, sind der Russe Kasimir Malewitsch und die Amerikanerin Georgia O'Keeffe. Aber af Klint scheint keine Verbindung zu diesen Künstlern gehabt zu

haben, die durch die allmähliche Vereinfachung der äußeren Bildwelt zur Abstraktion kamen.

Im Gegensatz dazu schuf af Klint ihre Form der abstrakten Kunst, hervorgerufen von den inneren Geistern, die sie leiteten, wie sie sagt, und zugleich als Antwort darauf. Als sie 1904 an einer

Séance teilnahm, kam sie zu der Überzeugung, dass die »Hohen Meister« ihr die Aufgabe zugewiesen hatten, das zu schaffen, was sie »The Paintings for the Temple« nannte; zwischen 1906 und 1915 schuf sie 193 abstrakte Tempelbilder. Die sehr großen Gemälde aus dem Jahr 1907, bekannt als *Die zehn Größten* (vorherige Seite), beschäftigen sich mit dem Zyklus des Lebens.

Da sie glaubte, die Öffentlichkeit sei noch nicht bereit für ihre nicht-figurativen Gemälde, und weil die »Hohen« ihr sagten, sie solle ihre Bilder weder ausstellen noch anderen zeigen, wurde in ihrem Testament festgelegt, dass deren Ausstellung bis lange nach ihrem Tod warten müsse. Als sie 1944 starb, lagerten mehr als 1.200 abstrakte Gemälde in ihrem Atelier in Kisten, die bis in die späten 1960er-Jahre ungeöffnet blieben. Die erste öffentliche Ausstellung ihrer Gemälde fand 1986 im Los Angeles County Museum of Art statt. In der Folgezeit erhielt sie Anerkennung für ihre Leistung als vermutlich früheste Malerin wirklich abstrakter Kunst.

Die Popularität der abstrakten Kunst beruht darauf, dass es auch ohne ein erkennbares Motiv möglich ist, durch die Verwendung visueller Elemente Emotionen zu vermitteln und hervorzurufen (S. 36–65). Kunst hat die Fähigkeit, Glück, Trauer, Aufregung, Ruhe und eine Reihe anderer menschlicher Emotionen zu suggerieren, ohne dass eine Bildsprache verwendet wird. Vielleicht ist dies vergleichbar mit der Art und Weise, in der Musik Emotionen ohne Worte hervorrufen kann.

Wenn selbst die einfachsten Formen und Farben eine Bedeutung vermitteln können, wie einfach kann dann ein Gemälde sein? Es ist fast unmöglich, ein Gemälde noch einfacher zu gestalten als Kasimir Malewitschs *Weiß auf Weiß* von 1918 (gegenüber) aus seiner Serie der Weiß-auf-Weiß-Bilder. Dieser russische Künstler assoziierte das weiße Quadrat mit einem Gefühl des Schwebens. Er verband Weiß mit Zeitlosigkeit und Unendlichkeit, weil es keine Ähnlichkeit mit einem erkennbaren Motiv – und damit Zeit oder Ort oder einem früheren künstlerischen Stil – hat.

Ihre Interpretation der abstrakten Kunst ist, da sie individuell und Ihre eigene ist, genauso wichtig und richtig wie die eines jeden anderen. Abstrakte Kunst trainiert Ihre Vorstellungskraft, denn wie Leonardo da Vinci empfahl: »Schauen Sie auf die Flecken an Wänden oder in die Asche eines Feuers oder in Wolken oder Schlamm oder ähnliche Stellen, in denen Sie, wenn Sie sie genau betrachten, wirklich wunderbare Ideen finden können ... denn durch unscharfe Dinge wird der Geist zu neuen Erfindungen angeregt.«

Kasimir Malewitsch
Weiß auf Weiß, 1918
Öl auf Leinwand,
79,4 x 79,4 cm
Museum of Modern Art,
New York

Der russische Suprematist Malewitsch reduzierte seine Malerei auf das Minimum an Farbe und Form, das notwendig ist, um als Gemälde zu gelten. Er sagte, unter »Suprematismus« verstehe er die Vorherrschaft des reinen Gefühls in der schöpferischen Kunst.

TATSACHE VERSUS MEINUNG

Zwar regt Kunst die Fantasie an, doch versuchen Sie bitte, Spekulationen in Ihrer Interpretation zu vermeiden. Kunsthistorische Schriften enthalten leider auch »Fake News«, in denen ein führender Autor oder Redner eine persönliche Meinung so präsentiert, als wäre sie eine unwiderlegbare, dokumentierte Tatsache. Aber Skepsis ist angebracht, wenn bestätigende Informationen, fotografische Beweise oder schriftliche Aufzeichnungen fehlen.

Das Problem zieht sich besonders bei der abstrakten Kunst durch die gesamte Kunstgeschichte. Bei der Sinnsuche in der prähistorischen Kunst gibt es keine Dokumente, die die ursprüngliche Intention des Künstlers klären. Es sind nur Vermutungen anhand von Vergleichen mit verwandten Werken möglich. Dennoch wird die kleine prähistorische Skulptur einer bauchigen nackten Frau,

Unbekannter Künstler
Venus von Willendorf,
ca. 28 000–25 000 v. Chr.
Oolithischer Kalkstein mit rotem Ocker,
Höhe 11,1 cm
Naturhistorisches Museum, Wien

Diese Steinfigur wurde als Fruchtbarkeitssymbol, als Muttergöttin, als anatomisches Ideal, als Selbstporträt, als Aphrodisiakum, als Glücksbringer und mehr bezeichnet. Dafür, dass diese Figur eine Idee »verkörpert«, spricht das Fehlen von Gesichtszügen, die auf die Darstellung einer bestimmten Person schließen lassen würden. Aber ohne schriftliche Dokumentation ist die einzige verlässliche Quelle für Informationen über prähistorische Kunst die Kunst selbst.

die um 28 000–25 000 v. Chr. gefertigt wurde, oft als die *Venus von Willendorf* (oben) bezeichnet. Ja, sie stammt aus Willendorf in Österreich. Aber gibt es einen Grund, sie Venus zu nennen, nach der römischen Göttin der Liebe? Manche meinen, sie sei schwanger und daher ein Fruchtbarkeitssymbol, aber ihre Anatomie ist nicht die einer schwangeren Frau. Handelt es sich stattdessen um ein Bild der Fettleibigkeit als Ideal in einer Zeit, in der Nahrung knapp war? Ihre Bedeutung, falls eine beabsichtigt war, bleibt eine unbeantwortete Frage. Versuchen Sie, der Tendenz zu widerstehen, Ideen, die in Ihrer eigenen Kultur heute aktuell sind, auf frühere oder fremde Kulturen zu übertragen.

Hinsichtlich der beabsichtigten Bedeutung eines Werkes ist der Künstler die ultimative Autorität. Nehmen wir Kay WalkingStick, ein Mitglied der Cherokee Nation of Oklahoma und eine Pionierin in der Kunst für amerikanische Ureinwohner. Sie schuf eine Serie von Landschafts-Diptychen, darunter *Oh, Canada!* (S. 128–29), 2018–19. Für WalkingStick ist die Kunst ein Weg, die Natur zu verstehen und, wie sie es ausdrückte, »die Erde zu ehren«. In *Oh, Canada!* malt WalkingStick die Schönheit der weiten und unberührten Felslandschaft des Mount Rundle, Banff National Park, Alberta. In Bezug auf das Diptychon-Format erklärt sie: »Ich sehe meine Bilder nicht als Landschaften per se, sondern eher als Bilder, die zwei Arten der Wahrnehmung der Erde beschreiben. Eine Sichtweise ist visuell und flüchtig und die andere ist abstrakt und ewig.« Durch die Abstraktion sucht WalkingStick nach der einfachsten Möglichkeit, einen tiefen Gedanken auszudrücken. Sie sagt: »Ich erwarte von der Abstraktion genauso wie von der Bildsprache, dass sie Bedeutung trägt.« Da sie sich mit der Geschichte der amerikanischen Ureinwohner befasst, hat WalkingStick das Muster der Symbole der Ureinwohner in ihr Werk einbezogen – zum einen wegen ihrer Verbindung zu den Stoney Nakoda, die noch immer auf diesem Land leben, und zum anderen als Erinnerung daran, dass dies alles Land der Ureinwohner ist. Sie betonte: »Wir sind alle verschieden und wir sind alle gleich.«

WICHTIGE IDEEN

Motivkategorien:

- Menschliche Figur
- Porträt
- Mythologie
- Religion
- Geschichte und Politik
- Genreszenen
- Landschaft
- Stillleben
- Abstrakte Kunst

Erzählerische Konventionen:

- Linearperspektive
- Relative Größe
- Fortlaufende Erzählung
- Körpersprache

Ikonografie – die Sprache der Symbole:

- Widersprüchliche Bedeutung
- Subtile Symbolik
- *Vanitas*- und *Memento-Mori*-Gemälde

Abstrakte Kunst:

- Hilma af Klint
- Validität der persönlichen Meinung eines jeden Betrachters

Fakt versus Meinung:

- Unbegründete Spekulationen vermeiden

Kay WalkingStick
Oh, Canada!, 2018–19
Öl auf Holztafel,
91,4 x 182,9 cm

Sammlung der Künstlerin

Die eigenen Worte der indigenen Künstlerin WalkingStick sind der direkteste Weg zum Verständnis ihrer Arbeit. Wie bei anderen Künstlern auch, besteht bei den Analysen, die selbst der scharfsinnigste Kritiker oder Kunsthistoriker verfasst, die Gefahr, Voreingenommenheit oder Fehlinformationen einzubringen, was umso wahrscheinlicher wird, je weiter wir von der Entstehung des Werks entfernt sind.

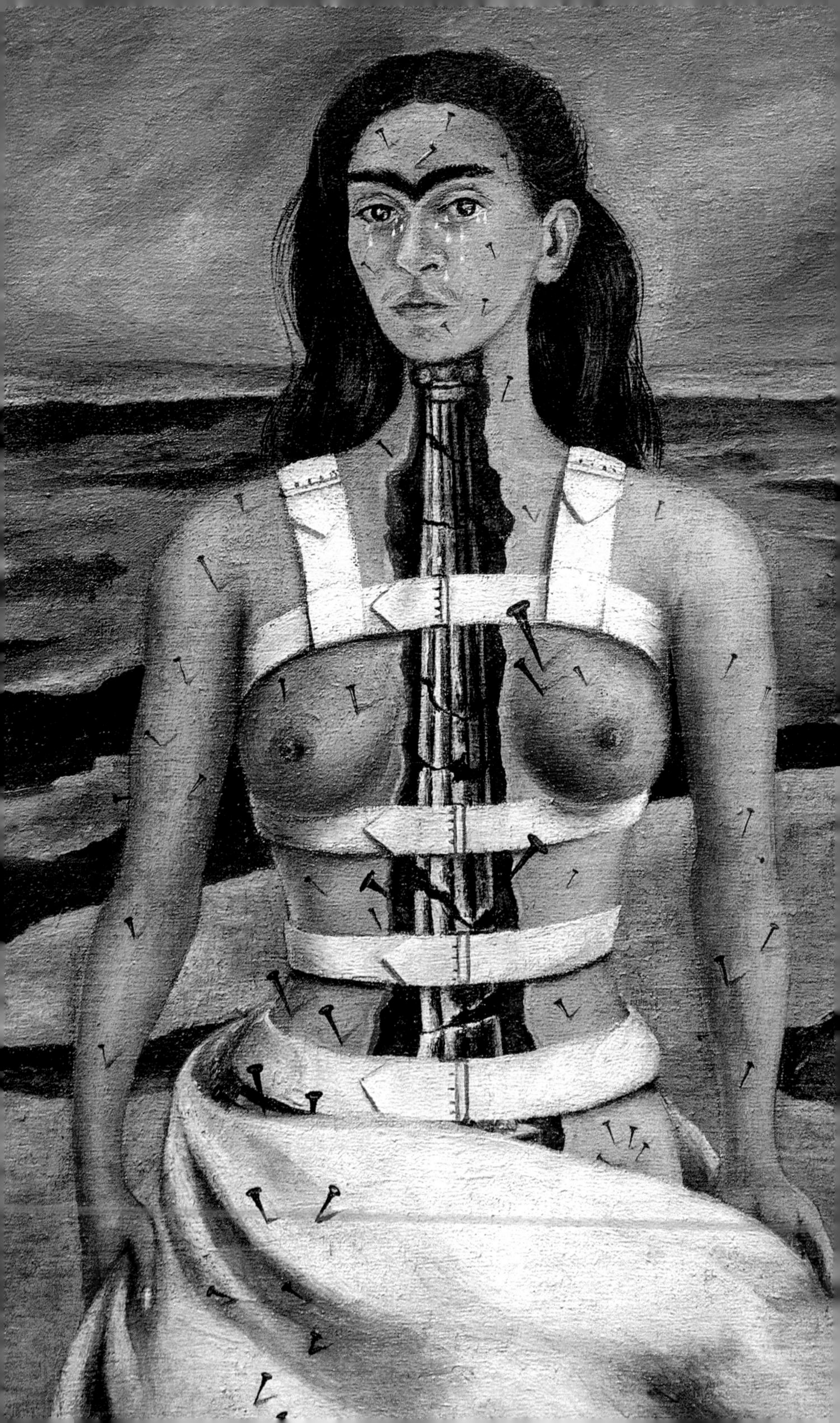

SECHS BESONDERE KÜNSTLERINNEN UND KÜNSTLER

-

Große Kunst wird bei dem einen durch Fleiß, bei dem anderen durch Studium, bei diesem durch Nachahmung, bei jenem durch Kenntnis der Wissenschaft geboren ... andere verwenden alle diese Dinge zusammen oder zumindest die meisten davon.

-

Giorgio Vasari
1568

Bestimmte Künstlerinnen und Künstler hatten besonderen Einfluss auf die Kunstgeschichte. Manche erlangen schon zu Lebzeiten große Bedeutung, aber bei den meisten erkennt die Öffentlichkeit leider erst nach ihrem Tod ihre Bedeutung oder gar Genialität. Dieses Kapitel bietet einen Überblick über das Leben und Werk von sechs innovativen Künstlerinnen und Künstlern. Sie wirkten vom späten 15. bis zum späten 20. Jahrhundert und kommen aus Italien, den Niederlanden, Frankreich, Mexiko, Spanien und den USA. Es sind Leonardo da Vinci, Rembrandt van Rijn, Vincent van Gogh, Frida Kahlo, Pablo Picasso und Andy Warhol.

LEONARDO DA VINCI (1452–1519)

Leonardo da Vinci, geboren in Vinci bei Florenz, war das Musterbeispiel dessen, was wir heute einen »Renaissance-Menschen« nennen. Dieser Universalgelehrte, der vor allem als Maler berühmt wurde, war auch Bildhauer, Architekt, Ingenieur, Anatom, Biologe, Geologe, Geograf, Erfinder, Bühnenbildner und Partyplaner.

Leonardo entwickelte zwei neue Methoden der Malerei: *Chiaroscuro* und *Sfumato*. *Chiaroscuro*, abgeleitet von den mit einander kombinierten italienischen Wörtern für »hell« und »dunkel« bzw. »klar« und »düster«, bezeichnet die besondere Verwendung von Licht- und Schattenbereichen. Das Licht hebt subtil hervor, was der Künstler dem Betrachter zeigen möchte, während die Schatten alles andere verdecken. In *Sfumato*, abgeleitet vom italienischen Wort für »Rauch«, werden die Umrisse der verschiedenen Formen weicher und verschmelzen mit dem Hintergrund, wodurch ein leicht dunstiger Effekt entsteht.

Leonardo da Vinci
Felsengrottenmadonna,
1483–86
Öl auf Tafel (übertragen auf Leinwand),
199 x 122 cm
Musée du Louvre, Paris

Leonardo da Vinci war wahrscheinlich der wissenschaftlichste Künstler seiner Zeit. Als einer der ersten Renaissance-Künstler sezierte Leonardo Leichen und fertigte detaillierte Zeichnungen der verschiedenen Körperteile und ihrer Funktionen an.

Wissenschaft und Kunst in der italienischen Renaissance

Leonardos innovativer Ansatz, Wissenschaft und Kunst zu verbinden, wird in seinem Gemälde der *Felsengrottenmadonna* (1483–86; gegenüber) deutlich. Die Ergebnisse seiner Forschung zeigen sich in den klassifizierbaren Pflanzen sowie den Stalagmiten und Stalaktiten der Grotte. Diese neuartige Darstellung von Maria und Jesus in einer Grotte suggeriert die Idee des Erdenschoßes, in dem Maria eine Muttergöttin ist. Sie beschützt den zukünftigen Johannes den Täufer, indem sie ihn unter ihren Mantel nimmt. Johannes repräsentiert die christliche Gemeinde, beschützt von Maria und gesegnet von Jesus.

Schönheit in der Kunst, so Leonardo, ist durch Geometrie, Arithmetik, Perspektive und wissenschaftliche Beobachtung zu erreichen. Diese Ideen prägen sein *Letztes Abendmahl* (S. 134–35), ein riesiges Wandgemälde, das zwischen 1495 und 1498 im Refektorium des Klosters Santa Maria delle Grazie in Mailand gemalt wurde.

Die Komposition stellt Jesus in den Mittelpunkt. Indem Leonardo den Raum, in dem das letzte Abendmahl stattfindet, in zentraler Ein-Punkt-Perspektive zeichnet, wobei alle diagonalen Fluchtlinien zu Jesus führen, lenkt er das Auge des Betrachters zu ihm. Jesus steht im Zentrum der fast zweiseitig symmetrischen Komposition und sein Oberkörper bildet ein gleichseitiges Dreieck, eine geometrische Form, die in der Renaissance wegen ihrer Stabilität beliebt war. Das größte der drei Fenster an der Rückwand befindet sich direkt hinter Jesus, rahmt ihn ein und hebt ihn hervor. Der Segmentgiebel über diesem Fenster ersetzt auf subtile Weise den Heiligenschein, den er in früheren Gemälden trug. Die zwölf Apostel sind zu je sechs auf jeder Seite angeordnet, fein säuberlich aufgeteilt in vier

Leonardo da Vinci
Letztes Abendmahl
1495–98
Verschiedene Materialien, 4,6 x 8,79 m
Refektorium, Kloster Santa Maria delle Grazie, Mailand

Leonardo unterschied zwischen verschiedenen Arten von Licht und schrieb: »Die Lichter, die undurchsichtige Körper beleuchten können, sind von vier Arten ... diffuses Licht, wie das der Atmosphäre ... direktes, wie das der Sonne ... reflektiertes Licht und ... das, das durch [halb]transparente Körper hindurchgeht, wie Leinen oder Papier, oder Ähnliches ...«

Gruppen zu je drei Figuren. Das Licht fällt sowohl von den Fenstern an der Rückwand als auch von der linken Seite ein, wobei die Seite mit dem Verräter Judas im Schatten liegt.

Leonardo experimentierte ständig, aber die Ergebnisse waren nicht immer erfolgreich. Der beklagenswerte Zustand des Abendmahl-Wandgemäldes ist auf die unerprobte Methode zurückzuführen, die er anwandte: Statt der üblichen buon-fresco-Technik, bei der auf nassen Kalkputz gemalt wird, malte er mit einer Kombination aus Öl und Tempera auf trockenem Putz. Die Farbe haftete nicht gut und begann sogar zu zerfallen, während er an ihr arbeitete. Das Abendmahl wurde mehrfach konserviert und restauriert, zuletzt von einem Expertenteam im Jahr 1999.

Das Interesse am Individuum ist typisch für die Renaissance und wurde von Künstlern in Porträts und Selbstporträts visuell sowie von Schriftstellern in Biografien und Autobiografien literarisch umgesetzt. Das berühmteste Beispiel eines Renaissance-Porträts, ja das berühmteste Gemälde der Welt, ist die von Leonardo da Vinci gemalte *Mona Lisa* (ca. 1503–19; gegenüber). Mona ist eine Kurzform von Madonna und bedeutet »meine Dame«. Die Dargestellte war die 1479 geborene Florentiner Adelige Lisa di Antonio Maria Gherardini, die im Alter von 15 Jahren mit dem aufstrebenden Florentiner Bürokraten Francesco del Giocondo, damals 29, verheiratet wurde. Folglich ist dieses Gemälde seiner dritten Frau auch als La Gioconda bekannt. Es ist umstritten, ob der Hintergrund einen realen Ort darstellt.

Der Ruhm der *Mona Lisa* beruht auf ihrem rätselhaften Blick.

Leonardo brach mit den starren, büstenlangen Profilporträts der Frührenaissance und etablierte mit dem Porträt der *Mona Lisa* eine neue Art der Darstellung einer Person. Seine Dargestellte erscheint in halber Länge, in Dreiviertelansicht, die Hände eingeschlossen, scheinbar entspannt und natürlich. Mona Lisa machte diese Art von Porträtformat populär, das während der Hochrenaissance und später immer wieder verwendet werden sollte.

Der Ruhm der Mona Lisa beruht auf dem Rätsel, das die Mehrdeutigkeit ihres Gesichtsausdrucks hervorruft. Lächelt sie oder ist sie traurig? Leonardo beschäftigte sich nicht nur mit dem Äußeren der Dargestellten, sondern auch mit dem Inneren, den psychologischen Feinheiten der einzelnen Persönlichkeiten. Ähnlich interessierte er sich bei der Sezierung von Leichen nicht nur für das Aussehen der inneren Organe, sondern auch für deren Funktion.

Leonardo da Vinci hinterließ der Nachwelt unzählige Seiten mit illustrierten Notizen, die er von rechts nach links mit der linken Hand schrieb. Darin enthalten sind Entwürfe für seine vielen Erfindungen, biologische und botanische Beobachtungen sowie architektonische Entwürfe (die nie gebaut wurden), die auf geometrischen Formen basieren. Er starb in seinem kleinen Schloss in Amboise, das er von seinem Gastgeber, dem französischen König Franz I., geschenkt bekommen hatte.

Leonardo da Vinci
Mona Lisa (Lisa Gherardini), ca. 1503–19
Öl auf Pappel,
77 x 53 cm
Musée du Louvre, Paris

Der Mode der Zeit enntsprechend deutet Lisa Gherardinis hochgezupfte und rasierte Stirn auf ihren Adelsstand hin, wobei das Fehlen der Augenbrauen den Effekt noch verstärkt. Neben der physischen Erscheinung seiner Porträtierten war für Leonardo auch ihr emotionaler Zustand von Interesse. Mona Lisas rätselhaftes Lächeln bringt den Betrachter dazu, sich zu fragen, was sie dachte (und vor allem, was sie fühlte), während sie für Leonardo posierte.

Rembrandt
Die Blendung Simsons,
1636
Öl auf Leinwand,
219,3 x 305 cm
Städel, Frankfurt am Main

Rembrandt wurde von der Dramatik der alttestamentarischen Ereignisse angezogen. Hier porträtiert er den schrecklichsten Teil dieser Geschichte, als Simsons Haare (die Quelle seiner Stärke) abgeschnitten und seine Augen ausgestochen werden.

REMBRANDT VAN RIJN (1606–69)

Der in Leiden geborene Rembrandt van Rijn ist zweifellos der berühmteste Maler des holländischen Barocks. Sein Studium der klassischen Literatur an der Universität Leiden brach er ab und widmete sich stattdessen der Malerei. Sein erstes Gruppenporträt, *Die Anatomie des Dr. Tulp* (1632; Mauritshuis, Den Haag), machte ihn zum beliebtesten Maler in Amsterdam. 1634 heiratete er Saskia van Ulenborch, die ihm große Freude bereitete, ihm oft Modell stand und aus einer wohlhabenden Familie stammte. Nun sehr glücklich verheiratet und mit vielen Aufträgen bedacht, besaß der wohlhabende Rembrandt ein großes Haus und eine Kunstsammlung in Amsterdam.

Das Goldene Zeitalter des niederländischen Barock

Rembrandts Gemälde der *Blendung Simsons* (1636; oben) demonstriert den künstlerischen Stil, der seinen Erfolg ausmacht. Der dramatische Moment, der für die Darstellung gewählt wurde, sowie die dynamischen Diagonalen, die die emotionale Spannung verstärken, entsprechen ganz dem niederländischen Barockgeschmack der Zeit. Rembrandt, der »Meister des Lichts« genannt wird, setzt auf starke Lichteffekte. *Chiaroscuro*, auf die Spitze getrieben, mit übertriebenen Hell-Dunkel-Kontrasten, wird zum Tenebrismus (von *tenebroso*, italienisch für »dunkel«), bei dem ein starkes Licht das

Zentrum des Interesses verstärkt, ausdrucksstarke Züge hervorhebt und unwichtige Details in den Schatten verbannt. Das Licht dient zwar mehreren Zwecken, ist aber nicht-naturalistisch und inkonsistent. Dennoch sind alle Gemälde Rembrandts in Bezug auf Licht und Dunkelheit perfekt ausbalanciert (was Sie testen können, indem Sie die Augen zusammenkneifen).

Saskias früher Tod im Jahr 1642, der Rembrandt mit ihrem kleinen Sohn Titus zurückließ, war der Wendepunkt im Leben des Künstlers. In diesem Jahr malte er die berühmte *Nachtwache* (S. 140–41), aber seine Popularität als Künstler begann zu sinken, weil sein Stil persönlicher wurde – und weniger leicht von seinen Gönnern verstanden. Seine finanziellen Schwierigkeiten begannen.

Anstatt jede Person gleichmäßig hervorzuheben, betonte Rembrandt die barocke dramatische Beleuchtung und diagonale Bewegungen.

Die Nachtwache ist ein riesiges Gruppenporträt der Bürgergarde in Amsterdam. Alle porträtierten Männer hatten gleichermaßen zu den Kosten beigetragen, was zu dem Problem führte, dass alle gleichmaßen prominent im Gemälde dargestellt werden wollten. Aber Hauptmann Frans Banninck Cocq und sein Leutnant Willem van Ruytenburch wurden am stärksten hervorgehoben, sodass sich die anderen – von denen zum Teil nur die Nasenspitzen aus der dunklen Barockbeleuchtung herausragen – betrogen fühlten. Rembrandt ging es vielmehr darum, eine barocke Komposition von sich auf Diagonalen bewegenden Handlungen zu schaffen und so das übliche Problem starrer Gesichtsreihen in Gruppenporträts zu vermeiden. Ursprünglich wurden der Hauptmann und der Leutnant nur einen Schritt von der Mitte der Komposition entfernt dargestellt. Dieses geschickte Mittel, Bewegung anzudeuten, das Giotto schon viele Jahre zuvor verwendete (S. 55), erfüllte auch bis zur Beschneidung des Gemäldes auf allen Seiten, besonders auf der linken Seite, seinen Zweck.

Das Gemälde zeigt die Mitglieder dieser Kompanie, wie sie am Morgen durch das Amsterdamer Stadttor kommen, um Marie dei Medici, Königin von Frankreich, zu begrüßen. Über die Identität des reich gekleideten Mädchens in der Menge wird bis heute debattiert; möglicherweise repräsentiert sie die Kloveniers-Miliz und trägt Embleme dieser Bürgergarde, darunter das Huhn, dessen Krallen eine Anspielung auf die Kloveniers sind, und einen Trinkbecher.

Rembrandt
Die Nachtwache, 1642
Öl auf Leinwand,
37,95 x 45,35 m
Rijksmuseum, Amsterdam

Rembrandts Gemälde erhielt im 18. Jahrhundert den Spitznamen »Nachtwache«, ursprünglich hieß es *Offiziere und andere Schützen des Bezirks II in Amsterdam, unter Führung von Hauptmann Frans Banninck Cocq und Leutnant Willem van Ruytenburch*. Doch es war nachgedunkelt und auch eine Reinigung half nicht. Das dargestellte Ereignis fand tatsächlich am Morgen statt.

Rembrandt sammelte Kunstwerke und andere Gegenstände und verwendete einige davon als Requisiten in seinen Gemälden. Aber er hatte einen extravaganten Geschmack und kaufte zwanghaft, auch als er sich das nicht mehr leisten konnte. Er besaß schließlich etwa 60 Abgüsse antiker Statuen und etwa 8.000 Drucke und Zeichnungen, darunter Werke von Raffael, Michelangelo, Tizian, Lucas van Leyden, Dürer, Holbein und Rubens. Seine Sammelleidenschaft, gepaart mit seiner Unfähigkeit, mit Geld umzugehen und seinem schwindenden Einkommen, führte zu einem finanziellen Desaster. Im Jahr 1656 erklärte Rembrandt seinen Bankrott.

Rembrandt
Selbstporträt im Alter von 63, 1669
Öl auf Leinwand, 86 x 70,5 cm
National Gallery, London

Selbstanalytisch stellt Rembrandt sich selbst als müde dar, sein Gesicht spiegelt den Intensität und die Tragik seines Lebens wider.

-

Rembrandts Stil wurde zunehmend introvertierter.

-

Es gab noch andere Probleme. Geertje Dircx, ursprünglich als Amme für Titus angestellt, wurde Rembrandts Geliebte. Doch die Beziehung zerbrach und endete mit einem Gerichtsprozess, in dem sie behauptete, er habe sein Eheversprechen gebrochen. Sie wurde inhaftiert und versuchte nach ihrer Freilassung, Rembrandt zu verklagen. Seine Zuneigung galt nun seiner Haushälterin Hendrickje Stoffels, die sein Modell, seine Geliebte und die Stiefmutter von Titus wurde. Stoffels brachte 1654 eine Tochter, Cornelia, zur Welt. 1660 gründeten Stoffels und der inzwischen 19-jährige Titus eine Kunsthandlung und gewährten Rembrandt im Tausch gegen seine Kunst Unterkunft und Verpflegung – eine Vereinbarung, die Rembrandt vor der Verfolgung durch seine Gläubiger bewahrte.

Er erhielt weiterhin wichtige Aufträge, doch sein Stil wurde zunehmend introvertierter, da er eher nach seinen eigenen Maßstäben als nach denen seiner Gönner arbeitete. Dennoch erfreute sein *Porträt der Vorsteher der Tuchmacherzunft* (Rijksmuseum, Amsterdam) von 1662 seine Auftraggeber.

-

Rembrandt hielt die Veränderungen in seinem Leben in etwa 80 Selbstporträts fest.

-

Rembrandt hielt die Veränderungen in seinem Leben in etwa 80 Selbstporträts fest. Gegenüber sehen Sie eines der letzten, gemalt im Jahr 1669, dem Jahr, in dem er starb. Er war einsam: Stoffels war 1663 gestorben, Titus 1668 im Alter von nur 26 Jahren ebenfalls.

Rembrandt selbst starb 13 Monate nach Titus und wurde in einem Armengrab beigesetzt. Bis zum Schluss bleibt Rembrandt der »Meister des Lichts«: Sein Umgang mit Farbe ist weiterhin meisterhaft, die verschiedenen Texturen werden betont, die Farben leuchten und glühen. Aber die Konturen werden lockerer, die Pinselstriche breiter, die Oberfläche ist nicht mehr so glatt wie in früheren Gemälden und der Einsatz von dickem Impasto nimmt zu.

VINCENT VAN GOGH (1853–90)

Vincent van Gogh, der Sohn eines Pfarrers, wurde in Zundert, Niederlande, geboren. Bevor er sich der Malerei widmete, probierte er viele verschiedene Berufe aus, darunter Kunsthändler, Lehrer und Laienpastor. Aber aufgrund seiner Schwierigkeiten, mit Menschen zurechtzukommen, folgte ein Misserfolg dem anderen. Alle Gemälde van Goghs stammen aus der Zeit zwischen 1880 und 1890, wobei die berühmtesten in den letzten Jahren seines kurzen Lebens entstanden.

Um 1880 begann Vincent auf Anraten seines jüngeren Bruders Theo, der selbst Kunsthändler war, eine formale Kunstausbildung in Brüssel. Seine frühen Gemälde, wie *Die Kartoffelesser* (1885; Van Gogh Museum, Amsterdam), konzentrierten sich auf das verarmte Leben der Landbevölkerung und waren in dunklen Farben gemalt.

Französischer Post-Impressionismus

1886 zog van Gogh nach Paris, wo er bei Theo wohnte. Er begann eine akademische Ausbildung und traf mehrere der Impressionisten und Post-Impressionisten. Kunsthistoriker ordnen ihn den französischen PostImpressionisten zu, weil er die meisten seiner Gemälde in Frankreich schuf und seine Interessen mit denen der Post-Impressionisten übereinstimmten. Van Goghs Farbpalette änderte sich und wurde lebendig und hell. Er malte 1887 in Paris eine Serie von Sonnenblumen, eine zweite Serie im Jahr 1888 in Arles in Südfrankreich. Vincent war in der Lage, dorthin zu ziehen, weil Theo ihn sowohl finanziell als auch emotional unterstützte.

-

Die Betonung von Umrissen und Silhouetten spiegelt Vincents Bewunderung für japanische Drucke wider.

-

Vincent malte oft seine persönliche Umgebung, wie z. B. sein Schlafzimmer in Arles (gegenüber) – die erste von drei Versionen. Die Betonung von Umrissen und Silhouetten spiegelt seine Bewunderung für japanische Drucke wider, ebenso wie die abrupten Übergänge zwischen leuchtenden Farben. Ähnlich verhält es sich bei *Das Nachtcafé* (Yale University Art Gallery, New Haven), das ebenfalls 1888 in Arles entstand. Hier werden die Farben nicht gemischt und gedämpft, sondern in maximaler Intensität aufgetragen.

Ängste und Verzweiflung

Seine Bilder spiegeln vor allem seine leidenschaftliche Persönlichkeit wider, seine nervöse Energie zeigt sich in den kurzen, abgehackten

Vincent van Gogh
Das Schlafzimmer des Künstlers im gelben Haus, 1888
Öl auf Leinwand, 72,4 x 91,3 cm
Van Gogh Museum, Amsterdam

Seine häufig wechselnde Umgebung sowie seine schwankenden Emotionen dokumentierte van Gogh immer wieder in seinen Bildern und in seinen Briefen an seinen Bruder Theo.

Pinselstrichen. Er legte seine eigenen Emotionen in jedes Gemälde, egal welches Thema. In diesem Sinne sind alle seine Gemälde Selbstporträts – nicht von seiner äußeren physischen Erscheinung, sondern von seinem inneren emotionalen Zustand.

Nach einem Streit mit Gauguin schnitt sich van Gogh den größten Teil seines linken Ohrs ab.

Der französische post-impressionistische Maler Paul Gauguin nahm van Goghs Einladung an, ihn in Arles zu besuchen. Van Gogh bewunderte Gauguin und sie beeinflussten sich gegenseitig in ihrer Kunst. Doch sie stritten sich fürchterlich, und nach einem Streit mit Gauguin schnitt sich van Gogh den größten Teil seines linken Ohrs ab (nach einer Zeichnung seines Arztes Félix Rey), wickelte es ein und ließ es seiner Prostituierten zukommen. Er litt unter Anfällen und Halluzinationen; im vollen Bewusstsein seines Zustandes ließ er sich freiwillig in Arles einweisen. Seine unmittelbare Umgebung hielt er weiterhin in Gemälden und Zeichnungen fest, wie z. B. in denen, die den Gemeinschaftsraum des Krankenhauses und den Klostergarten zeigen.

Vincent van Gogh
Sternennacht, 1889
Öl auf Leinwand,
73,7 x 92,1 cm
Museum of Modern Art,
New York

Landschaften werden normalerweise gemalt, um ein Gefühl von friedlicher Ruhe zu vermitteln. Aber Vincents Gemälde der *Sternennacht* ist vielleicht die emotionalste Landschaft, die je gemalt wurde, und zeigt eine Turbulenz, die selbst die Extreme der Natur übertrifft.

Van Gogh zog ins Sanatorium in Saint-Rémy, einer kleinen Stadt unweit von Arles, wo er von Mai 1889 bis Mai 1890 lebte. Während dieser Zeit malte er mit großer Geschwindigkeit und produzierte ungefähr 150 Bilder. Darunter, und vielleicht ist es das bekannteste aller Van-Gogh-Gemälde, auch *Sternennacht* (1889; gegenüber).

Die Natur ist stürmisch und aufgewühlt, strotzt vor Energie, pulsiert vor Vitalität, während der Himmel wirbelt, brodelt und schwirrt.

Vincents Briefe an Theo machen deutlich, dass er seinen emotionalen Zustand mit der Wahl seiner Farben und Pinselführung verband. Wenn er mit sich selbst im Reinen war, verwendete er ruhige Farben und keinen dicken Impasto. Offensichtlich fühlte er sich nicht gut, als er *Sternennacht* malte. In dieser explosiven Landschaft ist alles in Bewegung. Er trug die Farbe mit einem Pinsel auf, damit es schneller ging, auch mit einem Spachtel und drückte sogar Farbe direkt aus der Tube – als ob er seine Ideen so schnell wie möglich auf die Leinwand bringen wollte.

Die *Sternennacht* scheint spontan zu sein, wie in fieberhafter Eile gemalt. Die Natur ist stürmisch und aufgewühlt, strotzt vor Energie, pulsiert vor Vitalität, während der Himmel wirbelt, brodelt und schwirrt. In Wirklichkeit war *Sternennacht* jedoch geplant. Er schrieb an Theo und erklärte, dass er alles »bis ins letzte Detail« durchdenkt und dann schnell eine Reihe von Leinwänden malt, wobei er manchmal bis weit in die Nacht hinein arbeitet und dabei sogar das Essen vergisst.

Chronisch ruhelos, zog Vincent nach Auvers, in der Nähe von Paris, wo sich der Homöopath Dr. Paul Gachet, selbst ein Amateurkünstler, um ihn kümmerte. Er wohnte in der Auberge Ravoux, wo er wie ein Mitglied der Familie Ravoux behandelt wurde. 1890 malte Vincent die *Kirche von Auvers* (Musée d'Orsay, Paris). Er trug die dicke Farbe mit Pinselstrichen auf, die den gotischen Formen folgten, fügte Kurven zu ihren Konturen hinzu und ließ leblose Objekte dadurch lebendig wirken.

Sein letztes Bild dürfte *Weizenfeld mit Krähen* (1890; umseitig) gewesen sein. Am 19. Juli 1890 schoss er sich in dem Weizenfeld, das er mehrmals gemalt hatte, in die Brust oder den Unterleib. Vincent starb eineinhalb Tage später in Theos Armen, im Alter von 37 Jahren. Er erfuhr zu Lebzeiten nie Ruhm. Noch trauriger ist, dass Theo nur sechs Monate nach Vincent starb. Nun sind sie Seite an Seite in Auvers begraben.

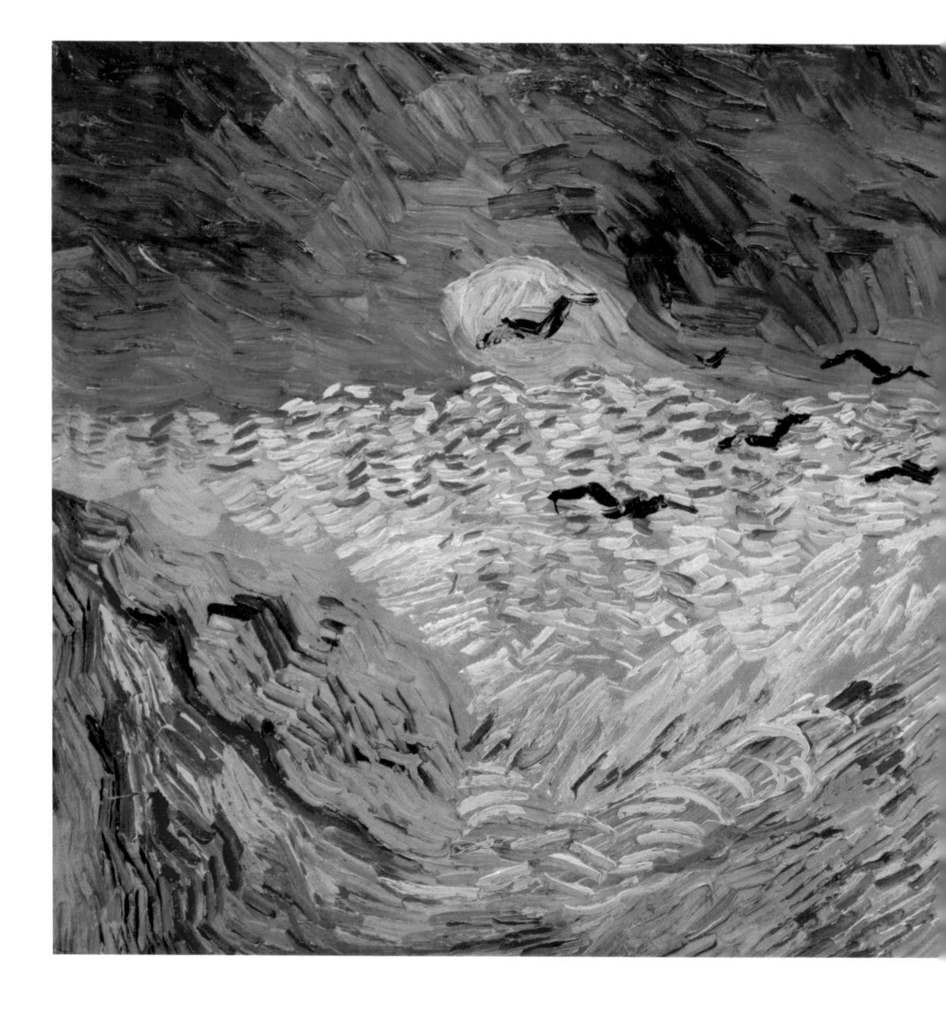

Vincent van Gogh
Weizenfeld mit Krähen,
1890
Öl auf Leinwand,
50,2 x 103 cm
Van Gogh Museum,
Amsterdam

Van Gogh setzte seinem Leben ein Ende, nachdem er sich wiederholt selbst verletzt und zuvor schon einen Selbstmordversuch unternommen hatte. Die jüngsten Annahmen, dass van Gogh von einem Teenager ermordet wurde oder sich versehentlich erschoss, erwiesen sich weitgehend als unglaubwürdig.

FRIDA KAHLO (1907–54)

Die faszinierende Malerin Frida Kahlo wurde in Coyoacán, Mexiko-Stadt, als Tochter einer mexikanischen Mutter und eines deutschstämmigen Vaters geboren. Ihre Bilder sind größtenteils autobiografisch und beziehen sich häufig auf ihre vielen körperlichen und emotionalen Probleme. Im Alter von sechs Jahren erkrankte sie an Kinderlähmung, die ihr rechtes Bein betraf. Ein Straßenbahnunfall im Alter von 18 Jahren beschädigte ihre Wirbelsäule, die inneren Organe und den rechten Fuß, sodass sie teilweise behindert war und unter chronischen Schmerzen litt. Ihr Äußeres war auffällig, vor allem durch ihre Augenbraue und den leichten Damenbart, und auch durch ihren Kleidungsstil zog sie Aufmerksamkeit auf sich. Sie war witzig, gesellig, aufgeschlossen und unprätentiös. Sie rauchte, trank, fluchte, sang unzüchtige Lieder und mochte schmutzige Witze. Sie hatte Talent, Ehrgeiz, Intelligenz und ein Gespür für das Dramatische. Sie heiratete den mexikanischen Maler Diego Rivera – zweimal. Keiner von beiden war treu, sie selbst hatte eine Affäre mit Leo Trotzki, Diego mit Fridas Schwester Cristina. Kurz vor ihrem Tod im Alter von 47 Jahren amputierten die Ärzte ihr rechtes Bein am Knie.

Frida Kahlo
Die zwei Fridas, 1939
Öl auf Leinwand,
171,9 x 171,9 cm
Museo de Arte Moderno,
Instituto Nacional de
Bellas Artes y Literatura,
Mexiko-Stadt

Vielleicht hat keine andere Künstlerin dem Betrachter jemals einen so vollständigen Zugang zu den vielen Schwierigkeiten ihres Lebens gegeben wie Kahlo. Hier zeigt sie die europäische (ihr Vater) und mexikanische (ihre Mutter) Hälfte ihrer Abstammung und die komplexe Beziehung zwischen ihnen.

Schmerzvolle Selbstporträts in Mexiko

Kahlo schuf 55 Selbstporträts, und die meisten ihrer anderen Gemälde beziehen sich direkt auf ihre Erfahrungen. Diese Gemälde präsentieren eine intime visuelle Autobiografie einer fesselnden Persönlichkeit und eines ungewöhnlich intensiven Lebens.

-

Das Herz der rechten Figur ist intakt, während das Herz der linken Figur aufgerissen ist.

-

Kahlos Selbstporträts dokumentieren gleichzeitig ihre körperlichen Merkmale und den Schmerz, den sie durchlebte. Unter ihren vielen Selbstporträts ist *Die zwei Fridas* (1939; gegenüber), gemalt kurz nach ihrer Scheidung von Diego Rivera, eine symbolische Darstellung ihres Leidens. Die beiden Fridas sitzen Seite an Seite und starren den Betrachter an. Das Doppelbild zeigt ihre Herkunft: Links trägt sie europäische viktorianische Kleidung – ein hochgeschlossenes Spitzenkleid. Rechts trägt sie farbenfrohe mexikanische Bauerntracht und hält ein winziges Porträt von Diego. Eine Arterie verläuft von Herz zu Herz – sie teilen das gleiche Blut und halten sich an den Händen. Das Herz der rechten Figur ist unversehrt, während das Herz der linken Figur aufgerissen ist.

Aufgrund von Komplikationen aus ihren Verletzungen nach dem Unfall verbrachte Kahlo einen Großteil ihres Lebens im Bett, entweder in einem Krankenhaus wegen einer Operation, häufig an der Wirbelsäule, oder sie war zu Hause , völlig unbeweglich, und erholte sich von einer Operation. Sie unterzog sich 30 bis 35 chirurgischen Eingriffen. Es gab 28 Gipskorsetts sowie andere Formen von Rückenstützen aus Leder und Metall, die in *The Broken Column* (1944; folgende Seite) zu sehen sind, in der ihre Wirbelsäule durch eine bröckelnde klassische ionische Säule ersetzt wird. Kahlo sagte:»Ich bin nicht krank ... Ich bin gebrochen ... aber ich bin glücklich, am Leben zu sein, solange ich malen kann ...«

Auf die Frage, warum sie sich so häufig selbst porträtierte, antwortete sie: »Weil ich ganz allein bin und weil ich das Motiv bin, das ich am besten kenne.« Der französische Schriftsteller und Begründer des

Surrealismus, André Breton, bezeichnete Kahlo als natürliche Surrealistin, aber Kahlo sagte, sie male ihre eigene Realität und nicht ihre Träume.

Fridas Mutter missbilligte Fridas Heirat mit Diego Rivera, dem zweimal geschiedenen Frauenhelden, der viel älter war – er war damals 42 und Frida 22 – und mit 1,85 m und etwa 136 Kilogramm viel größer als die zierliche Frida mit 1,60 m und 44,5 Kilogramm. Ihre Mutter beschrieb sie als eine Ehe zwischen einem Elefanten und einer Taube.

Gegenüber: Frida Kahlo
The Broken Column, 1944
Öl auf Masonit,
39,8 x 30,6 cm
Museo Dolores Olmedo,
Mexiko-Stadt

Die Schmerzen, die Kahlo Zeit ihres Lebens ertrug, resultierten aus der Kinderlähmung, die ein Bein betraf, den Schäden, die ihr Körper bei einem Straßenbahnunfall erlitt, und den vielen nachfolgenden Operationen und Korsetts, die ihre Wirbelsäule nicht reparieren konnten. Sie sagte: »Meine Malerei trägt die Botschaft des Schmerzes in sich.«

Sowohl Kahlo als auch Rivera hatten ein sprunghaftes Temperament und waren beide wiederholt untreu.
Aber er unterstützte ihre Malerei und lobte ihre Kunst. Mexiko verehrte Rivera, und seine Unterstützung für sie als Künstlerin bedeutete alles für Kahlo. In ihrem Gemälde *Diego und ich* (1949; unten) geht ihr Diego buchstäblich auf den Geist und Tränen fallen ihr aus den Augen, während ihr Haar sie zu erwürgen scheint.

In ihrer Kunst folgte Kahlo dem Rat Riveras und malte in ihrem ganz persönlichen Stil, anstatt der vorherrschenden Mode zu folgen. Die detaillierte dokumentarische Qualität ihrer Gemälde trägt zu ihrer Wirkung bei. Vielleicht haben die Beschreibungen der Kritiker, die ihren Stil als naiv oder Volkskunst bezeichnen, eine gewisse Berechtigung – aber es handelt sich um sehr anspruchsvolle naive Volkskunst, und dieser Effekt ist sicherlich beabsichtigt. Kahlos Selbstbewusstsein überlagert alles andere.

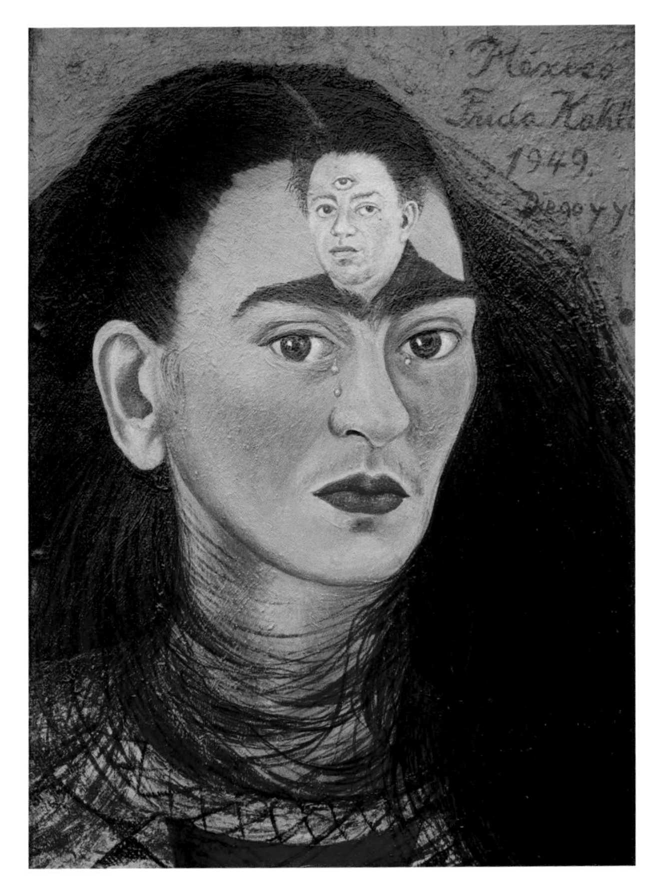

Frida Kahlo
Diego und ich, 1949
Öl auf Leinwand und Masonit, 29,5 x 22,4 cm
Privatsammlung

Die Hauptquelle für Kahlos emotionales Leiden war ihre Beziehung zu dem mexikanischen Maler Diego Rivera, mit dem sie zweimal verheiratet war. Kahlo sagte: »Es hat zwei große Unfälle in meinem Leben gegeben. Einer war die Straßenbahn und der andere war Diego. Diego war bei weitem der schlimmste.«

PABLO PICASSO (1881–1973)

Pablo Picasso wird aufgrund seines immensen Einflusses auf spätere Kunststile weithin als der bedeutendste Maler des 20. Jahrhunderts angesehen. Ständig auf der Suche nach neuen Ausdrucksmöglichkeiten, schuf er mehrere innovative Stile und wechselte seinen Stil fast ebenso oft, wie er während seiner 91 Jahre voller Vitalität, Energie und Produktivität seine Geliebten und Ehefrauen wechselte.

Ständige Innovation von Spanien bis Frankreich

Geboren in Málaga in Südspanien, erhielt Picasso eine konventionelle Kunstausbildung an der Königlichen Akademie in Madrid. Im Jahr 1900 zog er nach Paris und studierte dort den Impressionismus und Post-Impressionismus. Während Picassos früher Blauer Periode waren seine Gemälde buchstäblich blau in der Farbe und figurativ blau in der Stimmung, was sein mittelloses Leben widerspiegelt. In Gemälden wie *Die Tragödie* (1903; S. 59) und *The Old Guitarrist* (1903–04; gegenüber) sind die Körper ausgemergelt und kantig, die Linien grob und hart, die Wirkung starr und streng.

Als sich Picassos Leben verbesserte, wurden seine Farben heller und wärmer. Er ging allmählich in seine Rosa- oder Rosen-Periode über und malte mit kreidigen Rosa- und Terrakotta-Farben. Zunehmend mit ästhetischen Problemen befasst, malte Picasso 1907 *Les Demoiselles d'Avignon* (Museum of Modern Art, New York), in dem die Körper von fünf Frauen und der Hintergrund, gemalt in den für seine Rosa Periode typischen Farben, in kantige Scherben zerbrochen zu sein scheinen.

Pablo Picasso
The Old Guitarrist,
1903–04
Öl auf Holz,
122,9 x 82,6 cm
Art Institute of Chicago, Chicago

Picassos Blaue Periode stand im Zusammenhang mit dem Selbstmord seines Freundes, des Dichters und Malers Carles Casagemas, im Jahr 1901. Deprimiert und verarmt teilte Picasso mit dem Dichter Max Jacob ein Zimmer in Paris, in dem Picasso tagsüber schlief und nachts arbeitete, während Jacob nachts schlief und tagsüber arbeitete.

-

Ständig auf der Suche nach neuen Ausdrucksmöglichkeiten, schuf Picasso mehrere innovative Stile.

-

Les Demoiselles d'Avignon war ein Vorläufer des voll ausgebildeten Kubismus, der um 1908 in Paris auftauchte und von Picasso und anderen, insbesondere Georges Braque, entwickelt wurde. Die erste Stufe, der sogenannte Analytische Kubismus, beschäftigte sich mit der Erforschung von Kompositionsprinzipien und der Vereinfachung natürlicher Objekte zu geometrischen Formen, wie in Picassos *Girl with a Mandoline* (1910; S. 156). Die Formen werden in dünne, transparente Flächen zerlegt, die durch Linien und Winkel definiert, gekippt, nebeneinander gestellt und überlagert werden. Picasso gibt uns eine Reihe von fragmentarischen Ansichten, die verschiedene Aspekte der Form aus verschiedenen Blickwinkeln analysieren. Die Natur ist Picassos Aus-

Pablo Picasso
Girl with a Mandolin (Fanny Tellier), 1910
Öl auf Leinwand,
100,3 x 73,6 cm
Museum of Modern Art, New York

Der Analytische Kubismus wurde durch die Arbeit des französischen Post-Impressionisten Paul Cézanne beeinflusst, der sagte: »Behandle die Natur mithilfe des Zylinders, der Kugel und des Kegels, die alle in Perspektive gesetzt werden.« Der Kubismus sollte großen Einfluss auf spätere Stile haben.

gangspunkt, aber er bewegt sich so weit in Richtung Abstraktion, dass es einen Moment dauern kann, bis man die Figur findet. Kubistische Gemälde sind absichtlich fast monochrom, damit die Farbe nicht von dieser neuen Art der Analyse von Formen im Raum ablenkt.

Picassos nächste Phase war der Collage-Kubismus, repräsentiert durch sein 1912 entstandenes *Stillleben mit Stuhl* (Musée Picasso, Paris) aus Ölfarbe und Wachstuch auf Leinwand, das mit einem Seil gerahmt ist. Das Wort Collage kommt aus dem Französischen und bedeutet »Kleister« oder »Leim«, weil der Künstler verschiedene Materialien auf dem Bildträger anbringt (siehe S. 88, 90). Anstatt die natürlichen Formen in kleine Facetten und Flächen zu *zerlegen*, wie im Analytischen Kubismus, wird das Bild nun vom Künstler aufgebaut. Alle Formen befinden sich auf der Oberfläche und betonen die Zweidimensionalität der Bildebene.

Nach dem Collage-Kubismus ging Picasso mit anderen zum Synthetischen Kubismus über, der dritten Phase des Kubismus, repräsentiert durch Picassos *Drei Musikanten* (1921; unten). Frei zusammengesetzte flache geometrische Formen, dekorativer und farbiger als zuvor, bilden markante Muster. Clever und erfinderisch mit visuellen Wortspielen, zeigt dieses Gemälde drei Musiker und einen Hund. Obwohl es hier wenig Ähnlichkeit mit der Realität gibt, behält Picasso immer ein erkennbares Motiv bei. Jedes Objekt wird im Synthetischen Kubismus aus einem einzigen Blickwinkel dar-

Pablo Picasso
Drei Musikanten, 1921
Öl auf Leinwand
200,7 x 222,9 cm
Museum of Modern Art, New York

Der synthetische Kubismus war einer der vielen Stile Picassos. Diese Stile können sich überschneiden, da er in der Lage war, in mehr als einem Stil gleichzeitig zu arbeiten. Vielleicht ist dies analog dazu, wie er wiederholt Geliebte und Ehefrauen wechselte, er hatte auch mehrere gleichzeitig.

gestellt und nicht aus mehreren Blickwinkeln wie im Analytischen Kubismus.

Zur gleichen Zeit, als er im Stil des Synthetischen Kubismus malte, trat Picasso auch in seine Klassische Periode ein und arbeitete in einem naturalistischeren Stil mit Affinität zur klassischen griechischen Bildhauerei. Die Figuren hatten nun normale Proportionen und wurden schattiert, um dreidimensional zu wirken, wie zum Beispiel Picassos *Mutter mit Kind* von 1921 (Art Institute of Chicago, Chicago). Picasso blieb Zeit seines Lebens daran interessiert, traditionelle Themen zu malen.

Pablo Picasso
Guernica, 1937
Öl auf Leinwand,
3,49 x 7,77 m
Museo Nacional Centro de Arte Reina Sofía, Madrid

Durch die Größe des Bildes und die begrenzte Farbpalette konnte Picasso außerordentlich starke Emotionen vermitteln.

Picasso unterstützte die antifaschistische Seite des Spanischen Bürgerkriegs und kehrte nach Francos Sieg nicht mehr nach Spanien zurück. Entsprechend seinem Testament wurde Guernica erst nach Francos Tod nach Spanien gebracht. Picasso malte zerklüftete, unzusammenhängende, facettierte Formen in Kombination mit offener Mimik und Posen, um seine Empörung über diesen Krieg auszudrückn.

Zu den dramatischsten und eindringlichsten Antikriegsbildern, die je geschaffen wurden, gehört Picassos Guernica (unten), gemalt 1937 während des Spanischen Bürgerkriegs (1936–39), kurz nachdem deutsche Bomber Guernica, die Hauptstadt des Baskenlandes in Nordspanien, zerstört hatten. Durch die Größe des Bildes und die sehr begrenzte Farbpalette von nur Schwarz, Weiß und Grau war Picasso in der Lage, außerordentlich starke Emotionen zu vermitteln. Der zertrampelte Soldat in der unteren linken Ecke, der noch immer sein zerbrochenes Schwert hält, steht für die Männer, die bis zum Tod gekämpft haben. Über ihm befindet sich eine symbolische Pietà – eine Mutter, die das tote Kind in ihrem Schoß betrauert –, ein Hinweis auf Maria und Jesus. Die verzerrte, gebrochene, verdrehte Anatomie aller Figuren verstärkt die fesselnde Leidenschaft des Bildes.

ANDY WARHOL (1928–87)

So wie der Begriff Op Art eine Verkürzung von Optical Art ist, ist der Begriff Pop-Art eine Verkürzung von Popular Art. Andy Warhol ist der Inbegriff des Pop-Art-Künstlers, berühmt (oder berüchtigt) als Anführer einer neuen Kunstbewegung.

Er wurde als Andrew Warhola in Pittsburg, Pennsylvania, in einer Arbeiterfamilie geboren. Als guter Schüler machte er 1949 seinen Abschluss am Carnegie Institute of Technology (heute Carnegie Mellon University) mit einem Bachelor of Fine Arts in Pictorial Design. Er änderte seinen Namen in Warhol und zog nach New York City. Bald erschienen seine Illustrationen in der Zeitschrift *Glamour* für einen Artikel mit dem treffenden Titel »Success Is a Job in New York«. Warhol war talentiert, arbeitete ungewöhnlich hart und war als Werbegrafiker äußerst erfolgreich. Er kaufte sich ein Stadthaus in Manhattan, wo er mit seiner Mutter und einer großen Anzahl von Katzen (bis zu 25) lebte, die alle Sam hießen, bis auf eine.

King of American Pop Art

Das Bild, das am häufigsten mit Warhol in Verbindung gebracht wird, ist das der Campbell-Suppendosen (gegenüber). Dieses Beispiel stammt aus dem Jahr 1962. Pop-Art porträtiert alltägliche Gebrauchsgegenstände wie Suppendosen, Schachteln mit Brillo-Reinigungspads und Coca-Cola-Flaschen, die zuvor nicht als geeignetes Motiv für Künstler galten. Warhol stellt das Vertraute unpersönlich und unkommentiert dar: Pop-Art widersetzt sich nicht und kritisiert nicht. Stattdessen ermutigt die Pop-Art den Betrachter, gewöhnliche Dinge mit neuen Augen zu sehen.

Einige dieser Bilder hatten für Warhol einen sehr persönlichen Bezug. Über Campbell's Suppe sagte er: »Ich habe sie immer getrunken. Ich habe jeden Tag das gleiche gegessen, zwanzig Jahre lang. Ich schätze, immer wieder dasselbe.« Entsprechend schuf er in seiner Kunst das gleiche Bild »immer und immer wieder«. Und tatsächlich hatten auch andere kommerzielle Produkte für Warhol eine tiefere Bedeutung. Er betrachtete Coca-Cola als sozialen Gleichmacher, weil es etwas ist, das von Menschen aller Schichten geteilt wird, unabhängig von ihrem Status oder Reichtum, sagte er, vom Präsidenten über Liz Taylor bis hin zum Penner an der Ecke.

Prominente faszinierten Warhol von Kindheit an. Er strebte aktiv nach persönlichem Ruhm, nicht nur nach finanziellem Erfolg. Sein vielleicht am häufigsten wiederholtes Zitat lautet: »In der Zukunft wird jeder für 15 Minuten weltberühmt sein.« Neben der Suppendosenserie begann er 1962 mit einer Serie von Porträts von Filmstars. Das *Marilyn-Diptychon* (S. 162), das kurz nach ihrem Tod entstand, ist eines von vielen Werken, die er auf der Grundlage von Fotografien der Schauspielerin anfertigte. Als Elizabeth Taylor 1963 krank wurde, nahm Warhol sie in seinen Fokus. Ähnlich porträtierte Warhol ab 1963 Elvis Presley in mehreren Bildern.

Andy Warhol
Campbell's Soup Cans, 1962
Acryl- mit Metallic-Emaille-Farbe auf Leinwand, Gesamtinstallation
2,46 x 4,14 m
Museum of Modern Art, New York

Warhol erhebt einen gewöhnlichen Gebrauchsgegenstand auf die Ebene der Kunst und lädt uns damit ein, die Kunst im Gewöhnlichen zu erkennen. Er sagte: »Ich denke nicht, dass Kunst nur für wenige Auserwählte sein sollte«, erklärte er, »sie sollte für die Masse des amerikanischen Volkes sein.«

Besonders angezogen von Bildern der Tragödie, war Jackie Kennedy nach der Ermordung ihres Mannes, Präsident John F. Kennedy, im Jahr 1963 das Motiv mehrerer Drucke.

-

Warhol arbeitete nach Fotografien und verwendete Siebdruck, um mehrere, fast identische Bilder zu produzieren.

-

Warhols frühe Pop-Art-Bilder waren handgemalt, aber bald zeigten immer weniger seiner Arbeiten die physische Hand des Künstlers. Stattdessen arbeitete er nach Fotografien und verwendete Siebdruck, um mehrere, nahezu identische Bilder zu produzieren. Warhol brach die traditionelle, lange bestehende Barriere zwischen bildender Kunst und Werbung weiter auf, indem er Porträts berühmter Persönlichkeiten eher mit kommerziellen als mit traditionellen Techniken der bildenden Kunst produzierte.

Warhol war groß und sehr schlank, mit einem blassen Teint, den er noch weißer machte, indem er Make-up auftrug und zeitweise seine Augenbrauen weiß färbte. Seine natürliche Haarfarbe war braun, aber er bekam schon in jungen Jahren eine Glatze und trug Perücken – was er nicht zugeben wollte. Er ließ seine Perücken sogar von einem Friseur schneiden; einen Monat später setzte er eine andere, längere Perücke auf und ging wieder zum Friseur, um sie nachschneiden zu lassen. Menschen, die Warhol kannten, be-

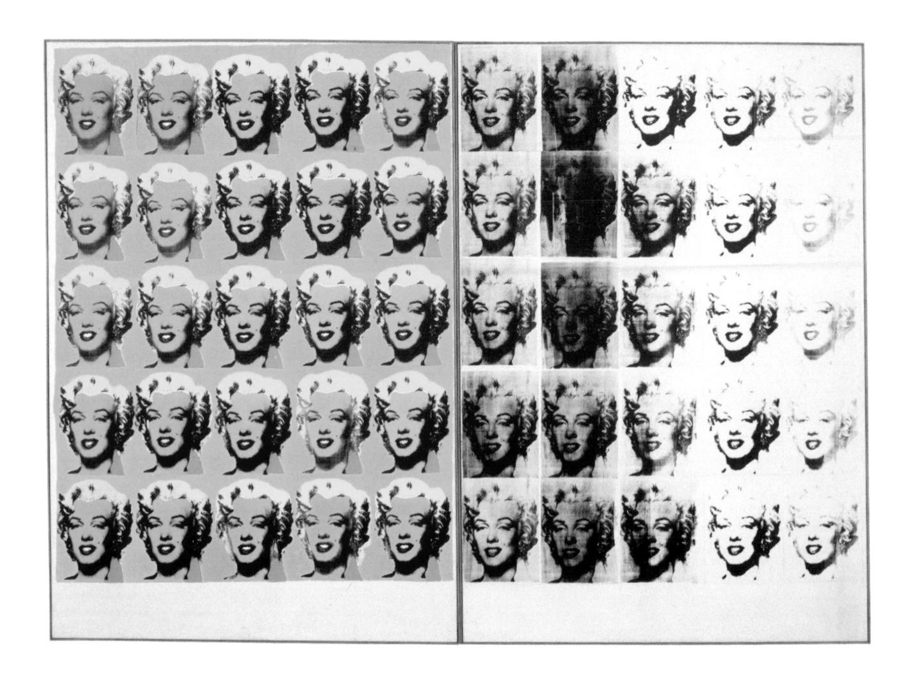

schrieben ihn als einen Workaholic mit außergewöhnlicher Energie. Sein Studio wurde wegen der Menge der dort produzierten Arbeiten »The Factory« genannt. Die Factory war auch der Ort wilder Partys und illegalen Drogenkonsums und der Treffpunkt für die Intelligenz, die Reichen und die Hollywood-Berühmtheiten sowie für Drag Queens und Menschen von der Straße.

Andy Warhol
Marilyn-Diptychon, 1962
Siebdruckfarbe und Acryl auf 2 Leinwänden
205,4 x 289,6 cm
Tate Collection, Großbritannien

Zu Warhols vielfältigen Interessen gehörte die Faszination für Berühmtheiten – und der Wunsch, selbst eine zu werden. Er war in vielen verschiedenen Projekten aktiv, darunter Musik, Film, Fernsehen und sogar Zeitschriften- und Buchpublikationen.

Alles änderte sich am 3. Juni 1968, als Valerie Solanas, radikale Feministin und Autorin von Off-Colour-Stücken, The Factory betrat und auf Warhol schoss. Die Kugel durchschlug beide Lungenflügel, seine Milz, den Magen, die Leber und die Speiseröhre. Er überlebte nur knapp, seine Gesundheit war dauerhaft beeinträchtigt.

Warhol erhielt 1984 den Auftrag, etwas zu schaffen, das auf Leonardo da Vincis berühmtem *Letzten Abendmahl* (S. 134–35) basiert, um es in einer Kunstgalerie gegenüber dem Kloster auszustellen, in dem sich Leonardos Wandbild befindet. Warhol war in der Tat tief religiös. Er kombinierte Leonardos Meisterwerk mit Bildern aus der populären kommerziellen Werbung und verschmolz so das Sakrale mit dem Profanen (S. 164–65). Respektlos? Vielleicht. Relevant für das zeitgenössische Leben? Auf jeden Fall. Die Ausstellung von Warhols *Abendmahl*-Serie wurde im Januar 1987 eröffnet. Es sollte sein letztes großes Projekt werden.

Im Februar 1987 unterzog er sich der Gallenblasenoperation, die er wegen seiner Angst vor Ärzten und Krankenhäusern aufgeschoben hatte. Obwohl die Operation reibungslos verlief, starb er am nächsten Tag im Alter von 58 Jahren im New Yorker Krankenhaus in Manhattan an einer Herzrhythmusstörung. Seine private Krankenschwester war eingeschlafen, während er intravenös Flüssigkeit erhielt, sodass er überhydriert war und aufgrund der Schusswunde nicht mehr normal atmen konnte.

Warhols Werk ruft eine Reihe von Reaktionen hervor, positive und negative. Auch wenn einige Kritiker seinem Werk gegenüber feindselig bleiben, besteht allgemeine Einigkeit darüber, dass er den Geist der amerikanischen Kultur seiner Zeit eingefangen hat.

WICHTIGE KÜNSTLER UND IDEEN

Leonardo da Vinci (1452–1519):

- Wissenschaft und Kunst vereinen sich in der italienischen Renaissance
- Studium der natürlichen Welt aus erster Hand
- Technische Neuerungen
- Chiaroscuro und Sfumato

Rembrandt (1606–69):

- Goldenes Zeitalter der Malerei in Holland
- Popularität der Porträtmalerei
- Selbstporträts
- Rembrandts persönlicher und beruflicher Aufstieg und Fall

Vincent van Gogh (1853–90):

- Post-Impressionismus in Frankreich
- Kunst und emotionale Ängste
- Impasto und lebhafte unnatürliche Farbe
- Beziehung zu seinem Bruder Theo

Frida Kahlo (1907–54):

- Malerei als visuelles Tagebuch in Mexiko
- Kinderlähmung, Straßenbahnunfall und Operationen
- Eheschließungen mit Diego Rivera

Pablo Picasso (1881–1973):

- Von Spanien nach Frankreich
- Die Blaue Periode und die Rosa oder Rosen-Periode
- Kubismus: analytisch, Collage und synthetisch
- Klassische Periode

Andy Warhol (1928–87):

- Pop-Art (Populäre Kunst) in Amerika
- Das Interesse am Gewöhnlichen finden
- Bildende Kunst und kommerzielle Kunst
- »The Factory« als kreatives Zentrum

Andy Warhol
The Last Supper, 1986
Siebdruck und
farbige Collage auf
handgeschöpftem Papier
59,7 x 80,6 cm
The Andy Warhol
Museum, Pittsburgh

Warhol hielt sein öffentliches und privates Leben ziemlich getrennt. Seine öffentliche Persona beinhaltete einen extremen Lebensstil, doch er war auch religiös, spendete Geld an Menschen in Not, lebte jahrelang bei seiner Mutter und hielt viele (sehr viele) Katzen sowie Hunde als Haustiere.

GLOSSAR

Acrylfarbe: siehe **Synthetische Farbe**.

Asymmetrie: siehe **Symmetrie**.

Bilaterale Symmetrie: siehe **Symmetrie**.

Bildebene: eine flache Oberfläche wie Papier, Leinwand oder eine Wand, auf die ein Bild gemalt oder gezeichnet wird.

Buchmalerei: Manuskripte sind handgeschriebene Bücher; die Illustrationen werden auch (vor allem, wenn sie Gold enthalten) als Illuminationen bezeichnet.

Buntglas: eine Technik, die vor allem bei der Gestaltung mittelalterlicher Kirchenfenster benutzt wurde. Flüssiges Glas ist von Natur aus grünlich, wird aber gelblich oder rötlich, wenn es länger gekocht wird. Durch Zusatz von Metalloxidpulvern lassen sich verschiedene Farben erzeugen.

Champlevé: siehe **Emaille**.

Chiaroscuro: aus der Kombination der italienischen Wörter für »hell« und »dunkel« oder »deutlich« und »undeutlich« abgeleiteter Begriff, der auf einen Malstil verweist, bei dem der Einsatz von Licht und Schatten eine besondere Rolle spielen.

Cloisonné: siehe **Emaille**.

Divisionismus: siehe **Pointillismus**.

Ei-Tempera: eine Maltechnik, die eine Emulsion aus Eigelb und Wasser als Bindemittel nutzt und ihren Höhepunkt im Mittelalter in Europa hatte.

Einheitlichkeit: eine wünschenswerte Eigenschaft in Kunstwerken, die alle Teile verbunden und kohäsiv erscheinen lässt. Kann durch Wiederholung von Formen, Pinselstrichen, Texturen Farben und anderen Elementen erreicht werden.

Emaille: eine künstlerische Technik, bei der farbiges Glaspulver oder -paste auf Metall aufgebracht wird. Die zwei Hauptarten sind **Cloisonné** auf Gold, bei der die Farben durch kleine erhöhte Ränder oder Zellen getrennt werden, und **Champlevé**, das ein vergoldetes Basismetall nutzt, in das Vertiefungen für die Farbe geritzt werden. In beiden Fällen wird das Objekt bei hohen Temperaturen gebrannt, sodass das Pulver verglast und leuchtende Farben erzeugt.

Enkaustik: eine Maltechnik, die heißes Wachs als Bindemittel verwendet.

Farbton: bezeichnet die eigentliche Farbe, wie Rot, Orange oder Lila.

Farbe: alle Arten von Farbe in Form gemahlener Teilchen aus farbigem Material und Bindemittel, also Kleber, der die Pigmentteilchen zusammenhält und sie auf einer Oberfläche haften lässt.

Fortlaufende Erzählung: ein visuelles Hilfsmittel zum Erzählen einer Geschichte, die mehrere separate Ereignisse umfasst. Der Betrachter weiß, dass diese Ereignisse nacheinander aufgetreten sind, der Künstler stellt sie dennoch gleichzeitig dar, ohne sie in verschiedene Bilder aufzuteilen.

Fresko: Maltechnik für Wandgemälde. Die zwei Grundtechniken sind ***buon fresco*** (auch ***fresco buono***), gemalt auf feuchten Putz, und ***fresco secco***, gemalt auf trockenen Putz.

Gebrochene Farbe: eine von den Impressionisten eingeführte Maltechnik, bei der jede Farbe in ihre Teilfarben zerlegt wird. Wenn ein Bereich also orange aussehen soll, werden gelbe und rote Flecken aufgebracht, die sich im Auge des Betrachters zu orange »vermischen«.

Gesso: dicke weiße Farbe, die auf Leinwand, Holztafeln oder Skulpturen aufgebracht wird, um die Oberfläche für das Bemalen vorzubereiten.

Gouache: siehe **Wasserfarbe und Gouache**.

Gravüre: siehe **Tiefdrucktechniken**.

Hervortretende und zurückweichende Farben: siehe **Warme und kalte Farben**.

Hohlbeitel: ein Schneidwerkzeug, das meist aus einem Holzgriff und einem Metallschaft besteht, der in einer U- oder V-förmigen Spitze endet und zum Entfernen kleiner Stücke Holz oder Metall dient, die für den Druck bearbeitet werden.

Holzschnitt: eine Technik zum Drucken auf Papier. Der Drucker schneidet den Entwurf in einen Holzblock, wobei er mit einem Beitel, Holzmeißel oder Messer die Bereiche entfernt, die nicht gedruckt werden sollen. Auf das verbleibende Relief wird die Tinte gerollt. Für einen **Holzschnitt** wird der Block mit der Faser, für einen **Holzstich** dagegen quer zur Faser geschnitten, sodass das Werkzeug in alle Richtungen den gleichen Widerstand erfährt.

Ikonografie: die Sprache der Symbole, eingesetzt, um Informationen zu vermitteln, ohne Wörter zu schreiben; oft in der religiösen Kunst zu finden.

Impasto: dicke Farbe, die auf eine Oberfläche aufgebracht wird.

Intensität oder **Sättigung**: beschreibt, wie lebhaft eine Farbe ist; das höchste Maß ist reine Farbe. Um die Intensität zu senken, fügen Sie die Komplementärfarbe hinzu.

Kaltnadelradierung: siehe **Tiefdrucktechniken**.

Kasein: Bindemittel aus getrockneten Quarkbrocken; wird zum Malen auf trockenem Gipsputz verwendet.

Kinetische Skulptur: Skulptur, die ihre Wirkung aufgrund von Bewegung erzielt, wie Alexander Calders Mobiles.

Komplementärfarben: Farbpaare, die einander auf dem normalen Farbrad gegenüberstehen und bei denen jedes Paar aus einer Primär- und einer Sekundärfarbe besteht. Daher Gelb und Lila, Rot und Grün, Blau und Orange.

Kontrapost: Aus dem Italienischen für »Gegensatz«; der Begriff für eine Pose, die im 5. Jahrhundert v. Chr. in Griechenland eingeführt wurde und bei der die Figur mit dem Gewicht auf einem Bein ruht, wobei eine Hüfte und die entgegengesetzte Schulter angehoben sind und die Wirbelsäule eine leichte S-Kurve beschreibt.

Lasur: eine dünne, transparente, glasartige Beschichtung.

Leinwand: schwerer Leinenstoff, der aus dem faserigen Gemeinen Lein (auch: Flachs) hergestellt wird und erstmals Anfang des 16. Jahrhunderts in Italien zum Bemalen mit Ölfarben verwendet wurde.

Auch das Leinöl in den Ölfarben stammt von dieser Pflanze.

Linearperspektive: ein Mittel zum Erzeugen der Illusion eines dreidimensionalen Raums auf einer zweidimensionalen **Bildebene**. Linien, die aussehen sollen, als würden sie in den Raum zurückweichen, laufen in einem oder mehreren Fluchtpunkten auf der Horizontlinie zusammen.

Lithografie: eine Technik zum Drucken auf Papier, bei der die Linien mit einer fettigen Substanz auf einen glatten Kalkstein gezeichnet werden. Die Behandlung der Steinfläche mit einer Mischung aus milder Säure und Gummi arabicum führt zu einer chemischen Änderung der nicht vom Fett geschützten Bereiche. Ölbasierte Tinte, die auf den Stein gerollt wird, haftet nur auf den fettigen Bereichen.

Luftperspektive: eine Maltechnik, die eine Illusion von Tiefe erreicht, indem sie das atmosphärische Phänomen nachahmt, das entfernte Objekte weniger deutlich und mit weniger Farbigkeit erscheinen lässt als nahegelegene Objekte.

Meisterstück: ein Kunstwerk, das außerordentliches Können beweist. Der Begriff stammt aus der Künstlerausbildung im Mittelalter und der Renaissance, bei der ein Schüler seine Fähigkeiten mit einem Meisterstück demonstrieren musste, bevor er selbst Meister werden und Schüler annehmen durfte.

Mischtechnik: eine Maltechnik aus dem 15. Jahrhundert als Übergang zwischen **Ei-Tempera** und **Ölfarbe**, bei der erst mit Ei-Tempera und darüber mit Ölfarbe gemalt wird, was die Vorteile beider Techniken ausnutzt. Da das eine wasser- und das andere ölbasiert ist, vermischen sich die Schichten nicht.

Mosaik: eine dem **Fresko** vergleichbare Technik, doch statt auf feuchten Putz zu malen, werden kleine Würfel aus farbigem Material (**Tesserae** vom griechischen Wort für »vier«, wegen der vier sichtbaren Ecken) in den feuchten Putz gedrückt. Tesserae können auch unregelmäßige Formen haben.

Narrative Konventionen: von Künstlern verwendete Mittel, um Bedeutung visuell zu transportieren, darunter nonverbale Bilder mit allgemein anerkannten Bedeutungen.

Ölmalerei: eine Maltechnik, die pflanzliches Öl (meist Leinöl) als Bindemittel nutzt. Wird viel Öl mit wenig Pigment gemischt, erhält man eine dünne **Lasur**; wenig Öl, gemischt mit viel Pigment ergibt ein dickes **Impasto**.

Orthogonale Linien: die diagonalen Linien in einer Zeichnung mit Linearperspektive, die in einem imaginierten Fluchtpunkt zu verschwinden scheinen.

Pergament: sorgfältig verarbeitete Tierhaut zum Schreiben und Illustrieren von Manuskripten. Pergament ist oft aus Kuhhaut, während das dünnere und feinere **Vellum** aus Kälberhaut ist.

Pointillismus: eine vom französischen Post-Impressionisten Georges Seurat entwickelte Maltechnik, bei der jede Farbe in ihre Bestandteile zerlegt und dann in Form kleiner Punkte aufgebracht wird. Auch als **Divisionismus** bezeichnet.

Predella: kleine Platten, die unter der Hauptplatte eines Altarbildes befestigt sind, meist mit Szenen zum gleichen Thema wie auf dem Hauptbild bemalt.

Primärfarben: die subtraktiven (oder Pigment) Primärfarben sind Gelb, Blau und Rot, mit denen sich alle anderen Farben bis auf Schwarz oder Weiß erzeugen lassen. Die additiven (oder Licht) Primärfarben sind Grün, Blau und Rot, sie werden bei Film und digitalen Formaten verwendet.

Proportion: die Beziehung zwischen der Größe der Elemente in einem Werk. Manche Proportionen wirken für das Auge angenehmer als andere. Künstler und Architekten nutzen seit Langem mathematische Verhältnisse, um gefällige Proportion z. B. für den menschlichen Körper und Gebäude zu schaffen.

Radierung: siehe **Tiefdrucktechniken**.

Reliefskulptur: Skulptur, in der dreidimensionale Formen von einem Hintergrund projiziert werden, dessen Teil sie sind. Je nach Grad der Projektion reicht ein Relief von Hochrelief bis Flachrelief (auch Basrelief).

Sättigung: siehe **Intensität**.

Schraffur: eine Zeichentechnik, bei der eine Reihe enger paralleler Linien eine Form bilden. Bei der **Kreuzschraffur** überkreuzen sich die Linien zu einem Raster.

Sekundärfarben: sind Grün, Lila und Orange, die jeweils durch Mischen zweier **Primärfarben** entstehen.

Serigrafie (Siebdruck): eine Technik zum Drucken auf Papier, bei der feiner Seidenstoff über einen Holzrahmen gespannt wird und eine Schablone die Bereiche blockiert, die nicht gedruckt werden sollen. Dicke Tinte, mit einem Rakel über den Stoff gezogen, durchdringt diesen und druckt auf das darunterliegende Papier. Heute werden synthetische Stoffe statt Seide benutzt.

Sfumato: ein vom italienischen Wort für »Rauch« abgeleiteter Begriff, der einen Malstil bezeichnet, bei dem die Umrisse weich in den Hintergrund übergehen, wodurch eine Art Dunst erzeugt wird, der die umgebende Atmosphäre andeutet.

Stichel: ein Schneidewerkzeug, das aus einem Holzgriff und einem in einer scharfen Spitze endenden Metalldorn besteht und für Radierungen verwendet wird.

Symmetrie: teilt eine Linie durch das Zentrum einer Komposition diese in zwei identische Spiegelbilder, erhält man perfekte **bilaterale Symmetrie**. Sind die zwei Seiten einer Komposition ähnlich, aber nicht völlig identisch, handelt es sich um **leichte bilaterale Symmetrie**. Bei zwei völlig verschiedenen Seiten einer Komposition liegt **Asymmetrie** vor (»ohne Symmetrie«).

Synthetische Farbe (Acryl-, Plastikfarbe): hier wird Pigment in einer Acrylpolymeremulsion verteilt. Mit den sehr vielseitigen synthetischen Farben lässt sich eine Vielzahl an Effekten erzielen. Feuchte synthetische Farben lösen sich in Wasser.

Tempera: eine Maltechnik, die eine Mischung aus erdfarbigen Pigmenten, einem Bindemittel pflanzlichen oder tierischen Ursprungs und Wasser benutzt und auf trockenen Putz ausgeführt wird.

Tenebrismus: von *tenebroso*, italienisch für »dunkel«, bezieht sich auf einen Malstil, bei dem starkes Licht das Zentrum des Interesses verstärkt, Wichtiges hervorhebt und Unwichtiges in den Schatten versteckt. Wird ***Chiaroscuro*** zum Äußersten getrieben, wird es zum **Tenebrismus**.

Terrakotta: italienisch für »gekochte Erde«, ein natürlicher Ton für Skulpturen und Töpferwaren, meist orange-braun.

Tesserae: siehe **Mosaik**.

Tiefdrucktechniken: zum Drucken auf Papier gebraucht. Bei allen Tiefdrucktechniken kommt die Tinte in Vertiefungen in einer Metallplatte. Für eine **Gravüre** (z. B. einen Kupferstich) werden mit einem Meißel oder Stichel Einschnitte in der Platte vorgenommen. Für eine **Kaltnadelradierung** schieben Sie ein spitzes Werkzeug über die Platte, ohne Metall zu entfernen. Stattdessen wird auf beiden Seiten der Linie ein Grat aufgeworfen. Um eine **Radierung** herzustellen, bedecken Sie die Oberfläche der Platte mit einer säurebeständigen, wachsartigen Schicht und kratzen Linien in diese; in einem milden Säurebad werden die herausgekratzten Linien geätzt. Weitere Tiefdrucktechniken sind **Aquatinta** und **Mezzotinto**, mit denen sich Grauschattierungen erreichen lassen.

Tonwert einer Farbe: bezeichnet, wie hell oder dunkel eine Farbe ist. Um den Tonwert zu erhöhen, fügen Sie Weiß hinzu. Dies ergibt eine Tönung oder Pastell; zum Verringern nutzen Sie Schwarz.

Vellum: siehe **Pergament**.

Visuelle Kraft: ein Mittel, um in einer Komposition Gleichgewicht zu erzielen. Es beruht auf der Tatsache, dass manche Dinge eher und länger die visuelle Aufmerksamkeit wecken als andere. Große, leuchtend gefärbte, deutlich texturierte und scheinbar bewegte Formen üben eine größere visuelle Kraft aus als solche, die klein, matt, undeutlich texturiert und statisch sind. Auch die Mitte einer Komposition übt Kraft aus, weil wir es gewohnt sind, unsere Aufmerksamkeit auf das physische Zentrum einer Komposition zu lenken.

Wachsausschmelzverfahren: eine auch als verlorene Form bezeichnete Methode zum Metallguss. Eine Wachsschicht bedeckt das Objekt und eine Gussform schließt das Ganze ein. Beim Erhitzen schmilzt das Wachs und geht »verloren« und der Hohlraum kann mit flüssigem Metall gefüllt werden.

Warme und kalte Farben (hervortretende und zurückweichende Farben): warme Farben wie Rot und Orange scheinen aus einem Gemälde hervorzutreten, während kalte Farben wie Grün und Blau in die Tiefe zurückzuweichen scheinen.

Wasserfarbe und Gouache: Malmedien, die aus Pigmenten bestehen, kombiniert mit Wasser, einem Bindemittel wie Gummi arabicum und Zutaten wie Glyzerin und/oder Honig zum Verbessern von Konsistenz und Farbe sowie Konservierungsstoffen. **Wasserfarbe** ist dünn und durchscheinend, während die größeren Partikel und der höhere Anteil an Pigmenten **Gouache** dicker und deckender machen.

LITERATUREMPFEHLUNGEN

Adamson, Glenn und Julia Bryan-Wilson, *Art in the Making: Artists and their Materials from the Studio to Crowdsourcing* (Thames & Hudson, London und New York, 2016)

Benton, Janetta Rebold und Robert DiYanni, *Arts and Culture: An Introduction to the Humanities* (Pearson, Upper Saddle River, 4th edn, 2012)

Benton, Janetta Rebold und Robert DiYanni, *Handbook for the Humanities* (Pearson, Upper Saddle River, 2014)

Brown, Matt, *Everything You Know About Art Is Wrong* (Batsford, London, 2017)

Dickerson, Madelynn, *The Handy Art History Answer Book* (Visible Ink Press, Detroit, 2013)

Goldwater, Robert und Marco Treves (Hrsg.), *Artists on Art from the XIV to the XX Century* (Pantheon Books, New York, 3rd edn, 1974)

Hodge, Susie, *Eine kurze Geschichte der Kunst* (Laurence King Verlag, 2018)

Hollein, Max (Vorwort), *Art = Discovering Infinite Connections in Art History* (Metropolitan Museum of Art, New York, und Phaidon Press, London, 2020)

Kilinski, Karl, *Greek Myth and Western Art: The Presence of the Past* (Cambridge University Press, Cambridge, 2012)

King, Ross (Vorwort), *Artists: Their Lives and Works* (Dorling Kindersley, London und New York, 2017)

Livingstone, Margaret, *Vision and Art: The Biology of Seeing* (Harry N. Abrams, New York, 2014)

Mayer, Ralph, *The Artist's Handbook of Materials and Techniques* (Erstveröff. 1940; Viking Press, New York, 5th edn, 1991)

Noey, Christopher und Thomas P. Campbell, *The Artist Project: What Artists See When They Look at Art* (Metropolitan Museum of Art, New York, und Phaidon Press, London, 2017)

Obrist, Hans Ulrich, *Lives of the Artists, Lives of the Architects* (Penguin, London, 2016)

Rideal, Liz, *How to Read Art: A Crash Course in Understanding and Interpreting Painting* (Bloomsbury, London, 2014 und Universel, New York, 2015)

Roberts, Helene E. (Hrsg.), *Encyclopedia of Comparative Iconography: Themes Depicted in Works of Art* (Routledge, Abingdon, 1998)

Schlam, Carolyn Dobkin, *The Joy of Art: How to Look At, Appreciate, and Talk about Art* (Allworth Press, New York, 2020)

Vasari, Giorgio, *Lebensläufe der berühmtesten Maler, Bildhauer und Architekten* (Manesse Bibliothek, 2020)

Wilson, Matt, *Symbols in Art* (Thames & Hudson, London und New York, 2020)

Woodford, Susan, *Kunst verstehen* (Midas Verlag, Zürich, 2018)

INDEX

Illustrationen sind *kursiv*.

abstrakte Kunst 34, 107, 122, 124–5, *125*
Acrylfarbe 78
Adam and Eve Reproached by God (Bronzerelief) 111, *111*
af Klint, *siehe* Klint
Akademien, Kunst 24–6

Banksy 116
Girl with Balloon 15–18, *17*
Bernini, Gianlorenzo 53
David 52–3, *53*
Bindemittel 73–4
Book of Kells 73, *74*
Bosch, Hieronymus: *Der Garten der Lüste* 116, *116*
Botero, Fernando 28
Stehende Frau 28, *29*
Botticelli, Sandro:
Die Geburt der Venus 40
Bouts, Dieric, der Ältere:
Abendmahl 108, *108*, 109
Boys' Club Federation 67
Brâncuşi, Constantin 47
Der Kuss 60, *61*
Der Vogel im Raum 47, *47*
Braque, Georges 154
Breton, André 151
Broederlam, Melchior 76
Mariä Verkündigung und Heimsuchung 76
Brüder von Limburg: *Les Très Riches Heures* 104
Bruegel, Pieter, der Ältere 10, *11*
Die Kinderspiele *11*, 104
Buchmalerei 73–4, *74*
Buntglas 86, 88

Calder, Alexander 97
Untitled *96*, 97
Carman, Bliss: *The Making of Personality* 30
Carracci-Familie 24–5
Cellini, Benvenuto 23, 24
Neptun und Erde *4*, *22*, 22–3
Cézanne, Paul 107
Chagall, Marc 99, 100
Chartres, Kathedrale von: Buntglasfenster 86, *87*
Chiaroscuro 132, 138
Claudel, Camille 34, 63
La Valse (Der Walzer) *63*
Cole, Thomas 52
The Oxbow 52, *52*, 107
Collage 88, 90

Daguerre, Louis 88
Dalí, Salvador 56
Das Abendmahl 56–7, *56–7*
Dalton, John 40
Daumier, Honoré 12
David, Jacques-Louis 118, 119
Der Tod des Marat 103, 118, *119*, 120
Der Tod des Sokrates 103, 118, *118*
dekorative Kunst 85
Dharmapala ... (tibetisch) 90, *91*
Diallo, Delphine 15
Hybrid *8*, *14*, 15
Dircx, Geertje 142
Divisionismus *siehe* Pointillismus
Drachen 114–15
Drachen-Robe (Qing) *114*
Drucke 80
Relieftechniken 80
Tiefdrucktechniken 80–81, 83
Duccio di Buoninsegna
Christi Geburt 74–5, *75*
Maestà *21*, 21–2
Dürer, Albrecht 139

Eiklar 73, 74
Einheitlichkeit (der Komposition) 57–8
Ei-Tempera, 64, 70, 74–5, 76, 77, 135
Emaille 85
Champlevé 85, 86
Cloisonné 85–6
glasartige 86, 88
Emotion in der Kunst 31–2, 38, 58
Enkaustik 68, 69
fortlaufende108, 110–11
Euphronios und Euxitheos: *Tod des Sarpedon* 23
Eyck, Jan van: *Arnolfini-Hochzeit* 18, *19*

Factory, The 162
Fairey, Shepard: *Obama Hope* 104, *105*
Farbe(n) 38–40
Intensität 40
kalte 40
Komplementär 38–9
Primär 38
psychologische Effekte 58
Sättigung 40
Sekundär 38
und Bedeutung 58
versus Linie 42–3
warme 40
Farbenblindheit 40
Farbrad *38*, 38–9
Farbtöne 40
Flavin, Dan: *Untitled (in honor of Harold Joachim) 3* 50, *50*, 54
Fluchtpunkt 108, 109
Fotografie 88
Frankenthaler, Helen
Grey Fireworks 66, 78, *78*
Fresken 69–71

Gachet, Dr. Paul 147
Gauguin, Paul 145
Genremalerei 104
Gérôme, Jean-Léon
Cupid und Psyche 102
Pygmalion und Galatea *2*, 102, *120*, 120–21
Giacometti, Alberto 28
Frau von Venedig III 28, *29*, 101
Giotto di Bondone 55
Jesu Einzug in Jerusalem 54, *55*, 139
Gleichgewicht (der Komposition) 54
Gogh, Theo van 144, 145, 147
Gogh, Vincent van 132, 144–5, 147
Das Nachtcafé 144
Das Schlafzimmer 144, *145*
Die Sternennacht 76, *146*, 147
Kartoffelesser 144
Sonnenblumen 144
Weizenfeld mit Krähen 147, *148–9*
Goldener Schnitt 56
Gorky, Arshile 35
The Liver Is the Cock's Comb 34, *35*
Gouache-Farbe 78–9
Goya, Francisco 81
Und es gibt kein Entrinnen 81, *81*, 104
»Graffiti-Kunst« 15
Gravüre 83
Grisaille 86
Größe, relative 108, 109–10
Grünewald, Matthias: *Isenheimer Altar* *31*, 31–2
Gummi arabicum 73
Guo Xi 107
Vorfrühling *106*, 107

H*aho-Triptychon* 85–6
Historiengemälde 103–4
Hogarth, William 12
Hokusai, Katsushika 80
Der Inume-Pass ... 80, *80*
Holbein, Hans, the Jüngere 24, 139
Holzschnitte 80, 83
Homer, Winslow: *Mending the Nets* 79, *79*
Hudson River School 52, 107

I*chthys* (christliches Fischsymbol) 112, *112*
Ikonografie 108, 112–17
Initiation des Kublai Khan ... (anon.) *20*, 20–21

Kahlo, Frida 101, 132, 150–53
Die gebrochene Säule *130*, 151, *152*
Die zwei Fridas 150, *151*
Diego und ich 153, *153*
Kaiserin Theodora ... 72, *72*
Kaltnadelradierung 83
Kandinsky, Wassily 122
Keats, John 9
Kennedy, Jackie 161
kinetische Skulptur 96, 97
Klint, Hilma af 122, 124
Die zehn Größten, Nr. 3, Jugend 107, *123*
Malereien für den Tempel 124
Koba (Wild Horse): *Warten auf Wild* 41, *41*

Kopf eines Oba (Edo) 95, 96
Komposition 38, 54, 56–8
Kontrapost 53
Körpersprache 108, 111
Kubismus 58, 60, 61, 154, 157
  Analytischer 154, 157
  Collage 157
  Synthetischer 157, 158
Kunst
  als Aufzeichnung der Geschichte 18, 20–22
  analysieren 62–5
  Definitionen 11–13, 15
  Stil(e) 60–2
  und Funktionalität 22–4
  und persönliche Vorlieben 10–11
  Werke vergleichen 62–3
  Zweck von 15–18

Landschaftsmalerei 16, 52, 104, 107
Lebrun, Charles 25
Leim, tierischer 73–4
Leinwände 76, 78
Leonardo da Vinci 63, 124–5, 132, 136
  Das Abendmahl 134–6, *134–5*, 162, *164–5*
  Der Vitruvianische Mensch 28
  Die Taufe Christi (Verrocchio) 63
  Felsgrottenmadonna 132, *133*
  Mona Lisa 102, 136, *137*
Leyden, Lucas van 139
Licht 38, 49–50
Linie(n) 38, 40–41
  implizierte 41–2
  versus Farbe 42–3
Lithografie 83
Löwen 115
Lysipp: *Apoxyomenos* 28

Malewitsch, Kasimir 122
  Weißes Quadrat 107, 124, *125*
Manzi-Schacht, Vera 94
  Remembrance 94, 95
Matisse, Henri 30
Memento-Mori-Gemälde 116, 117
menschliche Figur 28, 30, 101
Metallguss 95–6
Michelangelo Buonarroti 57, 60, 139
  Die Erschaffung Adams 70, *70–71*, 103
  David 5–3, *53*, *100*, 101, 103
  Sixtinische Kapelle, Decke *102–3*, 103
Minjemtimi (Ahnenfigur) *92*, 93
Mission der Apostel (Relief) 109–10, 112–13, *113*
Mondrian, Piet 32
  Komposition mit Gelb, Blau und Rot 32, *32*
Monet, Claude 49
  Kathedrale von Rouen: Das Portal (Sonnenlicht) *49*, 49–50, 58
Morisot, Berthe 30
  Die Schwestern 30, *30*
Mosaiken 64, *72*, 72–3
Motive 100–1
Museen, Kunst 11, 23, 64
mythologische Themen 102

Narmer-Palette 104
narrative Konventionen 108–11
Nebamun jagt ... (Grabmalerei) *27*, 27–8, 109
Nevelson, Louise 96
  Sky Cathedral 96–7
Newton, Isaac: Farbrad 38
Niépce, Nicéphore 88
Nikolaus von Verdun 85
  Noah und die Arche 85, 86

O'Keeffe, Georgia 122
Ölfarbe 64, 76–7
Oldenburg, Claes: *Two Cheeseburgers with Everything* 94

Palermo: Mosaiken der Palastkapelle 72–3
Pergament 73
Perspektive
  Einpunkt- 108, 134
  Linear- 108–9
  Luft- 52
Petit-Frère, Joanne 15
Picasso, Pablo 6, 12, 58, 62, 132, 154, 157–8
  Der alte Gitarrenspieler 154, *155*
  Die Tragödie 58, *59*, 62, 154
  Don Quijote und Sancho Pansa 121, 121–2
  Drei Musikanten 157, *157*
  Guernica 104, *158–9*, 159
  Les Demoiselles d'Avignon 154
  Mädchen mit Mandoline 154, *156*
  Mutter und Kind 158
  Pavian mit Jungem 12
  Stierkopf 12, *13*
  Stillleben mit Rohrstuhl 90, 157
Pigmente, Farbe 38, 70, 71
Pointillismus 45, 58
Politik, Kunst und 104
Polyklet: *Speerträger* 28
Porträt einer jungen Frau (Enkaustik) *68*, 101
Porträtmalerei 101–2, 136
Poussin, Nicolas 42
  Die Heilige Familie auf den Stufen 41–2, *42*
Poussinisten 43
prähistorische Kunst 126
Praxiteles 46
  Aphrodite von Knidos 45, *46*, *47*, *100*, 101
Proportion (der Komposition) 54, 56–7

Radierung 83
Raffael 51, 139
  Schule von Athen 51, *51*, 52, 54
Raum 38, 51–3
religiöse Kunst 102–3, 112
Rembrandt van Rijn 48, 62, 101, 132, 138–9, 142
  Die Anatomie des Doktor Tulp 138
  Die Blendung Simsons 138, *138*
  Die Nachtwache 76, 139, *140–41*
  Die Vorsteher ... 142
  Kreuzabnahme 48, 49, 54
  Selbstporträt mit 63, 142, *143*
Renoir, Pierre-Auguste 30, 31
  Ruderer in Chatou 39, *39*, 104
Reynolds, Sir Joshua 25
Rivera, Diego 150, 151–3
Rockwell, Norman 10
  Boys Playing Leapfrog 10
Rodin, Auguste 60, 63
  Der Gedanke 32, *33*, 34
  Der Kuss 60, *60*
Rowlandson, Thomas, und Pugin, Augustus: *Exhibition Room, Somerset House* 25
Rubénisten 43
Rubens, Peter Paul 42, 43, 139
  Heilige Familie ... 42–3, *43*
  Venus und Adonis 62
Ruysch, Rachel 116
  Stillleben mit Rosen ... 107, 117, *117*

Sasson, Steven 88
Schattierungen 40
Siebdruck 83–4
Senefelder, Alois 83
Seurat, Georges 45
  Ein Sonntagnachmittag auf der Insel La Grande Jatte 36, 45, *45*, 58
Sfumato 132
Sgraffito 86
Sherman, Cindy 88
  Untitled #475 89
Sitzender Ganesh (Elfenbein) 93, *93*
Sitzender Schreiber (Skulptur) 16, *16*, 101
Skulptur 53, 90
  Elfenbein 93
  Gips 94
  Holz 90, 93
  kinetische 96, 97
  Konstruktionen und Assemblagen 96
  Stein 90
  Terrakotta 94–5
Stilllebenmotive 107, 116–17
Stoffels, Hendrickje 142

Talbot, William Fox 88
Tempera 71
Tenebrismus 138
Teppich von Bayeux 110–11
Tesserae 72, 73
Textur 38, 44–5, 47, 64
Ti bei der Nilpferdjagd (Wandrelief) *26*, 27–8
Tintoretto, Jacopo 109
Abendmahl 109, *109*
Tizian 139
Der Raub der Europa 76, *77*
Venus und Adonis 62
Tönungen 40
Tonwerte (der Farbe) 40
Toulouse-Lautrec, Henri de 83
Divan Japonais 82, 83
Trajanssäule, Rom 110, *110*

unbetitelte Kunstwerke 122

Vanitas-Gemälde 116, 117
van Eyck, *siehe* Eyck
van Gogh, *siehe* Gogh
van Leyden, *siehe* Leyden
Vasarely, Victor 39
Vasari, Giorgio 63, 131
Velázquez, Diego 44
Die Alte beim Eierbraten 44, *44*
Vellum 73
Venus von Willendorf (prähistorisch) 126, *126*
Verkürzung 51
Vermeer, Jan 104
Das Konzert 104
Verrocchio, Andrea 63
Die Taufe Christi 63
Vitruvius 28

Wachsausschmelzverfahren 95
WalkingStick, Kay 37, 126–7
Oh, Canada! 98, 127, *128–9*
Warhol, Andy 12, 24, 84, 132, 160, 161–3
Abendmahl 162, *164–5*
Campbell's Soup Cans 84, *84*, 160, *161*
Marilyn Diptych 160–61, *162*
Wasserfarbe 78–9

Zünfte 23, 24, 25

BILDNACHWEISE

l links **r** rechts

2, 120 The Metropolitan Museum of Art, New York. Geschenk von Louis C. Raegner, 1927; **4** National Archives at College Park, Maryland. Still Picture Records Section, Special Media Archives Services Division. 306-NT-694A-1; **8, 14** Privatsammlung. Foto mit frdl. Genehmigung durch den Künstler; **10** Norman Rockwell Museum Collection, Stockbridge. Repr. gen. durch die Norman Rockwell Family Agency; **11** Kunsthistorisches Museum, Wien. Foto Superstock/A. Burkatovski/Fine Art Images; **13** Musée national Picasso, Paris. Foto © RMN-Grand Palais (Musée national Picasso-Paris)/Mathieu Rabeau. © Succession Picasso/DACS, London 2021; **16** Musée du Louvre, Paris. Foto © Musée du Louvre, Dist. RMN-Grand Palais/Christian Decamps; **17** Staatsgalerie, Stuttgart. Mit frdl. Genehmigung durch Banksy; **19** The National Gallery, London; **20** Rubin Museum of Art C2002.3.2 (HAR 65046); **21** Museo dell'Opera Metropolitana del Duomo, Siena; **22** Kunsthistorisches Museum, Wien; **25** The Metropolitan Museum of Art, New York. Harris Brisbane Dick Fund, 1917; **26** Foto © Araldo de Luca. *www.araldodeluca.com*; **27** British Museum, London. Foto The Trustees of the British Museum. Alle Rechte vorbehalten; **29l** Sammlung Fondation Alberto & Annette Giacometti, Paris. Foto Bridgeman Images. © The Estate of Alberto Giacometti (Fondation Giacometti, Paris und ADAGP, Paris), lizenziert in UK durch ACS und DACS, London 2021; **29r** Privatsammlung. Photo © Christie's Images/Bridgeman Images. © Fernando Botero; **30** National Gallery of Art, Washington, DC. Geschenk von Mrs. Charles S. Carstairs; **31** Unterlinden Museum, Colmar; **32** Tate, St Ives. Foto Tate; **33** Musée d'Orsay, Paris. Foto © RMN-Grand Palais (Musée d'Orsay)/René-Gabriel Ojéda; **35** Albright-Knox Art Gallery, Buffalo, New York. Geschenk von Seymour H. Knox, J., 1956. Foto Albright Knox Art Gallery/Art Resource, NY/Scala, Florenz; **36, 45** Art Institute of Chicago. Helen Birch Bartlett Memorial Collection; **39** National Gallery of Art, Washington, DC. Geschenk von Sam A. Lewisohn; **41** Division of Work and Industry, National Museum of American History, Smithsonian Institution; **42** Cleveland Museum of Art. Leonard C. Hanna, Jr Fund; **43** Art Institute of Chicago. Major Acquisitions Fund; **44** Scottish National Gallery, Edinburgh. Erworben mit Unterstützung des Art Fund and a Treasury Grant 1955; **46, 100l** Museo Pio-Clementino, Vatikanstadt. Foto © Scala, Florenz; **47** The Museum of Modern Art, New York. Anonymes Geschenk. Foto The Museum of Modern Art, New York/Scala, Florenz. © Succession Brancusi – Alle Rechte vorbehalten. ADAGP, Paris und DACS, London 2021; **48** National Gallery of Art, Washington, DC. Widdener Collection; **49** The Metropolitan Museum of Art, New York. Theodore M. Davis Collection, Nachlass von Theodore M. Davis, 1915; **50** The Dan Flavin Art Institute, Bridgehampton. Mit frdl. Genehmigung Dia Art Foundation, New York. Foto Bill Jacobson Studio, New York. © Stephen Flavin/Artists Rights Society (ARS), New York 2021; **51** Stanza della Segnatura, Apostolischer Palast, Vatikanstadt; **52** The Metropolitan Museum of Art, New York. Geschenk von Mrs. Russell Sage, 1908; **53l, 100r** Galleria dell'Accademia, Florenz. Foto © Scala, Florenz/mit frdl. Genehmigung Ministero per i Beni e le Attività Culturali e per il Turismo; **53r** Galleria Borghese, Rom. Mit frdl. Genehmigung Ministero per i Beni e le Attività Culturali e per il Turismo – Galleria Borghese; **55** Arenakapelle, Padua. Foto Granger Historical Picture Archive/ Alamy Stock Photo; **56–7** National Gallery of Art, Washington, DC. Chester Dale Collection. © Salvador Dalí, Fundació Gala-Salvador Dalí, DACS 2021; **59** National Gallery of Art, Washington, DC. Chester Dale Collection. © Succession Picasso/DACS, London 2021; **60** Musée Rodin, Paris. Foto Denis Chevalier/akg-images; **61** Philadelphia Museum of Art. The Louise and Walter Arensberg Collection, 1950. © Succession Brancusi – All rights reserved. ADAGP, Paris und DACS, London 2021; **63** Musée Camille Claudel, Nogent-sur-Seine. Foto © Marco Illuminati; **66, 78** Privatsammlung. Foto Rob McKeever. Mit frdl. Genehmigung Gagosian. © 2021 Helen

Frankenthaler Foundation, Inc./DACS, London; **68** The Metropolitan Museum of Art, New York. Rogers Fund, 1909; **70–71** Sixtinische Kapelle, Vatikanstadt; **72** Kirche San Vitale, Ravenna; **74** Trinity College Library, Dublin. Mit frdl. Genehmigung The Board of Trinity College Dublin; **75** National Gallery of Art, Washington, DC. Andrew W. Mellon Collection; **77** Isabella Stewart Gardner Museum, Boston. Foto Bridgeman Images; **79** National Gallery of Art, Washington, DC. Nachlass von Julia B. Engel; **80** The Metropolitan Museum of Art, New York. Henry L. Phillips Collection, Nachlass von Henry L. Phillips, 1939; **81** The Metropolitan Museum of Art, New York. Harris Brisbane Dick Fund, 1932; **82** The Metropolitan Museum of Art, New York. Nachlass von Clifford A. Furst, 1958; **84** The Andy Warhol Museum, Pittsburgh; Founding Collection, Contribution The Andy Warhol Foundation for the Visual Arts, Inc. © 2021 The Andy Warhol Foundation for the Visual Arts, Inc./Licensed by DACS, London; **85** Stift Klosterneuburg. Foto Peter Boettcher, IMAREAL Krems; **87** Kathedrale Notre-Dame, Chartres. Foto World History Archive/Alamy Stock Photo; **89** Mit frdl. Genehmigung des Künstlers und Metro Pictures, New York; **91** The Metropolitan Museum of Art, New York. Erwerb, Foundation of Fine Art of the Century Gift, 1985; **92** The Metropolitan Museum of Art, New York. The Michael C. Rockefeller Memorial Collection, Nachlass von Nelson A. Rockefeller, 1979; **93** The Metropolitan Museum of Art, New York. Geschenk von Mr. und Mrs. J. J. Klejman, 1964; **94** Collection of D'Achille-Rosone, Little Silver, NJ. Foto mit frdl. Genehmigung des Künstlers; **95** The Metropolitan Museum of Art, New York. The Michael C. Rockefeller Memorial Collection, Nachlass von Nelson A. Rockefeller, 1979; **96** Privatsammlung. Dauerleihgabe an die Tate. Foto Tate. © 2021 Calder Foundation, New York/DACS, London; **98, 128–9** Sammlung des Künstlers. Mit frdl. Genehmigung Froelick Gallery, Portland. Foto Ed Eckstein, Easton; **102–3** Sixtinische Kapelle, Vatikanstadt; **105** Obey Giant Art. Mit frdl. Genehmigung von Shepard Fairey/Obeygiant.com; **106** National Palace Museum, Taipei. Foto De Agostini/Getty Images; **108** Sint Pieterskirche, Leuven; **109** Basilika San Giorgio Maggiore, Venedig; **110** Trajans-Forum, Rom. Foto Araldo de Luca/Corbis via Getty Images; **111** Foto © Dommuseum Hildesheim. Foto Florian Monheim; **112** Museo Nazionale Romano, Terme di Diocleziano, Rom. Mit frdl. Genehmigung des Ministero per i beni e le attività culturali e per il turismo – Museo Nazionale Romano; **113** Sainte-Marie-Madeleine, Vézelay. Foto akg-images/Stefan Drechsel; **114** The Metropolitan Museum of Art, New York. Nachlass von Mrs. James W. Gerard, 1956; **116** Museo Nacional del Prado, Madrid. Foto Museo Nacional del Prado, Madrid/Scala, Florenz; **117** Privatsammlung; **118** The Metropolitan Museum of Art, New York. Catharine Lorillard Wolfe Collection, Wolfe Fund, 1931; **119** Königliche Museen der Schönen Künste, Brüssel; **121** © Succession Picasso/DACS, London 2021; **123** Hilma af Klint Foundation, Stockholm; **125** The Museum of Modern Art, New York. 1935 Erwerb bestätigt 1999 durch Übereinkunft mit dem Nachlass von Kasimir Malewitsch und ermöglicht mit Mitteln aus dem Nachlass von Mrs. John Hay Whitney (durch Austausch). Foto The Museum of Modern Art, New York/Scala, Florenz; **126** Naturhistorisches Museum, Wien; **130, 152** Museo Dolores Olmedo, Mexiko-Stadt. Foto Leonard de Selva/Bridgeman Images. © Banco de México Diego Rivera Frida Kahlo Museums Trust, Mexiko, D.F./DACS 2021; **133** Musée du Louvre, Paris. Foto Musée du Louvre, Dist. RMN-Grand Palais/Angèle Dequier; **134–5** Santa Maria delle Grazie, Mailand; **137** Musée du Louvre, Paris; **138** Städel Museum, Frankfurt am Main. Erworben 1905 mit Mitteln der Städelschen Stiftung, Städelscher Museums-Verein, der Stadt Frankfurt am Main und zahlreicher Freunde des Museums; **140–1** Rijksmuseum, Amsterdam. Leihgabe der Stadt Amsterdam; **143** National Gallery, London; **145** Van Gogh Museum, Amsterdam (Vincent van Gogh Foundation); **146** The Museum of Modern Art, New York. Erworben über den Nachlass Lillie Bliss (durch Austausch). Konservierung ermöglicht durch das Bank of America Art Conservation Project. Foto The Museum of Modern Art, New York/Scala, Florenz; **148–9** Van Gogh Museum, Amsterdam (Vincent van Gogh Foundation); **151** Collection Museo de Arte Moderno, Consejo Nacional para la Cultura y las Artes – Instituto Nacional de Bellas Artes, Mexiko-Stadt. © Banco de México Diego Rivera Frida Kahlo Museums Trust, Mexiko, D.F./DACS 2021; **153** Privatsammlung. Foto akg-images. © Banco de México Diego Rivera Frida Kahlo Museums Trust, Mexiko, D.F./DACS 2021; **155** Art Institute of Chicago. Helen Birch Bartlett Memorial Collection. Foto The Art Institute of Chicago/Art Resource, NY/ Scala, Florenz. © Succession Picasso/DACS, London 2021; **156** The Museum of Modern Art, New York. Nachlass Nelson A. Rockefeller. Foto The Museum of Modern Art, New York/Scala, Florenz. © Succession Picasso/DACS, London 2021; **157** The Museum of Modern Art, New York. Mrs Simon Guggenheim Fund. Foto The Museum of Modern Art, New York/ Scala, Florenz. © Succession Picasso/DACS, London 2021; **158–** Museo Nacional Centro de Arte Reina Sofía, Madrid. Photographic Archives Museo Nacional Centro de Arte Reina Sofía. © Succession Picasso/DACS, London 2021; **161** The Museum of Modern Art, New York. Teilgabe von Irving Blum. Zusätzliche Mittel bereitgestellt durch Nachlass Nelson A. Rockefeller, Geschenk von Mr. und Mrs. William A. M. Burden, Abby Aldrich Rockefeller Fund, Geschenk von Nina und Gordon Bunshaft, erworben durch Nachlass Lillie Bliss, Philip Johnson Fund, Nachlass Frances R. Keech, Geschenk von Mrs. Bliss Parkinson und Nachlass Florence B. Wesley (alle durch Austausch). Foto The Museum of Modern Art, New York/Scala, Florenz. © 2021 The Andy Warhol Foundation for the Visual Arts, Inc./ Lizenziert durch DACS, London; **162** Tate. Foto Tate. © 2021 The Andy Warhol Foundation for the Visual Arts, Inc./Lizenziert durch DACS, London; **164–5** The Andy Warhol Museum, Pittsburgh; Founding Collection, Contribution The Andy Warhol Foundation for the Visual Arts, Inc. © 2021 The Andy Warhol Foundation for the Visual Arts, Inc./Lizenziert durch DACS, London

www.artessentials.de
www.midascollection.com

IMPRESSUM

ISBN 978-3-03876-208-9

2. Auflage 2023

Herausgeber: Gregory C. Zäch
Übersetzung: Claudia Koch,
Kathrin Lichtenberg
Korrektorat: Sabine Müthing
Layout: Ulrich Borstelmann

Midas Verlag AG
Dunantstrasse 3
CH 8044 Zürich

www.midas.ch

Englische Originalausgabe:
How to Understand Art © 2021
Thames & Hudson Ltd, London
Text © Janetta Rebold Benton
Design by April

Die deutsche Nationalbibliothek verzeichnet diese Publikation in der Deutschen Nationalbibliografie; detaillierte bibliografische Daten sind im Internet abrufbar unter: http://www.dnb.de

QUELLENANGABEN

1. Umschlagseite: Flemish School, *Cognoscenti in a Room Hung with Pictures*, ca. 1620 (Detail). Öl auf Holztafel, 96 x 123,5 cm.
National Gallery, London

Titelseite: Jean-Léon Gérôme, *Pygmalion und Galatea*, ca. 1890 (Detail von S. 120)

S. 4: Ein Besucher der National Gallery of Art, Washington, DC, betrachtet Benvenuto Cellinis Salz- und Pfeffer-Gefäß (1540–43), ca. 1947. Foto. National Archives, College Park, MD

Kapitelanfangsseiten: **S. 8** Delphine Diallo, *Hybrid 8*, 2011 (Detail von S. 14); **S. 36** Georges Seurat, *Ein Sonntagnachmittag auf der Insel La Grande Jatte – 1884*, 1884–6 (Detail von S. 45); **S. 66** Helen Frankenthaler, *Grey Fireworks*, 1982 (Detail von S. 78); **S. 98** Kay WalkingStick, *Oh, Canada!*, 2018–19 (Detail von S. 128–9); **S. 130** Frida Kahlo, *Die gebrochene Säule*, 1944 (Detail von S. 152)

Zitate: **S. 9** John Keats, »Ode auf eine griechische Urne«, geschrieben Mai 1819, erstmals anonym veröffentlicht in *Annals of the Fine Arts*, vol. 4, no. 15, XX (Sherwood, Neely, and Jones, London, 1819), S. 639. Hathi Trust Digital Library, dt. Übertragung von Gisela Etzel; **S. 37** E-Mail von Kay WalkingStick an die Autorin, 5. November 2021; **S. 67** *Boys' Workers Round Table, A Magazine of Applied Ideals in Boycraft*, vol. 3 (Boys' Club Federation, New York City, Mittsommer 1923), S. 3, Spalte 2, ohne Zuschreibung. Hathi Trust Digital Library; **S. 97** James Johnson Sweeney, *Marc Chagall* (Museum of Modern Art, New York, NY, in Zusammenarbeit mit The Art Institute of Chicago, Chicago, Il, 1946), S. 7; **S. 131** Giorgio Vasari, *Le Vite de' più eccellenti pittori, scultori, ed architettori* (Lebensläufe der berühmtesten Maler, Bildhauer und Architekten) (Zweite erweiterte Ausgabe; Giunti, Florenz, 1568); Einführung zu Teil 2, S. 1, übersetzt von Janetta Rebold Benton, dt. von Claudia Koch.